Analysis for Financial Management

Analysis for Financial Management

Edited by Dr. G. C. R. Jaiswal

Clanrye International
www.clanryeinternational.com

Clanrye International,
750 Third Avenue, 9th Floor,
New York, NY 10017, USA

Edition: 2018 Clanrye International

ISBN: 978-1-63240-681-1

Cataloging-in-Publication Data

Analysis for financial management / edited by Dr. G. C. R. Jaiswal.
p. cm.
Includes bibliographical references and index.
ISBN 978-1-63240-681-1
1. Finance--Management. 2. Business enterprises--Finance. 3. Corporations--Finance.
I. Jaiswal, Dr. G. C. R.
HG173 .A53 2018
652.152--dc23

For information on all Clanrye International publications
visit our website at www.clanryeinternational.com

CLANRYE INTERNATIONAL

Printed in China.

Contents

Preface

Financial management refers to the optimum and careful management of money so that it is utilized in achieving the desired company objectives and goals. The two different types of financial management are personal finance and organizational finance. The most important aspects of financial management are better cash flow, minimize capital cost, maximize profit, increase wealth, etc. This book elucidates the concepts and innovative models around prospective developments with respect to financial management. It provides comprehensive insights into this vast field. This textbook is a valuable compilation of topics, ranging from the basic to the most complex theories and principles in the area of financial management. It will serve as a valuable source of reference for those interested in this subject.

A detailed account of the significant topics covered in this book is provided below:

Chapter 1- The process that an organization has to review its financial statements is known as financial statement analysis. It includes cash flow statement, income statement, statement of changes in equity and balance sheet. This chapter is an overview of the subject matter incorporating all the major aspects of financial statement analysis.

Chapter 2- Fundamental analysis studies the economic factors of an organization. Some of these factors are earnings, employment, management, interest rates, etc. The section strategically encompasses and incorporates the major components and key concepts of economic analysis, providing a complete understanding.

Chapter 3- Industry analysis is a tool that helps a company in developing an understanding of its position in the market. The processes involved in this are market analysis, balanced scorecard, growth-share matrix, Porter's five forces analysis and market environment. Industry analysis techniques are best understood in confluence with the major topics listed in the following chapter.

Chapter 4- Evaluating the theoretical value of a company is very important. This process is carried out by investors to assess products and services and to evaluate securities. This chapter has been carefully written to provide an easy understanding of the varied facets of company analysis.

Chapter 5- Security analysis is the analysis of the monetary contracts that occur between parties. It can be categorized into equities and debt securities or in a combination of both. The chapter closely examines the key concepts of technical analysis to provide an extensive understanding of the subject.

It gives me an immense pleasure to thank our entire team for their efforts. Finally in the end, I would like to thank my family and colleagues who have been a great source of inspiration and support.

Editor

1

Basics of Financial Statement Analysis

The process that an organization has to review its financial statements is known as financial statement analysis. It includes cash flow statement, income statement, statement of changes in equity and balance sheet. This chapter is an overview of the subject matter incorporating all the major aspects of financial statement analysis.

Financial Statements

Businesses are provided with funds from different financial stakeholders like equity shareholders and lenders. Besides such major stakeholders, other stakeholders like customers, suppliers, business partners etc. will like to know the performance of the business in order to justify their continuity or otherwise with the business and compare such business with other businesses. For this purpose, financial statements prepared and presented by companies are useful for all the stakeholders. Primarily the following statements are presented by the companies:

- Balance Sheet
- Income Statement
- Cash flow Statement

These statements pertaining to a particular accounting year are published as part of the annual report of companies. Abridged quarterly financial reports are also published by companies. To ensure that the financial statements are reliable and comparable over time and across firms, companies are required to follow generally accepted accounting principles (GAAP).

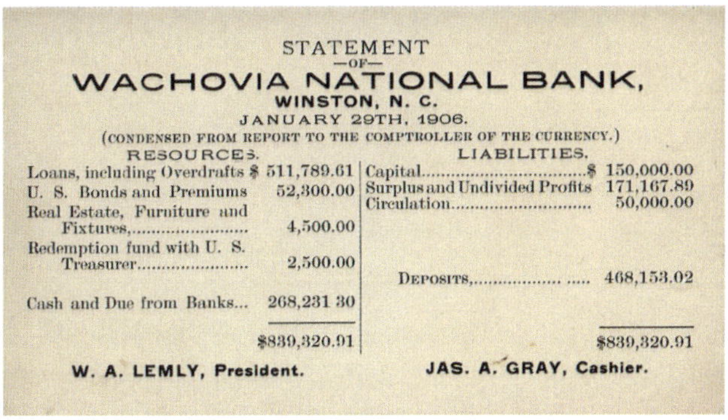
STATEMENT
—OF—
WACHOVIA NATIONAL BANK,
WINSTON, N. C.
JANUARY 29TH, 1906.
(CONDENSED FROM REPORT TO THE COMPTROLLER OF THE CURRENCY.)

RESOURCES.		LIABILITIES.	
Loans, including Overdrafts	$ 511,789.61	Capital	$ 150,000.00
U. S. Bonds and Premiums	52,300.00	Surplus and Undivided Profits	171,167.89
Real Estate, Furniture and Fixtures,	4,500.00	Circulation	50,000.00
Redemption fund with U. S. Treasurer	2,500.00	Deposits,	468,153.02
Cash and Due from Banks...	268,231 30		
	$839,320.91		$839,320.91

W. A. LEMLY, President. JAS. A. GRAY, Cashier.

Historical financial statements

Financial statements (or financial report) is a formal record of the financial activities and position of a business, person, or other entity.

Relevant financial information is presented in a structured manner and in a form easy to understand. They typically include basic financial statements, accompanied by a management discussion and analysis:

1. A balance sheet or statement of financial position, reports on a company's assets, liabilities, and owners equity at a given point in time.
2. An income statement or statement of comprehensive income, statement of revenue & expense, P&L or profit and loss report, reports on a company's income, expenses, and profits over a period of time. A profit and loss statement provides information on the operation of the enterprise. These include sales and the various expenses incurred during the stated period.
3. A Statement of changes in equityor equity statement or statement of retained earnings, reports on the changes in equity of the company during the stated period.
4. A cash flow statement reports on a company's cash flow activities, particularly its operating, investing and financing activities.

Purpose for Business Entities

"The objective of financial statements is to provide information about the financial position, performance and changes in financial position of an enterprise that is useful to a wide range of users in making economic decisions." Financial statements should be understandable, relevant, reliable and comparable. Reported assets, liabilities, equity, income and expenses are directly related to an organization's financial position.

Financial statements are intended to be understandable by readers who have "a reasonable knowledge of business and economic activities and accounting and who are willing to study the information diligently." Financial statements may be used by users for different purposes:

- Owners and managers require financial statements to make important business decisions that affect its continued operations. Financial analysis is then performed on these statements to provide management with a more detailed understanding of the figures. These statements are also used as part of management's annual report to the stockholders.
- Employees also need these reports in making collective bargaining agreements (CBA) with the management, in the case of labor unions or for individuals in discussing their compensation, promotion and rankings.
- Prospective investors make use of financial statements to assess the viability of investing in a business. Financial analyses are often used by investors and are prepared by professionals (financial analysts), thus providing them with the basis for making investment decisions.
- Financial institutions (banks and other lending companies) use them to decide whether to grant a company with fresh working capital or extend debt securities (such as a long-term bank loan or debentures) to finance expansion and other significant expenditures.

Consolidated

Consolidated financial statements are defined as "Financial statements of a group in which the assets, liabilities, equity, income, expenses and cash flows of the parent (company) and its subsidiaries are presented as those of a single economic entity", according to International Accounting Standard 27 "Consolidated and separate financial statements", and International Financial Reporting Standard 10 "Consolidated financial statements".

Government

The rules for the recording, measurement and presentation of government financial statements may be different from those required for business and even for non-profit organizations. They may use either of two accounting methods: accrual accounting, or cost accounting, or a combination of the two (OCBOA). A complete set of chart of accounts is also used that is substantially different from the chart of a profit-oriented business.

Personal

Personal financial statements may be required from persons applying for a personal loan or financial aid. Typically, a personal financial statement consists of a single form for reporting personally held assets and liabilities (debts), or personal sources of income and expenses, or both. The form to be filled out is determined by the organization supplying the loan or aid.

Audit and Legal Implications

Although laws differ from country to country, an audit of the financial statements of a public company is usually required for investment, financing, and tax purposes. These are usually performed by independent accountants or auditing firms. Results of the audit are summarized in an audit report that either provide an unqualified opinion on the financial statements or qualifications as to its fairness and accuracy. The audit opinion on the financial statements is usually included in the annual report.

There has been much legal debate over who an auditor is liable to. Since audit reports tend to be addressed to the current shareholders, it is commonly thought that they owe a legal duty of care to them. But this may not be the case as determined by common law precedent. In Canada, auditors are liable only to investors using a prospectus to buy shares in the primary market. In the United Kingdom, they have been held liable to potential investors when the auditor was aware of the potential investor and how they would use the information in the financial statements. Nowadays auditors tend to include in their report liability restricting language, discouraging anyone other than the addressees of their report from relying on it. Liability is an important issue: in the UK, for example, auditors have unlimited liability.

In the United States, especially in the post-Enron era there has been substantial concern about the accuracy of financial statements. Corporate officers (the chief executive officer (CEO) and chief financial officer (CFO)) are personally responsible for fair financial reporting allowing those reading the report to have a good sense of the organization.

Standards and Regulations

Different countries have developed their own accounting principles over time, making international comparisons of companies difficult. To ensure uniformity and comparability between financial statements prepared by different companies, a set of guidelines and rules are used. Commonly referred to as Generally Accepted Accounting Principles (GAAP), these set of guidelines provide the basis in the preparation of financial statements, although many companies voluntarily disclose information beyond the scope of such requirements.

Recently there has been a push towards standardizing accounting rules made by the International Accounting Standards Board ("IASB"). IASB develops International Financial Reporting Standards that have been adopted by Australia, Canada and the European Union (for publicly quoted companies only), are under consideration in South Africa and other countries. The United States Financial Accounting Standards Board has made a commitment to converge the U.S. GAAP and IFRS over time.

Inclusion in Annual Reports

To entice new investors, public companies assemble their financial statements on fine paper with pleasing graphics and photos in an annual report to shareholders, attempting to capture the excitement and culture of the organization in a "marketing brochure" of sorts. Usually the company's chief executive will write a letter to shareholders, describing management's performance and the company's financial highlights.

In the United States, prior to the advent of the internet, the annual report was considered the most effective way for corporations to communicate with individual shareholders. Blue chip companies went to great expense to produce and mail out attractive annual reports to every shareholder. The annual report was often prepared in the style of a coffee table book.

Notes in Financial Statements

Notes to financial statements (notes) are additional information added to the end of financial statements that help explain specific items in the statements as well as provide a more comprehensive assessment of a company's financial condition. Notes to financial statements can include information on debt, going concern criteria, accounts, contingent liabilities or contextual information explaining the financial numbers (e.g. to indicate a lawsuit).

The notes clarify individual statement line-items. For example, if a company lists a loss on a fixed asset impairment line in their income statement, notes could state the reason for the impairment by describing how the asset became impaired. Notes are also used to explain the accounting methods used to prepare the statements and they support valuations for how particular accounts have been computed.

In consolidated financial statements, all subsidiaries are listed as well as the amount of ownership (controlling interest) that the parent company has in the subsidiaries. Any items within the financial statements that are valuated by estimation are part of the notes if a substantial difference exists between the amount of the estimate previously reported and the actual result. Full disclosure of the effects of the differences between the estimate and actual results should be included.

Management Discussion and Analysis

Management discussion and analysis or MD&A is an integrated part of a company's annual financial statements. The purpose of the MD&A is to provide a narrative explanation, through the eyes of management, of how an entity has performed in the past, its financial condition, and its future prospects. In so doing, the MD&A attempt to provide investors with complete, fair, and balanced information to help them decide whether to invest or continue to invest in an entity.

The topic contains a description of the year gone by and some of the key factors that influenced the business of the company in that year, as well as a fair and unbiased overview of the company's past, present, and future.

MD&A typically describes the corporation's liquidity position, capital resources, results of its operations, underlying causes of material changes in financial statement items (such as asset impairment and restructuring charges), events of unusual or infrequent nature (such as mergers and acquisitions or share buybacks), positive and negative trends, effects of inflation, domestic and international market risks, and significant uncertainties.

Moving to Electronic

Financial statements have been created on paper for hundreds of years. The growth of the Web has seen more and more financial statements created in an electronic form which is exchangeable over the Web. Common forms of electronic financial statements are PDF and HTML. These types of electronic financial statements have their drawbacks in that it still takes a human to read the information in order to reuse the information contained in a financial statement.

More recently a market driven global standard, XBRL (Extensible Business Reporting Language), which can be used for creating financial statements in a structured and computer readable format, has become more popular as a format for creating financial statements. Many regulators around the world such as the U.S. Securities and Exchange Commission have mandated XBRL for the submission of financial information.

The UN/CEFACT created, with respect to Generally Accepted Accounting Principles, (GAAP), internal or external financial reporting XML messages to be used between enterprises and their partners, such as private interested parties (e.g. bank) and public collecting bodies (e.g. taxation authorities). Many regulators use such messages to collect financial and economic information.

Financial Statement Analysis

Financial statement analysis (or financial analysis) is the process of reviewing and analyzing a company's financial statements to make better economic decisions. These statements include the income statement, balance sheet, statement of cash flows, and a statement of changes in equity. Financial statement analysis is a method or process involving specific techniques for evaluating risks, performance, financial health, and future prospects of an organization.

It is used by a variety of stakeholders, such as credit and equity investors, the government, the public, and decision-makers within the organization. These stakeholders have different interests and apply a variety of different techniques to meet their needs. For example, equity investors are interested in the long-term earnings power of the organization and perhaps the sustainability and growth of dividend payments. Creditors want to ensure the interest and principal is paid on the organizations debt securities (e.g., bonds) when due.

Common methods of financial statement analysis include fundamental analysis, DuPont analysis, horizontal and vertical analysis and the use of financial ratios. Historical information combined with a series of assumptions and adjustments to the financial information may be used to project future performance. The Chartered Financial Analyst designation is available for professional financial analysts.

History

Benjamin Graham and David Dodd first published their influential book "Security Analysis" in 1934. A central premise of their book is that the market's pricing mechanism for financial securities such as stocks and bonds is based upon faulty and irrational analytical processes performed by many market participants. This results in the market price of a security only occasionally coinciding with the intrinsic value around which the price tends to fluctuate. Investor Warren Buffett is a well-known supporter of Graham and Dodd's philosophy.

The Graham and Dodd approach is referred to as Fundamental analysis and includes: 1) Economic analysis; 2) Industry analysis; and 3) Company analysis. The latter is the primary realm of financial statement analysis. On the basis of these three analyses the intrinsic value of the security is determined.

Horizontal and Vertical Analysis

Horizontal analysis compares financial information over time, typically from past quarters or years. Horizontal analysis is performed by comparing financial data from a past statement, such as the income statement. When comparing this past information one will want to look for variations such as higher or lower earnings.

Vertical analysis is a percentage analysis of financial statements. Each line item listed in the financial statement is listed as the percentage of another line item. For example, on an income statement each line item will be listed as a percentage of gross sales. This technique is also referred to as normalization or common-sizing.

Financial Ratio Analysis

Financial ratios are very powerful tools to perform some quick analysis of financial statements. There are four main categories of ratios: liquidity ratios, profitability ratios, activity ratios and leverage ratios. These are typically analyzed over time and across competitors in an industry.

- *Liquidity ratios* are used to determine how quickly a company can turn its assets into cash if it experiences financial difficulties or bankruptcy. It essentially is a measure of a company's ability to remain in business. A few common liquidity ratios are the current ratio and the liquidity index. The current ratio is current assets/current liabilities and measures how much liquidity is available to pay for liabilities. The liquidity index shows how quickly a company can turn assets into cash and is calculated by: (Trade receivables x Days to liquidate) + (Inventory x Days to liquidate)/Trade Receivables + Inventory.

- *Profitability ratios* are ratios that demonstrate how profitable a company is. A few popular profitability ratios are the breakeven point and gross profit ratio. The breakeven point calculates how much cash a company must generate to break even with their start up costs. The gross profit ratio is equal to (revenue - the cost of goods sold)/revenue. This ratio shows a quick snapshot of expected revenue.
- *Activity ratios* are meant to show how well management is managing the company's resources. Two common activity ratios are accounts payable turnover and accounts receivable turnover. These ratios demonstrate how long it takes for a company to pay off its accounts payable and how long it takes for a company to receive payments, respectively.
- *Leverage ratios* depict how much a company relies upon its debt to fund operations. A very common leverage ratio used for financial statement analysis is the debt-to-equity ratio. This ratio shows the extent to which management is willing to use debt in order to fund operations. This ratio is calculated as: (Long-term debt + Short-term debt + Leases)/ Equity.

DuPont analysis uses several financial ratios that multiplied together equal return on equity, a measure of how much income the firm earns divided by the amount of funds invested (equity).

A Dividend discount model (DDM) may also be used to value a company's stock price based on the theory that its stock is worth the sum of all of its future dividend payments, discounted back to their present value. In other words, it is used to value stocks based on the net present value of the future dividends.

Financial statement analyses are typically performed in spreadsheet software and summarized in a variety of formats.

Recasting Financial Statements

Investors typically are attempting to understand how much cash the company will generate in the future and its rate of profit growth, relative to the amount of capital deployed. Analysts may modify ("recast") the financial statements by adjusting the underlying assumptions to aid in this computation. For example, operating leases (treated like a rental transaction) may be recast as capital leases (indicating ownership), adding assets and liabilities to the balance sheet. This affects the financial statement ratios.

Recasting financial statements requires a solid understanding of accounting theory. Once the cash flow in future years is projected, a discount rate or interest rate will be applied to measure the value of the company and its stock or debt.

Certifications

Financial analysts typically have finance and accounting education at the undergraduate or graduate level. Persons may earn the Chartered Financial Analyst (CFA) designation through a series of challenging examinations.

Balance Sheet

In financial accounting, a balance sheet or statement of financial position is a summary of the financial balances of an individual or organisation, whether it be a sole proprietorship, a business partnership, a corporation, private limited company or other organization such as Government or not-for-profit entity. Assets, liabilities and ownership equity are listed as of a specific date, such as the end of its financial year. A balance sheet is often described as a "snapshot of a company's financial condition". Of the four basic financial statements, the balance sheet is the only statement which applies to a single point in time of a business' calendar year.

A standard company balance sheet has two sides: assets, on the left and financing, which itself has two parts, liabilities and ownership equity, on the right. The main categories of assets are usually listed first, and typically in order of liquidity. Assets are followed by the liabilities. The difference between the assets and the liabilities is known as equity or the net assets or the net worth or capital of the company and according to the accounting equation, net worth must equal assets minus liabilities.

Another way to look at the balance sheet equation is that total assets equals liabilities plus owner's equity. Looking at the equation in this way shows how assets were financed: either by borrowing money (liability) or by using the owner's money (owner's or shareholders' equity). Balance sheets are usually presented with assets in one section and liabilities and net worth in the other section with the two sections "balancing".

A business operating entirely in cash can measure its profits by withdrawing the entire bank balance at the end of the period, plus any cash in hand. However, many businesses are not paid immediately; they build up inventories of goods and they acquire buildings and equipment. In other words: businesses have assets and so they cannot, even if they want to, immediately turn these into cash at the end of each period. Often, these businesses owe money to suppliers and to tax authorities, and the proprietors do not withdraw all their original capital and profits at the end of each period. In other words, businesses also have liabilities.

Types

A balance sheet summarizes an organization or individual's assets, equity and liabilities at a specific point in time. Two forms of balance sheet exist. They are the report form and the account form. Individuals and small businesses tend to have simple balance sheets. Larger businesses tend to have more complex balance sheets, and these are presented in the organization's annual report. Large businesses also may prepare balance sheets for segments of their businesses. A balance sheet is often presented alongside one for a different point in time (typically the previous year) for comparison.

Personal

A personal balance sheet lists current assets such as cash in checking accounts and savings accounts, long-term assets such as common stock and real estate, current liabilities such as loan debt and mortgage debt due, or overdue, long-term liabilities such as mortgage and other loan debt. Securities and real estate values are listed at market value rather than at historical cost or cost basis. Personal net worth is the difference between an individual's total assets and total liabilities.

US Small Business

Sample Small Business Balance Sheet				
Assets (current)		**Liabilities and Owners' Equity**		
Cash	$6,600	**Liabilities**		
Accounts Receivable	$6,200	Notes Payable	$5,000	
Assets (non-current)		Accounts Payable $25,000		
Tools and equipment	$25,000	*Total liabilities*		$30,000
		Owners' equity		
		Capital Stock	$7,000	
		Retained Earnings	$800	
		Total owners' equity		$7,800
Total	$37,800	*Total*		$37,800

A small business balance sheet lists current assets such as cash, accounts receivable, and inventory, fixed assets such as land, buildings, and equipment, intangible assets such as patents, and liabilities such as accounts payable, accrued expenses, and long-term debt. Contingent liabilities such as warranties are noted in the footnotes to the balance sheet. The small business's equity is the difference between total assets and total liabilities.

Public Business Entities Structure

Guidelines for balance sheets of public business entities are given by the International Accounting Standards Board and numerous country-specific organizations/companies. The standard used by companies in the USA adhere to U.S. Generally Accepted Accounting Principles (GAAP). The Federal Accounting Standards Advisory Board (FASAB) is a United States federal advisory committee whose mission is to develop generally accepted accounting principles (GAAP) for federal financial reporting entities.

Balance sheet account names and usage depend on the organization's country and the type of organization. Government organizations do not generally follow standards established for individuals or businesses.

If applicable to the business, summary values for the following items should be included in the balance sheet: Assets are all the things the business owns. This will include property, tools, vehicles, furniture, machinery, and so on.

Assets

Non-current assets (Fixed assets)

1. Property, plant and equipment.
2. Investment property, such as real estate held for investment purposes.
3. Intangible assets such as (patents, copyrights and goodwill).
4. Financial assets (excluding investments accounted for using the equity method, accounts receivables, and cash and cash equivalents), such as notes receivables.
5. Investments accounted for using the equity method.
6. Biological assets, which are living plants or animals. Bearer biological assets are plants or animals which bear agricultural produce for harvest, such as apple trees grown to produce apples and sheep raised to produce wool.
7. Loan To (More than one financial period).

Current assets

1. Prepaid expenses for future services that will be used within a year.
2. Accounts receivable.
3. Cash and cash equivalents.
4. Cash at bank, Petty Cash, Cash On Hand.
5. Revenue Earned In Arrears (Accrued Revenue) for services done but not yet received for the year.
6. Loan To (Less than one financial period).

Liabilities

1. Accounts payable.
2. Provisions for warranties or court decisions (contingent liabilities that are both probable and measurable).
3. Financial liabilities (excluding provisions and accounts payables), such as promissory notes and corporate bonds.
4. Liabilities and assets for current tax.
5. Deferred tax liabilities and deferred tax assets.
6. Unearned revenue for services paid for by customers but not yet provided.
7. Interests on loan stock.

Equity / Capital

The net assets shown by the balance sheet equals the third part of the balance sheet, which is known as the shareholders' equity. It comprises:

1. Issued capital and reserves attributable to equity holders of the parent company (controlling interest)

2. Non-controlling interest in equity

Formally, shareholders' equity is part of the company's liabilities: they are funds "owing" to shareholders (after payment of all other liabilities); usually, however, "liabilities" is used in the more restrictive sense of liabilities excluding shareholders' equity. The balance of assets and liabilities (including shareholders' equity) is not a coincidence. Records of the values of each account in the balance sheet are maintained using a system of accounting known as double-entry bookkeeping. In this sense, shareholders' equity by construction must equal assets minus liabilities, and thus the shareholders' equity is considered to be a residual.

Regarding the items in equity section, the following disclosures are required:

1. Numbers of shares authorized, issued and fully paid, and issued but not fully paid

2. Par value of shares

3. Reconciliation of shares outstanding at the beginning and the end of the period

4. Description of rights, preferences, and restrictions of shares

5. Treasury shares, including shares held by subsidiaries and associates

6. Shares reserved for issuance under options and contracts

7. A description of the nature and purpose of each reserve within owners' equity

Substantiation

Balance sheet substantiation is the accounting process conducted by businesses on a regular basis to confirm that the balances held in the primary accounting system of record (e.g. SAP, Oracle, other ERP system's General Ledger) are reconciled (in balance with) with the balance and transaction records held in the same or supporting sub-systems.

Balance sheet substantiation includes multiple processes including reconciliation (at a transactional or at a balance level) of the account, a process of review of the reconciliation and any pertinent supporting documentation and a formal certification (sign-off) of the account in a predetermined form driven by corporate policy.

Balance sheet substantiation is an important process that is typically carried out on a monthly, quarterly and year-end basis. The results help to drive the regulatory balance sheet reporting obligations of the organization.

Historically, balance sheet substantiation has been a wholly manual process, driven by spreadsheets, email and manual monitoring and reporting. In recent years software solutions have been developed to bring a level of process automation, standardization and enhanced control to the balance sheet substantiation or account certification process. These solutions are suitable for organizations with a high volume of accounts and/or personnel involved in the Balance Sheet Substantiation process and can be used to drive efficiencies, improve transparency and help to reduce risk.

Balance sheet substantiation is a key control process in the SOX 404 top-down risk assessment.

Sample

The following balance sheet is a very brief example prepared in accordance with IFRS. It does not show all possible kinds of assets, liabilities and equity, but it shows the most usual ones. Because it shows goodwill, it could be a consolidated balance sheet. Monetary values are not shown, summary (subtotal) rows are missing as well.

Under IFRS items are always shown based on liquidity from the least liquid assets at the top, usually land and buildings to the most liquid, i.e. cash. Then liabilities and equity continue from the most immediate liability to be paid (usual account payable) to the least i.e. long term debt such a mortgages and owner's equity at the very bottom.

Consolidated Statement of Finance Position of XYZ, Ltd.

As of 31 December 2015

ASSETS

Non-Current Assets (Fixed Assets)

Property, Plant and Equipment (PPE)

Less : Accumulated Depreciation

Goodwill

Intangible Assets (Patent, Copyright, Trademark, etc.)

Less : Accumulated Amortization

Investments in Financial assets due after one year

Investments in Associates and Joint Ventures

Other Non-Current Assets, e.g. Deferred Tax Assets, Lease Receivable and Receivables due after one year

Current Assets

Inventories

Prepaid Expenses

Investments in Financial assets due within one year

Non-Current and Current Assets Held for sale

Accounts Receivable (Debtors) due within one year

Less : Allowances for Doubtful debts

Cash and Cash Equivalents

TOTAL ASSETS (this will match/balance the total for Liabilities and Equity below)

LIABILITIES and EQUITY

Current Liabilities (Creditors: amounts falling due within one year)

Accounts Payable

Current Income Tax Payable

Current portion of Loans Payable

Short-term Provisions

Other Current Liabilities, e.g. Deferred income, Security deposits

Non-Current Liabilities (Creditors: amounts falling due after more than one year)

Loans Payable

Issued Debt Securities, e.g. Notes/Bonds Payable

Deferred Tax Liabilities

Provisions, e.g. Pension Obligations

Other Non-Current Liabilities, e.g. Lease Obligations

EQUITY

Paid-in Capital

Share Capital (Ordinary Shares, Preference Shares)

Share Premium

Less: Treasury Shares

Retained Earnings

Revaluation Reserve

Other Accumulated Reserves

Accumulated Other Comprehensive Income

Non-Controlling Interest

TOTAL LIABILITIES and EQUITY (this will match/balance the total for Assets above)

Balance Sheet: Balance sheet is statement of 'Assets' and 'Liabilities & Equities' at a particular moment of time. That is why it is also known as position statement rather statement of financial position. Assets can be defined as what a business owns and liabilities mean what a business owes to non-owners, equities means what a business owes to owners. Assets are also known as resources and Liabilities and Equities can be otherwise known as sources of resources.

Income Statement

An income statement or profit and loss account (also referred to as a *profit and loss statement* (P&L), *statement of profit or loss*, *revenue statement*, *statement of financial performance*, *earnings statement*, *operating statement*, or *statement of operations*) is one of the financial statements of a company and shows the company's revenues and expenses during a particular period. It indicates how the revenues (money received from the sale of products and services before expenses are taken out, also known as the "top line") are transformed into the net income (the result after all revenues and expenses have been accounted for, also known as "net profit" or the "bottom line"). The purpose of the income statement is to show managers and investors whether the company made or lost money during the period being reported.

One important thing to remember about an income statement is that it represents a period of time like the cash flow statement. This contrasts with the balance sheet, which represents a single moment in time.

Charitable organizations that are required to publish financial statements do not produce an income statement. Instead, they produce a similar statement that reflects funding sources compared against program expenses, administrative costs, and other operating commitments. This statement is commonly referred to as the statement of activities. Revenues and expenses are further categorized in the statement of activities by the donor restrictions on the funds received and expended.

The income statement can be prepared in one of two methods. The Single Step income statement takes the simpler approach, totaling revenues and subtracting expenses to find the bottom line. The more complex Multi-Step income statement (as the name implies) takes several steps to find the bottom line, starting with the gross profit. It then calculates operating expenses and, when deducted from the gross profit, yields income from operations. Adding to income from operations is the difference of other revenues and other expenses. When combined with income from operations, this yields income before taxes. The final step is to deduct taxes, which finally produces the net income for the period measured.

Usefulness and Limitations of Income Statement

Income statements should help investors and creditors determine the past financial performance of the enterprise, predict future performance, and assess the capability of generating future cash flows through report of the income and expenses.

However, information of an income statement has several limitations:

- Items that might be relevant but cannot be reliably measured are not reported (*e.g.*, brand recognition and loyalty).
- Some numbers depend on accounting methods used (*e.g.*, using FIFO or LIFO accounting to measure inventory level).
- Some numbers depend on judgments and estimates (*e.g.*, depreciation expense depends on estimated useful life and salvage value).

- INCOME STATEMENT GREENHARBOR LLC -

For the year ended DECEMBER 31 2010

	€	€
	Debit	Credit
Revenues		
GROSS REVENUES (including INTEREST income)		296,397

Expenses:		
ADVERTISING	6,300	
BANK & CREDIT CARD FEES	144	
BOOKKEEPING	2,350	
SUBCONTRACTORS	88,000	
ENTERTAINMENT	5,550	
INSURANCE	750	
LEGAL & PROFESSIONAL SERVICES	1,575	

LICENSES	632	
PRINTING, POSTAGE & STATIONERY	320	
RENT	13,000	
MATERIALS	74,400	
TELEPHONE	1,000	
UTILITIES	1,491	

TOTAL EXPENSES		(195,512)

NET INCOME		100,885

Guidelines for statements of comprehensive income and income statements of business entities are formulated by the International Accounting Standards Board and numerous country-specific organizations, for example the FASB in the U.S.

Names and usage of different accounts in the income statement depend on the type of organization, industry practices and the requirements of different jurisdictions.

If applicable to the business, summary values for the following items should be included in the income statement:

Operating Section

- Revenue - Cash inflows or other enhancements of assets (including accounts receivable) of an entity during a period from delivering or producing goods, rendering services, or other activities that constitute the entity's ongoing major operations. It is usually presented as sales minus sales discounts, returns, and allowances. Every time a business sells a product or performs a service, it obtains revenue. This often is referred to as gross revenue or sales revenue.

- Expenses - Cash outflows or other using-up of assets or incurrence of liabilities (including accounts payable) during a period from delivering or producing goods, rendering services, or carrying out other activities that constitute the entity's ongoing major operations.

    - Cost of Goods Sold (COGS) / Cost of Sales - represents the direct costs attributable to goods produced and sold by a business (manufacturing or merchandizing). It includes *material costs*, *direct labour*, and *overhead costs* (as in absorption costing), and excludes operating costs (period costs) such as selling, administrative, advertising or R&D, etc.

    - Selling, General and Administrative expenses (SG&A or SGA) - consist of the combined payroll costs. SGA is usually understood as a major portion of non-production related costs, in contrast to production costs such as direct labour.

  - Selling expenses - represent expenses needed to sell products (e.g., *salaries of sales people, commissions and travel expenses, advertising, freight, shipping, depreciation of sales store buildings and equipment*, etc.).

  - General and Administrative (G&A) expenses - represent expenses to manage the business (*salaries of officers / executives, legal and professional fees, utilities, insurance, depreciation of office building and equipment, office rents, office supplies*, etc.).

- Depreciation / Amortization - the charge with respect to fixed assets / intangible assets that have been capitalised on the balance sheet for a specific (accounting) period. It is a systematic and rational allocation of cost rather than the recognition of market value decrement.

- Research & Development (R&D) expenses - represent expenses included in research and development.

Expenses recognised in the income statement should be analysed either by nature (raw materials, transport costs, staffing costs, depreciation, employee benefit etc.) or by function (cost of sales, selling, administrative, etc.). (IAS 1.99) If an entity categorises by function, then additional information on the nature of expenses, at least, – depreciation, amortisation and employee benefits expense – must be disclosed. (IAS 1.104) The major exclusive of costs of goods sold, are classified as operating expenses. These represent the resources expended, except for inventory purchases, in generating the revenue for the period. Expenses often are divided into two broad sub classicifications selling expenses and administrative expenses.

Non-operating Section

- Other revenues or gains - revenues and gains from other than primary business activities (e.g., *rent, income from patents*, goodwill). It also includes unusual gains that are either unusual or infrequent, but not both (e.g., *gain from sale of securities* or *gain from disposal of fixed assets*)

- Other expenses or losses - expenses or losses not related to primary business operations, (e.g., *foreign exchange loss*).

- Finance costs - costs of borrowing from various creditors (e.g., *interest expenses, bank charges*).

- Income tax expense - sum of the amount of tax payable to tax authorities in the current reporting period (current tax liabilities/ tax payable) and the amount of deferred tax liabilities (or assets).

Irregular Items

They are reported separately because this way users can better predict future cash flows - irregular items most likely will not recur. These are reported *net of taxes*.

- Discontinued operations is the most common type of irregular items. Shifting business location(s), stopping production temporarily, or changes due to technological improvement do not qualify as discontinued operations. Discontinued operations *must* be shown separately.

Cumulative effect of changes in accounting policies (principles) is the difference between the book value of the affected assets (or liabilities) under the old policy (principle) and what the book value would have been if the new principle had been applied in the prior periods. For example, valuation of inventories using LIFO instead of weighted average method. The changes should be applied retrospectively and shown as adjustments to the *beginning* balance of affected components in Equity. All comparative financial statements should be restated. (IAS 8)

However, *changes in estimates* (e.g., estimated useful life of a fixed asset) only requires prospective changes. (IAS 8)

No items may be presented in the income statement as extraordinary items under IFRS regulations, but are permissible under US GAAP. (IAS 1.87) *Extraordinary items* are both unusual (abnormal) and infrequent, for example, unexpected natural disaster, expropriation, prohibitions under new regulations.

Additional items may be needed to fairly present the entity's results of operations. (IAS 1.85)

Disclosures

Certain items must be disclosed separately in the notes (or the statement of comprehensive income), if material, including: (IAS 1.98)

- Write-downs of inventories to net realisable value or of property, plant and equipment to recoverable amount, as well as *reversals* of such write-downs
- Restructurings of the activities of an entity and *reversals* of any provisions for the costs of restructuring
- Disposals of items of property, plant and equipment
- Disposals of investments
- Discontinued operations
- Litigation settlements
- Other reversals of provisions

Earnings Per Share

Because of its importance, earnings per share (EPS) are required to be disclosed on the face of the income statement. A company which reports any of the irregular items must also report EPS for these items either in the statement or in the notes.

$$\text{Earnings per share} = \frac{\text{Net income} - \text{Preferred stock dividends}}{\text{Weighted average of common stock shares outstanding}}$$

There are two forms of EPS reported:

- Basic: in this case "weighted average of shares outstanding" includes only actual stocks outstanding.
- Diluted: in this case "weighted average of shares outstanding" is calculated as if all stock options, warrants, convertible bonds, and other securities that could be transformed into shares *are* transformed. This increases the number of shares and so EPS decreases. Diluted EPS is considered to be a more reliable way to measure EPS.

Sample Income Statement

The following income statement is a very brief example prepared in accordance with IFRS. It does not show all possible kinds of accounts, but it shows the most usual ones. Please note the difference between IFRS and US GAAP when interpreting the following sample income statements.

Fitness Equipment Limited

INCOME STATEMENTS

(in millions)

Year Ended March 31,	2009	2008	2007
Revenue	$14,580.2	$11,900.4	$8,290.3
Cost of sales	(6,740.2)	(5,650.1)	(4,524.2)
Gross profit	*7,840.0*	*6,250.3*	*3,766.1*
SGA expenses	(3,624.6)	(3,296.3)	(3,034.0)

Operating profit	***$ 4,215.4***	***$ 2,954.0***	***$ 732.1***
Gains from disposal of fixed assets	46.3	-	-
Interest expense	(119.7)	(124.1)	(142.8)
Profit *before* tax	4,142.0	2,829.9	589.3
Income tax expense	(1,656.8)	(1,132.0)	(235.7)
Profit (or loss) for the year	***$ 2,485.2***	***$ 1,697.9***	***$ 353.6***

DEXTERITY INC. AND SUBSIDIARIES

CONSOLIDATED STATEMENTS OF OPERATIONS

(In millions)

Year Ended December 31,	2009	2008	2007
Revenue	$36,525.9	$29,827.6	$21,186.8

Cost of sales	(18,545.8)	(15,858.8)	(11,745.5)
Gross profit	*17,980.1*	*13,968.8*	*9,441.3*
Operating expenses:			
Selling, general and administrative expenses	(4,142.1)	(3,732.3)	(3,498.6)
Depreciation	(602.4)	(584.5)	(562.3)
Amortization	(209.9)	(141.9)	(111.8)
Impairment loss	(17,997.1)	—	—
Total operating expenses	(22,951.5)	(4,458.7)	(4,172.7)
Operating profit (or loss)	***$ (4,971.4)***	***$ 9,510.1***	***$ 5,268.6***
Interest income	25.3	11.7	12.0
Interest expense	(718.9)	(742.9)	(799.1)

Profit (or loss) from continuing operations *before* tax, share of profit (or loss) from associates and non-controlling interest	$ (5,665.0)	$ 8,778.9	$ 4,481.5
Income tax expense	(1,678.6)	(3,510.5)	(1,789.9)
Profit (or loss) from associates, *net of tax*	(20.8)	0.1	(37.3)
Profit (or loss) from non-controlling interest, *net of tax*	(5.1)	(4.7)	(3.3)
Profit (or loss) from continuing operations	**$ (3960.5)**	**$ 5,263.8**	**$ 2,651.0**
Profit (or loss) from discontinued operations, *net of tax*	(1,090.3)	(802.4)	164.6
Profit (or loss) for the year	***$ (2,870.2)***	***$ 4,461.4***	***$ 2,486.4***

Bottom Line

"Bottom line" is the net income that is calculated after subtracting the expenses from revenue. Since this forms the last line of the income statement, it is informally called "bottom line." It is important to investors as it represents the profit for the year attributable to the shareholders.

After revision to IAS 1 in 2003, the Standard is now using profit or loss for the year rather than *net profit or loss* or *net income* as the descriptive term for the bottom line of the income statement.

Requirements of IFRS

On 6 September 2007, the International Accounting Standards Board issued a revised *IAS 1: Presentation of Financial Statements,* which is effective for annual periods beginning on or after 1 January 2009.

A business entity adopting IFRS must include:

- a statement of comprehensive income or
- *two* separate statements comprising:
  1. an income statement displaying components of profit or loss *and*
  2. a *statement of comprehensive income* that *begins* with profit or loss (bottom line of the income statement) and displays the items of other comprehensive income for the reporting period. (IAS1.81)

All non-owner changes in equity (i.e., *comprehensive income*) shall be presented in either in the statement of comprehensive income (or in a separate income statement and a statement of comprehensive income). Components of comprehensive income may not be presented in the statement of changes in equity.

Comprehensive income for a period includes profit or loss (net income) for that period and other comprehensive income recognised in that period.

All items of income and expense recognised in a period must be included in profit or loss unless a Standard or an Interpretation requires otherwise. (IAS 1.88) Some IFRSs require or permit that some components to be excluded from profit or loss and instead to be included in other comprehensive income. (IAS 1.89)

Items and Disclosures

The statement of comprehensive income should include: (IAS 1.82)

1. Revenue
2. Finance costs (including interest expenses)
3. Share of the profit or loss of associates and joint ventures accounted for using the equity method
4. Tax expense
5. A *single* amount comprising the total of (1) the *post-tax* profit or loss of *discontinued operations* and (2) the *post-tax* gain or loss recognised on the disposal of the assets or disposal group(s) constituting the *discontinued operation*

6. Profit or loss
7. Each component of other comprehensive income classified by nature
8. Share of the other comprehensive income of associates and joint ventures accounted for using the equity method
9. Total comprehensive income

The following items must also be disclosed in the statement of comprehensive income as allocations for the period: (IAS 1.83)

- Profit or loss for the period attributable to non-controlling interests and owners of the parent
- Total comprehensive income attributable to non-controlling interests and owners of the parent

No items may be presented in the statement of comprehensive income (or in the income statement, if separately presented) or in the notes as *extraordinary items*.

Income Statement: The major components of income statement are:

- Income
  - Sales
  - Other income
- Expenses
  - Operating expenses
  - Financial expenses
  - Tax provision
  - Net profit
- Appropriation of net profit
  - Transfer to reserves
  - Distribution of profit as dividend

Table below provides an abridged version of the income statement of Natco Pharma Ltd.

Natco Pharma Ltd. **Income Statement for the period: [in Rs. Crore]**			
	2008-09	2007-08	2006-07
INCOME :			
Sales Turnover	273.79	235.91	193.23

Excise Duty	4.1	6.87	8.45
Net Sales	269.69	229.04	184.78
Other Income	11.5	18.39	18.21
Stock Adjustments	7.1	4.05	6.25
Total Income	288.29	251.48	209.24
EXPENDITURE :			
Raw Materials	96.6	91.93	79.32
Power & Fuel Cost	15.24	11.02	10.13
Employee Cost	35.68	29.28	25.06
Other Manufacturing Expenses	17.03	14.14	11.19
Selling and Administration Expenses	40.63	29.21	23.99
Miscellaneous Expenses	4.3	3.04	5.55
Total Expenditure	209.48	178.62	155.24
Operating Profit (PBDIT)	78.81	72.86	54.00
Interest	15.05	9.73	6.61
PBDT	63.76	63.13	47.39
Depreciation	10.35	8.59	7.61
Profit Before Tax	53.41	54.54	39.78
Tax	10.67	14.49	9.32
Reported Net Profit	42.74	40.05	30.46
Extraordinary Items	0.06	-0.38	8.69
Adjusted Net Profit	42.68	40.43	21.77
P & L Balance brought forward	81.97	49.43	25.84
Appropriations	7.1	7.51	6.87
P & L Balance carried down	117.61	81.97	49.43
Dividend	3.5	3.43	3.4

Cash flow Statement: Cash is considered as life blood of a business. Cash flow statement of a company provides the inflow and outflow of cash during a particular period. Several questions which are not answered by balance sheet and income statement can possibly be answered by looking at the cash flow statement. The cash flow statement classifies the cash flow into three parts:

- Cash flow from operating activities: The profit adjusted for depreciation, gains and/or losses on sale of non-current assets, tax paid, and working capital changes. For a running organization this is supposed to be the most vital source of cash flow.
- Cash flow from investment activities: Purchases of non-current assets and proceeds on the sale of non-current assets.
- Cash flow from financing activities: Proceeds on the issue of equity/preference shares and loans/debentures and the redemption of redeemable preference shares and loan/ debentures. Payment of interest and dividend are considered as application of cash in this category.

Statement of Changes in Equity

A Statement of changes in equity and similarly the statement of changes in owner's equity for a sole trader, statement of changes in partners' equity for a partnership, statement of changes in Shareholders' equity for a Company or statement of changes in Taxpayers' equity for Government financial statements is one of the four basic financial statements.

The statement explains the changes in a company's Share Capital, accumulated reserves and retained earnings over the reporting period. It breaks down changes in the owners' interest in the organization, and in the application of retained profit or surplus from one accounting period to the next. Line items typically include profits or losses from operations, dividends paid, issue or redemption of shares, revaluation reserve and any other items charged or credited to accumulated other comprehensive income. In also includes the Non-Controlling Interest attribuable to other individuals and organisations.

The statement is expected under the generally accepted accounting principles and explains the owners' equity shown on the balance sheet, where:

owners' equity = assets – liabilities.

Requirements of the U.S. GAAP

In the United States this is called a *statement of retained earnings* and it is required under the U.S. Generally Accepted Accounting Principles (U.S. GAAP) whenever comparative balance sheets and income statements are presented. It may appear in the balance sheet, in a combined income statement and changes in retained earnings statement, or as a separate schedule.

Therefore, the statement of retained earnings uses information from the income statement and provides information to the balance sheet.

Retained earnings are part of the balance sheet (another basic financial statement) under "stockholders equity (shareholders' equity)" and is mostly affected by net income earned during a period of time by the company less any dividends paid to the company's owners / stockholders. The retained earnings account on the balance sheet is said to represent an "accumulation of earnings" since net profits and losses are added/subtracted from the account from period to period.

Retained Earnings are part of the "Statement of Changes in Equity". The general equation can be expressed as following:

Ending Retained Earnings = *Beginning* Retained Earnings – Dividends Paid + Net Income

This equation is necessary to use to find the Profit Before Tax to use in the Cash Flow Statement under Operating Activities when using the indirect method. This is used whenever a comprehensive income statement is not given but only the balance sheet is given.

Requirements of IFRS

IAS 1 requires a business entity to present a *separate statement of changes in equity* (SOCE) as one of the components of financial statements.

The statement shall show: (IAS1.106)

1. total comprehensive income for the period, showing separately amounts attributable to owners of the parent and to non-controlling interests
2. the effects of retrospective application, when applicable, for each component
3. reconciliations between the carrying amounts at the *beginning* and the *end* of the period for each component of equity, separately disclosing:
    - profit or loss
    - each item of other comprehensive income
    - transactions with owners, showing separately contributions by and distributions to owners and changes in ownership interests in subsidiaries that *do not result in a loss of control*

However, the amount of dividends recognised as distributions, and the related amount per share, *may* be presented in the notes instead of presenting in the statement of changes in equity. (IAS1.107)

For small and medium enterprises (SMEs), the statement of changes in equity should show all changes in equity including:

- total comprehensive income
- owners' investments
- dividends
- owners' withdrawals of capital
- treasury share transactions

They can omit the statement of changes in equity if the entity has no owner investments or withdrawals other than dividends, and elects to present a combined statement of comprehensive income and retained earnings.

Financial Analysis

Financial analysis (also referred to as financial statement analysis or accounting analysis or Analysis of finance) refers to an assessment of the viability, stability and profitability of a business, sub-business or project.

It is performed by professionals who prepare reports using ratios that make use of information taken from financial statements and other reports. These reports are usually presented to top management as one of their bases in making business decisions. Financial analysis may determine if a business will:

- Continue or discontinue its main operation or part of its business;
- Make or purchase certain materials in the manufacture of its product;
- Acquire or rent/lease certain machineries and equipment in the production of its goods;
- Issue stocks or negotiate for a bank loan to increase its working capital;
- Make decisions regarding investing or lending capital;
- Make other decisions that allow management to make an informed selection on various alternatives in the conduct of its business.

Goals

Financial analysts often assess the following elements of a firm:

1. Profitability - its ability to earn income and sustain growth in both the short- and long-term. A company's degree of profitability is usually based on the income statement, which reports on the company's results of operations;
2. Solvency - its ability to pay its obligation to creditors and other third parties in the long-term;
3. Liquidity - its ability to maintain positive cash flow, while satisfying immediate obligations;

   Both 2 and 3 are based on the company's balance sheet, which indicates the financial condition of a business as of a given point in time.

4. Stability - the firm's ability to remain in business in the long run, without having to sustain significant losses in the conduct of its business. Assessing a company's stability requires the use of both the income statement and the balance sheet, as well as other financial and non-financial indicators. etc.

Method

Financial analysts often compare financial ratios (of solvency, profitability, growth, etc.):

- Past Performance - Across historical time periods for the same firm (the last 5 years for example),
- Future Performance - Using historical figures and certain mathematical and statistical techniques, including present and future values, This extrapolation method is the main source of errors in financial analysis as past statistics can be poor predictors of future prospects.
- Comparative Performance - Comparison between similar firms.

These ratios are calculated by dividing a (group of) account balance(s), taken from the balance sheet and / or the income statement, by another, for example :

Net income / equity = return on equity (ROE)

Net income / total assets = return on assets (ROA)

Asset Management Ratios gauge how efficiently a company can change assets into sales.

Stock price / earnings per share = P/E ratio

Comparing financial ratios is merely one way of conducting financial analysis. Financial ratios face several theoretical challenges:

- They say little about the firm's prospects in an absolute sense. Their insights about relative performance require a reference point from other time periods or similar firms.
- One ratio holds little meaning. As indicators, ratios can be logically interpreted in at least two ways. One can partially overcome this problem by combining several related ratios to paint a more comprehensive picture of the firm's performance.
- Seasonal factors may prevent year-end values from being representative. A ratio's values may be distorted as account balances change from the beginning to the end of an accounting period. Use average values for such accounts whenever possible.
- Financial ratios are no more objective than the accounting methods employed. Changes in accounting policies or choices can yield drastically different ratio values.
- Fundamental analysis.

Financial analysts can also use percentage analysis which involves reducing a series of figures as a percentage of some base amount. For example, a group of items can be expressed as a percentage of net income. When proportionate changes in the same figure over a given time period expressed as a percentage is known as horizontal analysis. Vertical or common-size analysis, reduces all items on a statement to a "common size" as a percentage of some base value which assists in comparability with other companies of different sizes. As a result, all Income Statement items are divided by Sales, and all Balance Sheet items are divided by Total Assets.

Another method is comparative analysis. This provides a better way to determine trends. Comparative analysis presents the same information for two or more time periods and is presented side-by-side to allow for easy analysis.

Sources of Financial Information

- ✓ Annual Reports of Companies
- ✓ Secondary databases/ information services
- ✓ Stock exchanges
- ✓ Periodicals and Newspapers
- ✓ Websites companies and other investment advisory firms.

Tools of FSA

- Trend Analysis: Comparison of major financial figures over a time period and observing a trend in the same;
- Comparative Statements:
  - Comparison of financial performance between current year and previous year
  - Comparison with other companies in the same industry/ sector
- Common Size Statements: A financial statement presented by representing each item as a percentage to the total amount of which it is a part.
  - Common size balance sheet: Constructed by showing each item of asset as a percentage of total assets, similarly each item of liability and owner's equity is shown as a percentage of total liabilities and owners equity.
  - Common size income statement: Here one can show the net sales as 100% and each of the components of expenses and profits as a percentage of net sales.
- Ratio Analysis: Ratio is a relationship between two items taken from one or more financial statement or market data. The items are expected to be related to justify the calculation. One can measure and comment on the profitability, solvency, efficiency and market standing of the company by using financial ratios.

Financial Ratio

A financial ratio or accounting ratio is a relative magnitude of two selected numerical values taken from an enterprise's financial statements. Often used in accounting, there are many standard ratios used to try to evaluate the overall financial condition of a corporation or other organization. Financial ratios may be used by managers within a firm, by current and potential shareholders (owners) of a firm, and by a firm's creditors. Financial analysts use financial ratios to compare the strengths and weaknesses in various companies. If shares in a company are traded in a financial market, the market price of the shares is used in certain financial ratios.

Ratios can be expressed as a decimal value, such as 0.10, or given as an equivalent percent value, such as 10%. Some ratios are usually quoted as percentages, especially ratios that are usually or always less than 1, such as earnings yield, while others are usually quoted as decimal numbers, especially ratios that are usually more than 1, such as P/E ratio; these latter are also called multiples. Given any ratio, one can take its reciprocal; if the ratio was above 1, the reciprocal will be below 1, and conversely. The reciprocal expresses the same information, but may be more understandable: for instance, the earnings yield can be compared with bond yields, while the P/E ratio cannot be: for example, a P/E ratio of 20 corresponds to an earnings yield of 5%.

Sources of Data for Financial Ratios

Values used in calculating financial ratios are taken from the balance sheet, income statement, statement of cash flows or (sometimes) the statement of changes in equity. These comprise the firm's "accounting statements" or financial statements. The statements' data is based on the accounting method and accounting standards used by the organisation.

Purpose and Types of Ratios

Financial ratios quantify many aspects of a business and are an integral part of the financial statement analysis. Financial ratios are categorized according to the financial aspect of the business which the ratio measures. Liquidity ratios measure the availability of cash to pay debt. Activity ratios measure how quickly a firm converts non-cash assets to cash assets. Debt ratios measure the firm's ability to repay long-term debt. Profitability ratios measure the firm's use of its assets and control of its expenses to generate an acceptable rate of return. Market ratios measure investor response to owning a company's stock and also the cost of issuing stock. These are concerned with the return on investment for shareholders, and with the relationship between return and the value of an investment in company's shares.

Financial ratios allow for comparisons

- between companies
- between industries
- between different time periods for one company
- between a single company and its industry average

Ratios generally are not useful unless they are benchmarked against something else, like past performance or another company. Thus, the ratios of firms in different industries, which face different risks, capital requirements, and competition are usually hard to compare.

Accounting Methods and Principles

Financial ratios may not be directly comparable between companies that use different accounting methods or follow various standard accounting practices. Most public companies are required by law to use generally accepted accounting principles for their home countries, but private companies, partnerships and sole proprietorships may not use accrual basis accounting. Large multi-national corporations may use International Financial Reporting Standards to produce their financial statements, or they may use the generally accepted accounting principles of their home country.

There is no international standard for calculating the summary data presented in all financial statements, and the terminology is not always consistent between companies, industries, countries and time periods.

Abbreviations and Terminology

Various abbreviations may be used in financial statements, especially financial statements summarized on the Internet. Sales reported by a firm are usually net sales, which deduct returns, allowances, and early payment discounts from the charge on an invoice. Net income is always the amount *after* taxes, depreciation, amortization, and interest, unless otherwise stated. Otherwise, the amount would be EBIT, or EBITDA.

Companies that are primarily involved in providing services with labour do not generally report "Sales" based on hours. These companies tend to report "revenue" based on the monetary value of income that the services provide.

Note that Shareholders' Equity and Owner's Equity are *not* the same thing, Shareholder's Equity represents the total number of shares in the company multiplied by each share's book value; Owner's Equity represents the total number of shares that an individual shareholder owns (usually the owner with controlling interest), multiplied by each share's book value. It is important to make this distinction when calculating ratios.

Abbreviations

(*Note:* These are not ratios, but values in currency.)

- COGS = Cost of goods sold, or cost of sales.
- EBIT = Earnings before interest and taxes
- EBITDA = Earnings before interest, taxes, depreciation, and amortization
- EPS = Earnings per share

Ratios

Profitability Ratios

Profitability ratios measure the company's use of its assets and control of its expenses to generate an acceptable rate of return.

Gross margin, Gross profit margin or Gross Profit Rate

$$\frac{\text{Gross Profit}}{\text{Net Sales}} \text{ ::: OR ::: } \frac{\text{Net Sales -- COGS}}{\text{Net Sales}}$$

Operating margin, Operating Income Margin, Operating profit margin or Return on sales (ROS)

$$\frac{\text{Operating Income}}{\text{Net Sales}}$$

Note: Operating income is the difference between operating revenues and operating expenses, but it is also sometimes used as a synonym for EBIT and operating profit. This is true if the firm has no non-operating income. (Earnings before interest and taxes / Sales).

Profit margin, net margin or net profit margin

$$\frac{\text{Net Profit}}{\text{Net Sales}}$$

Return on equity (ROE)

$$\frac{\text{Net Income}}{\text{Average Shareholders Equity}}$$

Return on assets (ROA ratio or Du Pont Ratio)

$$\frac{\text{Net Income}}{\text{Average Total Assets}}$$

Return on assets (ROA)

$$\frac{\text{Net Income}}{\text{Total Assets}}$$

Return on assets Du Pont (ROA Du Pont)

$$\left(\frac{\text{Net Income}}{\text{Net Sales}}\right)\left(\frac{\text{Net Sales}}{\text{Total Assets}}\right)$$

Return on Equity Du Pont (ROE Du Pont)

$$\left(\frac{\text{Net Income}}{\text{Net Sales}}\right)\left(\frac{\text{Net Sales}}{\text{Average Assets}}\right)\left(\frac{\text{Average Assets}}{\text{Average Equity}}\right)$$

Return on net assets (RONA)

$$\frac{\text{Net Income}}{\text{Fixed Assets + Working Capital}}$$

Return on capital (ROC)

$$\frac{\text{EBIT (1–Tax Rate)}}{\text{Invested Capital}}$$

Risk adjusted return on capital (RAROC)

$$\frac{\text{Expected Return}}{\text{Economic Capital}} \text{ ::: OR ::: } \frac{\text{Expected Return}}{\text{Value at Risk}}$$

Return on capital employed (ROCE)

$$\frac{\text{EBIT}}{\text{Capital Employed}}$$

Note: this is somewhat similar to (ROI), which calculates Net Income per Owner's Equity

Cash flow return on investment (CFROI)

$$\frac{\text{Cash Flow}}{\text{Market Recapitalisation}}$$

Efficiency ratio

$$\frac{\text{Non-Interest expense}}{\text{Revenue}}$$

Net gearing

$$\frac{\text{Net debt}}{\text{Equity}}$$

Basic Earnings Power Ratio

$$\frac{\text{EBIT}}{\text{Total Assets}}$$

Liquidity Ratios

Liquidity ratios measure the availability of cash to pay debt.

Current ratio (Working Capital Ratio)

$$\frac{\text{Current Assets}}{\text{Current Liabilities}}$$

Acid-test ratio (Quick ratio)

$$\frac{\text{Current Assets -- (Inventories + Prepayments)}}{\text{Current Liabilities}}$$

Cash ratio

$$\frac{\text{Cash and Marketable Securities}}{\text{Current Liabilities}}$$

Operating cash flow ratio

$$\frac{\text{Operating Cash Flow}}{\text{Total Debts}}$$

Activity Ratios (Efficiency Ratios)

Activity ratios measure the effectiveness of the firm's use of resources.

Average collection period

$$\frac{\text{Accounts Receivable}}{\text{Annual Credit Sales} \div 365\text{ Days}}$$

Degree of Operating Leverage (DOL)

$$\frac{\text{Percent Change in Net Operating Income}}{\text{Percent Change in Sales}}$$

DSO Ratio.

$$\frac{\text{Accounts Receivable}}{\text{Total Annual Sales} \div 365\text{ Days}}$$

Average payment period

$$\frac{\text{Accounts Payable}}{\text{Annual Credit Purchases} \div 365\text{ Days}}$$

Asset turnover

$$\frac{\text{Net Sales}}{\text{Total Assets}}$$

Stock turnover ratio

$$\frac{\text{Cost of Goods Sold}}{\text{Average Inventory}}$$

Receivables Turnover Ratio

$$\frac{\text{Net Credit Sales}}{\text{Average Net Receivables}}$$

Inventory conversion ratio

$$\frac{365\text{ Days}}{\text{Inventory Turnover}}$$

Inventory conversion period (essentially same thing as above)

$$\left(\frac{\text{Inventory}}{\text{Cost of Goods Sold}}\right)365\text{ Days}$$

Receivables conversion period

$$\left(\frac{\text{Receivables}}{\text{Net Sales}}\right)365\text{ Days}$$

Payables conversion period

$$\left(\frac{\text{Accounts Payables}}{\text{Purchases}}\right)365\text{ Days}$$

Cash Conversion Cycle

Inventory Conversion Period + Receivables Conversion Period - Payables Conversion Period

Debt Ratios (Leveraging Ratios)

Debt ratios quantify the firm's ability to repay long-term debt. Debt ratios measure financial leverage.

Debt ratio

$$\frac{\text{Total Liabilities}}{\text{Total Assets}}$$

Debt to equity ratio

$$\frac{\text{Long-term Debt} + \text{Value of Leases}}{\text{Average Shareholders Equity}}$$

Long-term Debt to equity (LT Debt to Equity)

$$\frac{\text{Long-term Debt}}{\text{Average Shareholders Equity}}$$

Times interest earned ratio (Interest Coverage Ratio)

$$\frac{\text{EBIT}}{\text{Annual Interest Expense}}$$

OR

$$\frac{\text{Net Income}}{\text{Annual Interest Expense}}$$

Debt service coverage ratio

$$\frac{\text{Net Operating Income}}{\text{Total Debt Service}}$$

Market Ratios

Market ratios measure investor response to owning a company's stock and also the cost of issuing stock. These are concerned with the return on investment for shareholders, and with the relationship between return and the value of an investment in company's shares.

Earnings per share (EPS)

$$\frac{\text{Net Earnings}}{\text{Number of Shares}}$$

Payout ratio

$$\frac{\text{Dividends}}{\text{Earnings}}$$

OR

$$\frac{\text{Dividends}}{\text{EPS}}$$

Dividend cover (the inverse of Payout Ratio)

$$\frac{\text{Earnings per Share}}{\text{Dividend per Share}}$$

P/E ratio

$$\frac{\text{Market Price per Share}}{\text{Diluted EPS}}$$

Dividend yield

$$\frac{\text{Dividend}}{\text{Current Market Price}}$$

Cash flow ratio or Price/cash flow ratio

$$\frac{\text{Market Price per Share}}{\text{Present Value of Cash Flow per Share}}$$

Price to book value ratio (P/B or PBV)

$$\frac{\text{Market Price per Share}}{\text{Balance Sheet Price per Share}}$$

Price/sales ratio

$$\frac{\text{Market Price per Share}}{\text{Gross Sales}}$$

PEG ratio

$$\frac{\text{Market Price per Share}}{\text{Gross Sales}}$$

Other Market Ratios

EV/EBITDA

$$\frac{\text{Enterprise Value}}{\text{EBITDA}}$$

EV/Sales

$$\frac{\text{Enterprise Value}}{\text{Net Sales}}$$

Cost/Income ratio

Sector-specific ratios

EV/capacity

EV/output

Capital Budgeting Ratios

In addition to assisting management and owners in diagnosing the financial health of their company, ratios can also help managers make decisions about investments or projects that the company is considering to take, such as acquisitions, or expansion.

Many formal methods are used in capital budgeting, including the techniques such as

- Net present value
- Profitability index
- Internal rate of return
- Modified internal rate of return
- Equivalent annuity

Debt-to-equity Ratio

The debt-to-equity ratio (D/E) is a financial ratio indicating the relative proportion of shareholders' equity and debt used to finance a company's assets. Closely related to leveraging, the ratio is also known as risk, gearing or leverage. The two components are often taken from the firm's balance sheet or statement of financial position (so-called book value), but the ratio may also be calculated using market values for both, if the company's debt and equity are publicly traded, or using a combination of book value for debt and market value for equity financially.

Usage

Preferred stock can be considered part of debt or equity. Attributing preferred shares to one or the other is partially a subjective decision but will also take into account the specific features of the preferred shares.

When used to calculate a company's financial leverage, the debt usually includes only the Long Term Debt (LTD). Quoted ratios can even exclude the current portion of the LTD. The composition of equity and debt and its influence on the value of the firm is much debated and also described in the Modigliani-Miller theorem.

Financial economists and academic papers will usually refer to all liabilities as debt, and the statement that equity plus liabilities equals assets is therefore an accounting identity (it is, by definition, true). Other definitions of debt to equity may not respect this accounting identity, and should be carefully compared. Generally speaking, a high ratio may indicate that the company is much resourced with (outside) borrowing as compared to funding from shareholders.

Formula

In a general sense, the ratio is simply debt divided by equity. However, what is classified as debt can differ depending on the interpretation used. Thus, the ratio can take on a number of forms including:

- Debt / Equity
- Long-term Debt / Equity
- Total Liabilities / Equity

In a basic sense, Total Debt / Equity is a measure of all of a company's future obligations on the balance sheet relative to equity. However, the ratio can be more discerning as to what is actually a borrowing, as opposed to other types of obligations that might exist on the balance sheet under the liabilities section. For example, often only the liabilities accounts that are actually labelled as "debt" on the balance sheet are used in the numerator, instead of the broader category of "total liabilities". In other words, actual borrowings like bank loans and interest-bearing debt securities are used, as opposed to the broadly inclusive category of total liabilities which, in addition to debt-labelled accounts, can include accrual accounts like unearned revenue.

Another popular iteration of the ratio is the long-term-debt-to-equity ratio which uses only long-term debt in the numerator instead of total debt or total liabilities. Total debt includes both long-term debt and short-term debt which is made up of actual short-term debt that has actual short-term maturities and also the portion of long-term debt that has become short-term in the current period because it is now nearing maturity. This second classification of short-term debt is carved out of long-term debt and is reclassified as a current liability called *current portion of long-term debt* (or a similar name). The remaining long-term debt is used in the numerator of the long-term-debt-to-equity ratio.

A similar ratio is debt-to-capital (D/C), where capital is the sum of debt and equity:

D/C = total liabilities / total capital = debt / (debt + equity)

The relationship between D/E and D/C is:

D/C = D/(D+E) = D/E / (1 + D/E)

The debt-to-total assets (D/A) is defined as

D/A = total liabilities / total assets = debt / (debt + equity + non-financial liabilities)

It is a problematic measure of leverage, because an increase in non-financial liabilities reduces this ratio. Nevertheless, it is in common use.

In the financial industry (particularly banking), a similar concept is equity to total assets (or equity to risk-weighted assets), otherwise known as capital adequacy.

Background

On a balance sheet, the formal definition is that debt (liabilities) plus equity equals assets, or any equivalent reformulation. Both the formulas below are therefore identical:

A = D + E

E = A – D or D = A – E.

Debt to equity can also be reformulated in terms of assets or debt:

D/E = D /(A – D) = (A – E) / E.

Example

General Electric Co.

- Debt / equity: 4.304 (total debt / stockholder equity) (340/79). Note: This is often presented in percentage form, for instance 430.4.
- Other equity / shareholder equity: 7.177 (568,303,000/79,180,000)
- Equity ratio: 12% (shareholder equity / all equity) (79,180,000/647,483,000)

Current Ratio

The current ratio is a liquidity ratio that measures whether or not a firm has enough resources to meet its short-term obligations. It compares a firm's current assets to its current liabilities, and is expressed as follows:

$$\text{Current ratio} = \frac{\text{Current Assets}}{\text{Current Liabilities}}$$

The current ratio is an indication of a firm's liquidity. Acceptable current ratios vary from industry to industry. In many cases a creditor would consider a high current ratio to be better than a low current ratio, because a high current ratio indicates that the company is more likely to pay the creditor back. Large current ratios are not always a good sign for investors. If the company's current ratio is too high it may indicate that the company is not efficiently using its current assets or its short-term financing facilities.

If current liabilities exceed current assets the current ratio will be less than 1. A current ratio of less than 1 indicates that the company may have problems meeting its short-term obligations. Some types of businesses can operate with a current ratio of less than one however. If inventory turns into cash much more rapidly than the accounts payable become due, then the firm's current ratio can comfortably remain less than one. Inventory is valued at the cost of acquiring it and the firm intends to sell the inventory for more than this cost. The sale will therefore generate substantially more cash than the value of inventory on the balance sheet. Low current ratios can also be justified for businesses that can collect cash from customers long before they need to pay their suppliers

Limitations of Current Ratio

1. The ratio is only useful when two companies are compared within industry because inter industry business operations differ substantially.
2. To determine liquidity, the current ratio is not as helpful as the quick ratio, because it includes all those assets that may not be easily liquidated, like prepaid expenses and inventory.

Quick Ratio

In finance, the acid-test or quick ratio or liquidity ratio measures the ability of a company to use its *near cash* or quick assets to extinguish or retire its current liabilities immediately. Quick assets include those current assets that presumably can be quickly converted to cash at close to their book values. It is the ratio between quick or liquid assets and current liabilities.

A normal liquid ratio is considered to be 1:1. A company with a quick ratio of less than 1 cannot currently fully pay back its current liabilities.

This ratio is considered to be much better and reliable as a tool for assessment of liquidity position of firms.

Formula

$$\text{Liquid Ratio} = \frac{\text{Liquid Assets}}{\text{Current Liabilities}}$$

Formula

$$\text{Quick (Acid Test) Ratio} = \frac{\text{Cash and Cash Equivalent} + \text{Marketable Securities} + \text{Accounts Receivable}}{\text{Current Liabilities}}$$

Note that inventory is excluded from the sum of assets in the quick ratio, but included in the current ratio. Ratios are tests of viability for business entities but do not give a complete picture of the business' health. If a business has large amounts in accounts receivable which are due for payment after a long period (say 120 days), and essential business expenses and accounts payable due for immediate payment, the quick ratio may look healthy when the business is actually about to run out of cash. In contrast, if the business has negotiated fast payment or cash from customers, and long terms from suppliers, it may have a very low quick ratio and yet be very healthy.

Generally, the acid test ratio should be 1:1 or higher, however this varies widely by industry. In general, the higher the ratio, the greater the company's liquidity (i.e., the better able to meet current obligations using liquid assets).

Return on Equity

In corporate finance, the return on equity (ROE) is a measure of the profitability of a business in relation to the book value of shareholder equity, also known as *net assets* or *assets minus liabilities*. ROE is a measure of how well a company uses investments to generate earnings growth.

The Formula

$$\text{ROE} = \frac{\text{Net Income}}{\text{Shareholder Equity}} \times 100$$

ROE is equal to a fiscal year net income (after preferred stock dividends, before common stock dividends), divided by total equity (excluding preferred shares), expressed as a percentage.

Usage

ROE is especially used for comparing the performance of companies in the same industry. As with return on capital, a ROE is a measure of management's ability to generate income from the equity available to it. ROEs of 15-20% are generally considered good.

ROEs are also a factor in stock valuation, in association with other financial ratios. In general, stock prices are influenced by earnings per share (EPS), so that stock of a company with a 20% ROE will generally cost twice as much as one with a 10% ROE.

ROE and Sustainable Growth

The benefit of low ROEs comes from reinvesting earnings to aid company growth. The benefit can also come as a dividend on common shares or as a combination of dividends and company reinvestment. ROE is less relevant if earnings are not reinvested.

- The sustainable growth model shows that when firms pay dividends, earnings growth lowers. If the dividend payout is 20%, the growth expected will be only 80% of the ROE rate.
- The growth rate will be lower if earnings are used to buy back shares. If the shares are

bought at a multiple of book value (a factor of x times book value), the incremental earnings returns will be reduced by that same factor (ROE/x).

- New investments may not be as profitable as the existing business. Ask "what is the company doing with its earnings?"
- ROE is calculated from the company perspective, on the company as a whole. Since much financial manipulation is accomplished with new share issues and buyback, the investor may have a different recalculated value 'per share' (earnings per share/book value per share).

The DuPont Formula

The DuPont formula, also known as the strategic profit model, is a common way to break down ROE into three important components. Essentially, ROE will equal the net profit margin multiplied by asset turnover multiplied by financial leverage. Splitting return on equity into three parts makes it easier to understand changes in ROE over time. For example, if the net margin increases, every sale brings in more money, resulting in a higher overall ROE. Similarly, if the asset turnover increases, the firm generates more sales for every unit of assets owned, again resulting in a higher overall ROE. Finally, increasing financial leverage means that the firm uses more debt financing relative to equity financing. Interest payments to creditors are tax deductible, but dividend payments to shareholders are not. Thus, a higher proportion of debt in the firm's capital structure leads to higher ROE. Financial leverage benefits diminish as the risk of defaulting on interest payments increases. So if the firm takes on too much debt, the cost of debt rises as creditors demand a higher risk premium, and ROE decreases. Increased debt will make a positive contribution to a firm's ROE only if the matching Return on assets (ROA) of that debt exceeds the interest rate on the debt.

$$\text{ROE} = \frac{\text{Net income}}{\text{Sales}} \times \frac{\text{Sales}}{\text{Total Assets}} \times \frac{\text{Total Assets}}{\text{Shareholder Equity}}$$

Profit Margin

Profit margin, net margin, net profit margin or net profit ratio is a measure of profitability. It is calculated by finding the net profit as a percentage of the revenue.

$$\text{net profit margin} = \frac{\text{net profit}}{\text{revenue}}$$

Net profit is revenue minus cost.

Overview

Profit margin is calculated with selling price (or revenue) taken as base times 100. It is the percentage of selling price that is turned into profit, whereas "profit percentage" or "markup" is the percentage of cost price that one gets as profit on top of cost price. While selling something one should know what percentage of profit one will get on a particular investment, so companies calculate profit percentage to find the ratio of profit to cost.

The profit margin is used mostly for internal comparison. It is difficult to accurately compare the net profit ratio for different entities. Individual businesses' operating and financing arrangements vary so much that different entities are bound to have different levels of expenditure, so that comparison of one with another can have little meaning. A low profit margin indicates a low margin of safety: higher risk that a decline in sales will erase profits and result in a net loss, or a negative margin.

Profit margin is an indicator of a company's pricing strategies and how well it controls costs. Differences in competitive strategy and product mix cause the profit margin to vary among different companies.

- If an investor makes $10 revenue and it cost him $1 to earn it, when he takes his cost away he is left with 90% margin. He made 900% profit on his $1 investment.
- If an investor makes $10 revenue and it cost him $5 to earn it, when he takes his cost away he is left with 50% margin. He made 100% profit on his $5 investment.
- If an investor makes $10 revenue and it cost him $9 to earn it, when he takes his cost away he is left with 10% margin. He made 11.11% profit on his $9 investment.

Profit Percentage

On the other hand, profit percentage is calculated with cost price taken as base

$$\text{profit percentage} = \frac{\text{net profit}}{\text{cost price}} * 100\%$$

Suppose that something is bought for $50 and sold for $100.

Cost price = $50

Selling price (revenue) = $100

Profit = $100 – $50 = $50

Profit percentage (profit divided by cost) = $50/$50 = 100%

Return on investment multiple = $50 / $50 (profit divided by cost).

If the revenue is the same as the cost, profit percentage is 0%. The result above or below 100% can be calculated as the percentage of return on investment. In this example, the return on investment is a multiple of 0.5 of the investment, resulting in a 50% gain.

Profitability Ratios

Generation of profit by business is taken as a sound objective of business organization. This also acts as an incentive for stakeholders like investors and management. Profitability ratios are of two types viz. those related to revenue and those related to investment.

- Gross profit margin: Gross profit is defined as the difference between sales and cost of goods sold. For companies in manufacturing sector this ratio indicates the coverage of major expenses particularly with respect to manufacturing of products.

- Operating profit margin: Operating profit is calculated after subtracting other operating expenses (like selling and distribution expenses) from gross profit. Operating profit is also known as earnings before interest and tax (EBIT). Operating profit margin is the ration between operating profit and sales. Higher operating profit margin indicates the efficiency of organization and makes companies more comfortable in meeting non- operating expenses like interest.
- Net profit margin: This ratio indicates the profit meant for shareholders – both preference and equity and is measured as a ratio of net profit to sales. This is also another measure of business efficiency.
- Return on investment or Earning Power: Earnings before interest and taxes (EBIT) to Total Assets: This ratio indicates the return available to all investors together irrespective of proportion of different types of capital. This ratio is ideal for comparison across firms since it is not affected by capital structure and tax policy of the firms. It reflects the earning power of assets.
- Return on equity: This is the return available for equity shareholders, the residual owners of the business. The return on equity is measured as below:

$$\text{Return on Equity } (\text{RoE}) = \frac{\text{Net profit}}{\text{Average net worth}}$$

  Net worth includes equity, reserves and surplus adjusted for any fictitious assets. The net worth of current year and previous year are averaged for the purpose. Besides profitability, RoE is affected by leverage, i.e. presence of debt in capital structure. Under good conditions, leverage magnifies RoE compared to an unlevered company.
- Earnings per share (EPS): This ratio is measured by dividing net profit [available for equity shareholders] with number equity shares. This is an absolute measure and indicated in the currency. This measure can be misleading while comparing between different companies when their equity capital structure in terms of amount of paid-up capital or face value share are different.

$$\text{EPS (in Rs.)} = \frac{\text{Profit after tax less preference dividend(if any)}}{\text{Number of equity shares}}$$

- Dividend per share (DPS): This is measured as below:

$$\text{DPS} = \frac{\text{Equity dividend}}{\text{Number of equity shares}}$$

Investors like senior citizens and pension funds prefer higher dividend since such income is considered as a regular source of income. Besides, declaration of dividend is considered normally as a healthy sign since it denotes liquidity and profitability of the companies.

Efficiency Ratios: Such ratios (also known as turnover ratios) indicate efficiency in asset utilization and in broad terms are expressed as a relationship between sales and assets.

- Total assets turnover ration (TATR): This ratio measures the revenue generation in comparison to the funds deployed by the investors. Higher the ratio is always better. This reflects overall efficiency in utilization of assets.

$$\text{TATR} = \frac{\text{Net sales}}{\text{Average total assets}}$$

- Similarly to know the efficiency of a particular type of asset the TATR is modified to reflect the average value of particular asset. The other asset turnover rations that are used by analysts:
    - Fixed assets turnover
    - Current assets turnover
    - Inventory turnover
    - Receivables or debtors turnover

The Du Pont financial analysis: This is propounded by Du Pont Company of the US and is widely appreciated. This analysis combines two major aspects of business performance: profitability in terms of net profit margin and asset utilization in terms of total assets turnover ratio.

$$\text{Return on Assets (RoA)} = \frac{\text{Net profit}}{\text{Average total assets}} = \frac{\text{Net profit}}{\text{Net sales}} \times \frac{\text{Net sales}}{\text{Average total assets}}$$

For improving RoA, firms need to focus on increased profit margin [i.e. cost reduction] and better utilization of assets. Du Pont analysis can be extended to measure the return on equity and its components.

The Du Pont framework is revised to reflect the factors affecting return on equity. In the revised formula, the leverage effect (asset to equity ratio) is considered.

$$\text{Return on Equity (RoE)} = \frac{\text{Net profit}}{\text{Average net worth}} = \frac{\text{Net profit}}{\text{Net sales}} \times \frac{\text{Net sales}}{\text{Average total assets}} \times \frac{\text{Average total assets}}{\text{Average net worth}}$$

Liquidity or Short Term Solvency: Liquidity ratios measure the firm's ability to meet short term obligations.

- Current Ratio: this is the ratio between current assets and current liabilities. A current ratio of 2 indicates that the company has two rupees of current assets to meet one rupee of current liability. Although higher current ratio indicates better short term solvency or liquidity, very high current ratio can be due to idle current assets like inventories. Current assets include cash, bank, short term deposits, inventories, receivables, prepaid expenses. Current liabilities include creditors for supplies and other inputs, payables, provisions for tax, proposed dividend, and outstanding expenses.
- Quick Ratio: Also known as acid test ratio, this is a stringent measure of liquidity and is measured as a ratio between quick assets and current liabilities. As part of quick assets, all current assets except inventory are considered. Inventories are considered less liquid in comparison to other current assets.
- Inventory turnover ratio (ITR) and inventory conversion period: ITR This ratio measures the efficiency of inventory utilization and is measured as:

$$\text{ITR(in times)} = \frac{\text{Cost of goods sold}}{\text{Average inventory}}$$

Higher inventory turnover ratio indicates that the company holds less inventory to meet the sales. By dividing 365 with ITR, inventory conversion period can be found. With an ITR of 5 times, inventory conversion period is calculated as 73 days. Thus, it takes 73 days on an average to convert inventory into sales.

- Receivables or Debtors turnover ratio (DTR) and average collection period: DTR is calculated as below:

$$\text{DTR (in times)} = \frac{\text{Net Credit Sales}}{\text{Average receivables}}$$

Higher debtor turnover ratio indicates stringent credit policy and terms as well as timely collection of receivables. Average collection period is calculated by dividing 365 with DTR.

Long Term Solvency: Companies depend upon borrowing for financing the business. While borrowing leads to leverage and helps in magnifying earnings available for equity shareholders, it can also lead to problems of solvency. Higher borrowing ratio can invite higher interest charges by bankers and other lenders. Hence companies try to have an optimal borrowing level. The different measures of long term solvency are discussed below.

- Debt-to-equity ratio: This ratio is calculated as Debt / Net worth. Debt consists of interest bearing liabilities. A debt-equity ratio of 1.5 indicates that the company has borrowed Rs.1.5 for every one rupee contributed by the owners.

- Liabilities-to-equity ratio: This ratio is like debt to equity ratio but for the fact that in this case, in numerator, all liabilities – whether interest bearing or not – are considered.

- Total debt to total capital (debt + equity): this is a variety of debt-equity ratio and is indicated in terms of %. A debt equity ratio 2:1 is essentially a debt to total capital ratio of 66.67% [2 / (2+1)].

- Interest coverage ratio (EBIT / Interest, expressed in 'times'): this ratio indicates the comfort level of the firms in the ability to pay interest. Bankers attach a lot of importance to this coverage ratio while appraising a loan.

- Fixed charges coverage ratio: This ratio measures the ability of company to honour all the debt obligation like interest and repayment of debt.

$$\text{Fixed charges coverage ratio(in times)} = \frac{\text{EBIT} + \text{Depreciation}}{\text{Interest} + \dfrac{\text{Repayment of debt}}{1 - \text{Tax rate}}}$$

In the above formula repayment of debt is adjusted for tax since unlike interest, this is not a tax deductible payment.

Capital Market Standing

- Price-earnings (P/E) ratio: P/E ratio, a very popular ratio for financial market players, is a relative valuation measure for equity share and is measured as Market price per share to EPS. P/E ratio is essentially compared with an average P/E ratio of stocks of similar industry or benchmark index. High P/E ratio in comparison to benchmark or average P/E indicates over valuation and vice versa.
- Enterprise value / EBIDTA or EBIDTA multiple: Enterprise value is combination of market value of equity and debt; EBIDTA: Earnings before interest, tax, depreciation and amortization. EBIDTA multiple neutralizes the effect of capital structure, new or old company [i.e. new or old assets thus leading to different depreciation] and corporate tax effect. This ratio indicates the value of the company unlike P/E ratio which indicates the value of equity.
- Price-to-book ratio: Measured as Market price per share to book value per share this is another realative valuation ratio. This ratio is appropriate for companies that depend on assets held as value driver. However for companies that has intangibles [not reflected in balance sheet like, brand, image, human resources, etc.] this ratio is not appropriate. The book value of share is measured as 'Net worth / Number of equity shares'.
- Dividend-yield: Measured as Dividend per share to Market price per share, dividend yield indicates the return in terms of dividend for the stockholders on the equity shares. Certain investors prefer high dividend yield stocks.

Although ratio analysis help investors in identifying suitable companies for investment and also provides alert in advance, the mechanism suffers from different limitations viz. historical nature of financial statements, different accounting policies followed by companies, window dressing among other things.

Price–earnings Ratio

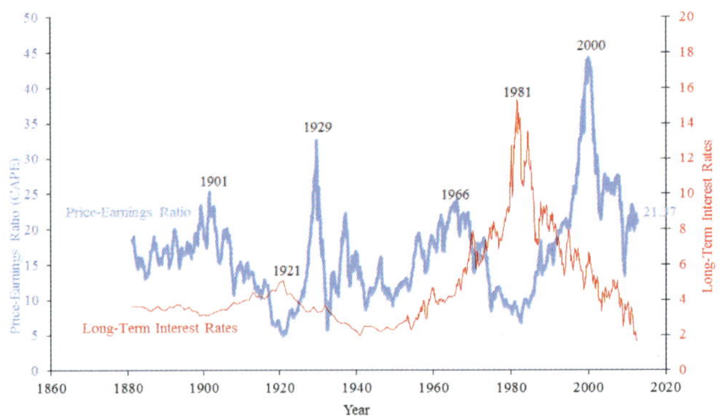

The price/earnings ratio (often shortened to the P/E ratio or the PER) is the ratio of a company's stock price to the company's earnings per share. The ratio is used in valuing companies.Robert Shiller's plot of the S&P composite real price–earnings ratio and interest rates (1871–2012), from *Irrational Exuberance*, 2d ed. In the preface to this edition, Shiller warns that "the stock market has not come down to historical levels: the price–earnings ratio as I define it in this book is still, at this writing [2005], in the mid-20s, far higher than the historical average. ... People still place too much confidence in the markets and have too strong a belief that paying attention to the gyrations in their investments will someday make them rich, and so they do not make conservative preparations for possible bad outcomes."

Versions

There are multiple versions of the P/E ratio, depending on whether earnings are projected or realized, and the type of earnings.

- "Trailing P/E" uses the weighted average number of common shares in issue divided by the net income for the most recent 12-month period. This is the most common meaning of "P/E" if no other qualifier is specified. Monthly earnings data for individual companies are not available, and in any case usually fluctuate seasonally, so the previous four quarterly earnings reports are used and earnings per share are updated quarterly. Note, each company chooses its own financial year so the timing of updates varies from one to another.

- "Trailing P/E from continued operations" uses operating earnings, which exclude earnings from discontinued operations, extraordinary items (e.g. one-off windfalls and write-downs), and accounting changes.

- "Forward P/E": Instead of net income, this uses estimated net earnings over next 12 months. Estimates are typically derived as the mean of those published by a select group of analysts (selection criteria are rarely cited).

As an example, if stock A is trading at $24 and the earnings per share for the most recent 12-month period is $3, then stock A has a P/E ratio of 24/3 or 8. Put another way, the purchaser of the stock is investing $8 for every dollar of earnings. Companies with losses (negative earnings) or no profit have an undefined P/E ratio (usually shown as "not applicable" or "N/A"); sometimes, however, a negative P/E ratio may be shown.

Some people mistakenly use the formula market capitalization / net income to calculate the P/E ratio. This formula often gives the same answer as market price / earnings per share, but if new capital has been issued it gives the wrong answer, as market capitalization = market price × *current* number of shares whereas earnings per share= net income / *weighted average* number of shares.

Variations on the standard trailing and forward P/E ratios are common. Generally, alternative P/E measures substitute different measures of earnings, such as rolling averages over longer periods of time (to attempt to "smooth" volatile or cyclical earnings, for example), or "corrected" earnings figures that exclude certain extraordinary events or one-off gains or losses. The definitions may not be standardized. For companies that are loss-making, or whose earnings are expected to change dramatically, a "primary" P/E can be used instead, based on the earnings projections made for the next years to which a discount calculation is applied.

Interpretation

The price/earnings ratio (PER) is the most widely used method for determining whether shares are "correctly" valued in relation to one another. But the PER does not in itself indicate whether the share is a bargain. The PER depends on the market's perception of the risk and future growth in earnings. A company with a low PER indicates that the market perceives it as higher risk or lower growth or both as compared to a company with a higher PER. The PER of a listed company's share is the result of the collective perception of the market as to how risky the company is and what its earnings growth prospects are in relation to that of other companies. Investors use the PER to compare their own perception of the risk and growth of a company against the market's collective perception of the risk and growth as reflected in the current PER. If the investor feels that his perception is superior to that of the market, he can make the decision to buy or sell accordingly.

Historical P/E Ratios for the U.S. Stock Market

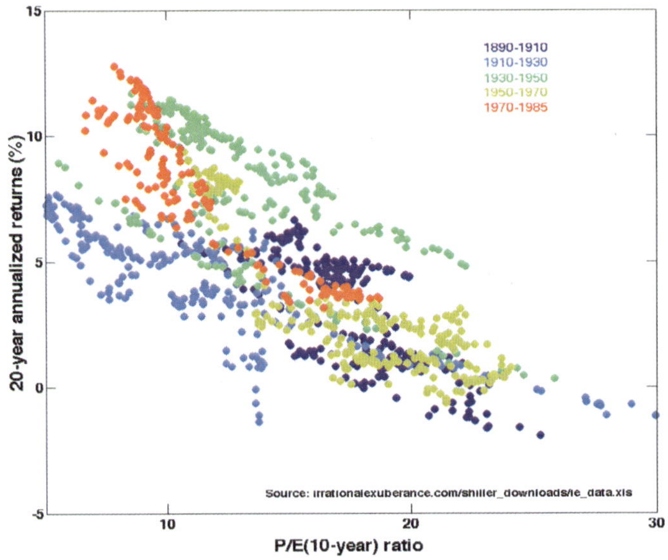

Price-Earnings ratios as a predictor of twenty-year returns based upon the plot by Robert Shiller. The horizontal axis shows the real price-earnings ratio of the S&P Composite Stock Price Index as computed in *Irrational Exuberance* (inflation adjusted price divided by the prior ten-year mean of inflation-adjusted earnings). The vertical axis shows the geometric average real annual return on investing in the S&P Composite Stock Price Index, reinvesting dividends, and selling twenty years later. Data from different twenty-year periods is color-coded as shown in the key. Shiller stated in 2005 that this plot "confirms that long-term investors—investors who commit their money to an investment for ten full years—did do well when prices were low relative to earnings at the beginning of the ten years. Long-term investors would be well advised, individually, to lower their exposure to the stock market when it is high, as it has been recently, and get into the market when it is low."

Since 1900, the average P/E ratio for the S&P 500 index has ranged from 4.78 in Dec 1920 to 44.20 in Dec 1999. However, except for some brief periods, during 1920–1990 the market P/E ratio was mostly between 10 and 20.

The average P/E of the market varies in relation with, among other factors, expected growth of earnings, expected stability of earnings, expected inflation, and yields of competing investments. For example, when U.S. treasury bonds yield high returns, investors pay less for a given earnings per share and P/E's fall.

The average U.S. equity P/E ratio from 1900 to 2005 is 14 (or 16, depending on whether the geometric mean or the arithmetic mean, respectively, is used to average).

Jeremy Siegel has suggested that the average P/E ratio of about 15 (or earnings yield of about 6.6%) arises due to the long term returns for stocks of about 6.8%. In *Stocks for the Long Run*,

(2002 edition) he had argued that with favorable developments like the lower capital gains tax rates and transaction costs, P/E ratio in “low twenties” is sustainable, despite being higher than the historic average.

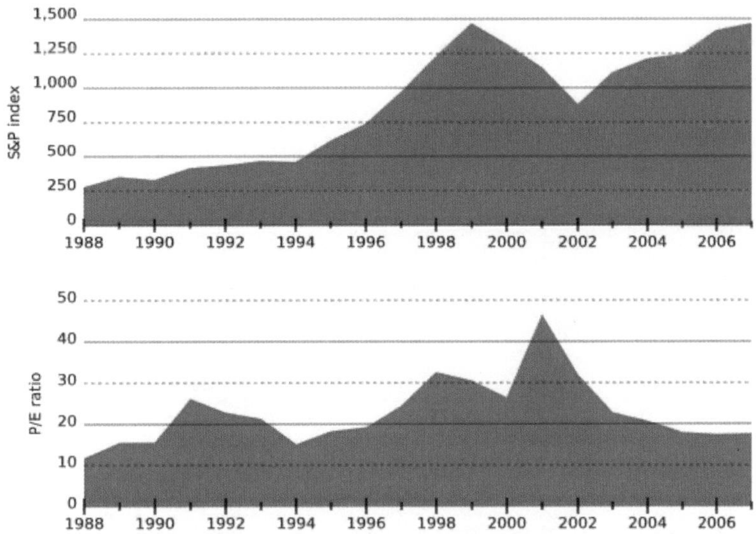

Set out below are the recent year end values of the S&P 500 index and the associated P/E as reported. For a list of recent contractions (recessions) and expansions.

Date	Index	P/E	EPS growth %	Comment
2009-06-30	919.32	122.41	–	
2009-03-31	797.87	116.31	–	
2008-12-31	903.25	60.70	–	
2007-12-31	1468.36	22.19	1.4	
2006-12-31	1418.30	17.40	14.7	
2005-12-31	1248.29	17.85	13.0	
2004-12-31	1211.92	20.70	23.8	
2003-12-31	1111.92	22.81	18.8	
2002-12-31	879.82	31.89	18.5	
2001-12-31	1148.08	46.50	−30.8	2001 contraction resulting in P/E peak
2000-12-31	1320.28	26.41	8.6	Dot-com bubble burst: 10 March 2000
1999-12-31	1469.25	30.50	16.7	
1998-12-31	1229.23	32.60	0.6	
1997-12-31	970.43	24.43	8.3	
1996-12-31	740.74	19.13	7.3	
1995-12-31	615.93	18.14	18.7	
1994-12-31	459.27	15.01	18.0	Low P/E due to high recent earnings growth.

Date	Index	P/E	EPS growth %	Comment
1993-12-31	466.45	21.31	28.9	
1992-12-31	435.71	22.82	8.1	
1991-12-31	417.09	26.12	−14.8	
1990-12-31	330.22	15.47	−6.9	July 1990 – March 1991 contraction.
1989-12-31	353.40	15.45	.	
1988-12-31	277.72	11.69	.	Bottom (Black Monday was 19 Oct 1987)

The height of the Dot-com bubble P/E had risen to 32. The collapse in earnings caused P/E to rise to 46.50 in 2001. It has declined to a more sustainable region of 17. Its decline in recent years has been due to higher earnings growth.

The P/E Ratio in Business Culture

The P/E ratio of a company is a major focus for many managers. They are usually paid in company stock or options on their company's stock (a form of payment that is supposed to align the interests of management with the interests of other stock holders). The stock price can increase in one of two ways: either through improved earnings or through an improved multiple that the market assigns to those earnings. In turn, the primary drivers for multiples such as the P/E ratio is through higher and more sustained earnings growth rates.

Consequently, managers have strong incentives to boost earnings per share, even in the short term, and/or improve long term growth rates. This can influence business decisions in several ways:

- If a company wants to acquire companies with a higher P/E ratio than its own, it usually prefers paying in cash or debt rather than in stock. Though in theory the method of payment makes no difference to value, doing it this way offsets or avoids earnings dilution.
- Conversely, companies with higher P/E ratios than their targets are more tempted to use their stock to pay for acquisitions.
- Companies with high P/E ratios but volatile earnings may be tempted to find ways to smooth earnings and diversify risk—this is the theory behind building conglomerates.
- Conversely, companies with low P/E ratios may be tempted to acquire small high growth businesses in an effort to "rebrand" their portfolio of activities and burnish their image as growth stocks and thus obtain a higher PE rating.
- Companies try to smooth earnings, for example by "slush fund accounting" (hiding excess earnings in good years to cover for losses in lean years). Such measures are designed to create the image that the company always slowly but steadily increases profits, with the goal to increase the P/E ratio.
- Companies with low P/E ratios are usually more open to leveraging their balance sheet. As seen above, this mechanically lowers the P/E ratio, which means the company looks

cheaper than it did before leverage, and also improves earnings growth rates. Both of these factors help drive up the share price.

- Strictly speaking, the ratio is measured in years, since the price is measured in dollars and earnings are measured in dollars per year. Therefore, the ratio demonstrates how many years it takes to cover the price, if earnings stay the same.

Earnings Before Interest, Taxes, Depreciation, and Amortization

A company's earnings before interest, taxes, depreciation, and amortization is an accounting measure calculated using a company's net earnings, before interest expenses, taxes, depreciation and amortization are subtracted, as a proxy for a company's current operating profitability (i.e., how much profit it makes with its present assets and its operations on the products it produces and sells, as well as providing a proxy for cash flow).

Usage

Although EBITDA is not a financial measure recognized in generally accepted accounting principles, it is widely used in many areas of finance when assessing the performance of a company, such as securities analysis. It is intended to allow a comparison of profitability between different companies, by discounting the effects of interest payments from different forms of financing (by ignoring interest payments), political jurisdictions (by ignoring tax), collections of assets (by ignoring depreciation of assets), and different takeover histories (by ignoring amortization often stemming from goodwill). EBITDA is a financial measurement of cash flow from operations that is widely used in mergers and acquisitions of small businesses and businesses in the middle market. It is not unusual for adjustments to be made to EBITDA to normalize the measurement allowing buyers to compare the performance of one business to another.

A negative EBITDA indicates that a business has fundamental problems with profitability and with cash flow. A positive EBITDA, on the other hand, does not necessarily mean that the business generates cash. This is because EBITDA ignores changes in working capital (usually needed when growing a business), in capital expenditures (needed to replace assets that have broken down), in taxes, and in interest.

Some analysts do not support omission of capital expenditures when evaluating the profitability of a company: capital expenditures are needed to maintain the asset base which in turn allows for profit. Warren Buffett famously asked: “Does management think the tooth fairy pays for capital expenditures?”

Margin

EBITDA margin refers to EBITDA divided by total revenue (or “total output”, “output” differing “revenue” by the changes in inventory).

Misuse

Over time, EBITDA has mostly been used as a calculation to describe the performance in its intrinsic nature, which means ignoring every cost that does not occur in the normal course of business.

In spite of the fact this simplification can be quite useful, it is often misused, since it results in considering too many cost items as unique, and thus boosting profitability. Instead, in case these sort of unusual costs get downsized, the resulting calculation ought to be called "adjusted EBITDA" or similar.

Because EBITDA (and its variations) are not measures generally accepted under U.S. GAAP, the U.S. Securities and Exchange Commission requires that companies registering securities with it (and when filing its periodic reports) reconcile EBITDA to net income in order to avoid misleading investors.

P/B ratio

The price-to-book ratio, or P/B ratio, is a financial ratio used to compare a company's current market price to its book value. It is also sometimes known as a Market-to-Book ratio. The calculation can be performed in two ways, but the result should be the same each way. In the first way, the company's market capitalization can be divided by the company's total book value from its balance sheet. The second way, using per-share values, is to divide the company's current share price by the book value per share (i.e. its book value divided by the number of outstanding shares).

As with most ratios, it varies a fair amount by industry. Industries that require more infrastructure capital (for each dollar of profit) will usually trade at P/B ratios much lower than, for example, consulting firms. P/B ratios are commonly used to compare banks, because most assets and liabilities of banks are constantly valued at market values. A higher P/B ratio implies that investors *expect* management to create more value from a given set of assets, all else equal (and/or that the market value of the firm's assets is significantly higher than their accounting value). P/B ratios do not, however, directly provide any information on the ability of the firm to generate profits or cash for shareholders.

This ratio also gives some idea of whether an investor is paying too much for what would be left if the company went bankrupt immediately. For companies in distress, the book value is usually calculated without the intangible assets that would have no resale value. In such cases, P/B should also be calculated on a "diluted" basis, because stock options may well vest on sale of the company or change of control or firing of management.

It is also known as the market-to-book ratio and the price-to-equity ratio (which should not be confused with the price-to-earnings ratio), and its inverse is called the book-to-market ratio.

Total Book Value vs Tangible Book Value

Technically, P/B can be calculated either including or excluding intangible assets and goodwill. When intangible assets and goodwill are excluded, the ratio is often specified to be "price to tangible book value" or "price to tangible book".

Value and Limitations

Except in the case of a small minority of companies like property companies and investment trusts that are asset based, book values bear little or no relationship to true values of the companies. The items on the balance sheet are the result of various transactions, recorded using double entry at a particular point in time, to the extent that they do not form part of the profit and loss account to that point in time. The assets and liabilities comprising the book value are mainly stated at historic cost though a few items therein may be stated at valuations.

In many of today's companies, their most valuable assets are not shown on the balances sheet and are therefore not included in the book value. Book values are meaningless in companies such as Apple, Microsoft, Google, Facebook, GlaxoSmithKline, etc. where their intellectual capital, internally generated goodwill, etc. are much more valuable than the assets per their balance sheets but are not included therein.

In Benjamin Graham's days, book values were more relevant as most companies then had significant investments in tangible assets and such assets comprised the bulk of the value of the company. The value of today's companies, other than asset based companies like investment trusts and property companies, is very different from the book values and there is no relationship between their intrinsic values and their book values. That is why Warren Buffett said "In all cases, what is clear is that book value is meaningless as an indicator of value" in his 2000 annual report.

Despite the theoretical limitations of the price-book ratio, academic research has persistently shown that stocks with low price-book ratios persistently outperform stocks with high price-book ratios. Fama and French incorporated a price-book term in their influential three factor model. Penman Richardson and Tuna (2013) show how the ratio can be decomposed into financing and operating components. Foye and Mramor (2016) show that while stocks with low price-book ratios normally outperform, the ratios decomposed elements exhibit a different relationship with returns in different countries, implying that the price-book ratio may have a country-specific interpretation.

Dividend Yield

The dividend yield or dividend-price ratio of a share is the dividend per share, divided by the price per share. It is also a company's total annual dividend payments divided by its market capitalization, assuming the number of shares is constant. It is often expressed as a percentage.

Dividend yield is used to calculate the earning on investment (shares) considering only the returns in the form of total dividends declared by the company during the year.

Its reciprocal is the Price/Dividend ratio.

Preferred Share Dividend Yield

Dividend payments on preferred stocks ("preference shares" in the UK) are set out in the prospectus. The name of the preferred share will typically include its nominal yield: for example, a 6% preferred share. However, the dividend may under some circumstances be passed or reduced. The current yield is the ratio of the annual dividend to the current market price, which will vary.

Common Share Dividend Yield

Unlike preferred stock, there is no stipulated dividend for common stock ("ordinary shares" in the UK). Instead, dividends paid to holders of common stock are set by management, usually with regard to the company's earnings. There is no guarantee that future dividends will match past dividends or even be paid at all. The historic yield is calculated using the following formula:

$$\text{Current Dividend Yield} = \frac{\text{Most Recent Full-Year Dividend}}{\text{Current Share Price}}$$

For example, take a company which paid dividends totaling $1 per share last year and whose shares currently sell for $20. Its dividend yield would be calculated as follows:

$$\begin{aligned}\text{Current Dividend Yield} &= \frac{\text{Most Recent Full-Year Dividend}}{\text{Current Share Price}}\\ &= \frac{\$1}{\$20}\\ &= 0.05\\ &= 5\%\end{aligned}$$

The yield for the S&P 500 is reported this way. US newspaper and web listings of common stocks apply a somewhat different calculation: they report the latest quarterly dividend multiplied by 4 divided by the current price. Others try to estimate the next year's dividend and use it to derive a prospective dividend yield. Such a scheme is used for the calculation of the *FTSE UK Dividend+ Index*. Estimates of future dividend yields are by definition uncertain.

Trailing Dividend Yield

Trailing dividend yield gives the dividend percentage paid over a prior period, typically one year. A trailing twelve month dividend yield, denoted as "TTM", includes all dividends paid during the past year in order to calculate the dividend yield. While a trailing dividend can be indicative of future dividends, it can be misleading as it does not account for dividend increases or cuts, nor does it account for a special dividend that may not occur again in the future.

Forward Dividend Yield

Forward dividend yield is some estimation of the future yield of a stock. This may be an analyst estimate, or just using the company's guidance. For example, if a company has announced a dividend increase, even though nothing has been paid, this may be assumed to be the payment for the next year. Similarly, if a company has said that it will suspend its dividend, the yield would be assumed to be zero.

The calculation is done by taking the first dividend payment and annualizing it and then divide that number by the current stock price. In other words, if the first quarterly dividend was $0.04 and the current stock price was $10.00 the forward dividend yield would be (.04*4)/10= 1.6%.

The trailing dividend yield is done in reverse by taking the last dividend annualized divided by the current stock price.

Related Measures

The reciprocal of the dividend yield is the Price/Dividend ratio. The dividend yield is related to the earnings yield via:

- earnings yield = dividend yield · dividend cover, and
- dividend yield = earnings yield · dividend payout ratio.

Desirability

Historically, a higher dividend yield has been considered to be desirable among many investors. A high dividend yield can be considered to be evidence that a stock is underpriced or that the company has fallen on hard times and future dividends will not be as high as previous ones. Similarly a low dividend yield can be considered evidence that the stock is overpriced or that future dividends might be higher. Some investors may find a higher dividend yield attractive, for instance as an aid to marketing a fund to retail investors, or maybe because they cannot get their hands on the capital, which may be tied up in a trust arrangement. In contrast some investors may find a higher dividend yield unattractive, perhaps because it increases their tax bill.

Dividend yield fell out of favor somewhat during the 1990s because of an increasing emphasis on price appreciation over dividends as the main form of return on investments.

The importance of the dividend yield in determining investment strength is still a debated topic. The persistent historic low in the Dow Jones dividend yield during the early 21st century is considered by some investors as indicative that the market is still overvalued.

Dow Industrials

The dividend yield of the Dow Jones Industrial Average, which is obtained from the annual dividends of all 30 companies in the average divided by their cumulative stock price, has also been considered to be an important indicator of the strength of the U.S. stock market. Historically, the Dow Jones dividend yield has fluctuated between 3.2% (during market highs, for example in 1929) and around 8.0% (during typical market lows). The highest ever Dow Jones dividend yield occurred in 1932 when it yielded over 15%, which was years after the famous stock market collapse of 1929, when it yielded only 3.1%.

With the decreased emphasis on dividends since the mid-1990s, the Dow Jones dividend yield has fallen well below its historical low-water mark of 3.2% and reached as low as 1.4% during the stock market peak of 2000.

The Dogs of the Dow is a popular investment strategy which invests in the ten highest dividend yield Dow stocks at the beginning of each calendar year.

S&P 500

In 1982 the dividend yield on the S&P 500 Index reached 6.7%. Over the following 16 years, the dividend yield declined to just a percentage value of 1.4% during 1998, because stock prices increased faster than dividend payments from earnings, and public company earnings increased slower than stock prices. During the 20th century, the highest growth rates for earnings and dividends over any 30-year period were 6.3% annually for dividends, and 7.8% for earnings.

Yield on Cost

Yield is sometimes computed based on the amount *paid* for a stock. For example, if stock X was bought for $20 per share, and it split 2:1 three times, and it is now trading for $50, and it pays a dividend of $2 per year, then the yield on cost is 80%. The yield with the current price is 4%.

References

- Williams, Jan R.; Susan F. Haka; Mark S. Bettner; Joseph V. Carcello (2008). Financial & Managerial Accounting. McGraw-Hill Irwin. p. 40. ISBN 978-0-07-299650-0
- "US Small Business Administration sample spreadsheet for a small business". Archived from the original on 2007-07-15. Retrieved 2003-08-10
- Epstein, Barry J.; Eva K. Jermakowicz (2007). Interpretation and Application of International Financial Reporting Standards. John Wiley & Sons. p. 931. ISBN 978-0-471-79823-1
- "Balance sheet comparing two year-end balance sheets". Archived from the original on 2007-10-19. Retrieved 2010-05-08
- Helfert, Erich A. (2001). "The Nature of Financial Statements: The Income Statement". Financial Analysis - Tools and Techniques - A Guide for Managers. McGraw-Hill. p. 40. doi:10.1036/0071395415
- Harry I. Wolk, James L. Dodd, Michael G. Tearney. Accounting Theory: Conceptual Issues in a Political and Economic Environment (2004). ISBN 0-324-18623-1
- Williams, Jan R.; Susan F. Haka; Mark S. Bettner; Joseph V. Carcello (2008). Financial & Managerial Accounting. McGraw-Hill Irwin. p. 266. ISBN 978-0-07-299650-0

2

Fundamental and Economic Analysis

Fundamental analysis studies the economic factors of an organization. Some of these factors are earnings, employment, management, interest rates, etc. The section strategically encompasses and incorporates the major components and key concepts of economic analysis, providing a complete understanding.

Fundamental Analysis

Fundamental analysis, in accounting and finance, is the analysis of a business's financial statements (usually to analyze the business's assets, liabilities, and earnings); health; and its competitors and markets. When applied to futures and forex, it focuses on the overall state of the economy, and considers factors including interest rates, production, earnings, employment, GDP, housing, manufacturing and management. When analyzing a stock, futures contract, or currency using fundamental analysis, there are two basic approaches that can be used: bottom up analysis and top down analysis. These terms are used to distinguish such analysis from other types of investment analysis, such as quantitative and technical.

Fundamental analysis is performed on historical and present data, but with the goal of making financial forecasts. There are several possible objectives:

- to conduct a company stock valuation and predict its probable price evolution.
- to make a projection on its business performance.
- to evaluate its management and make internal business decisions and/or to calculate its credit risk.
- to find out the intrinsic value of the share.

The two Analytical Models

There are two basic methodologies investors rely upon when the objective of the analysis is to determine what stock to buy and at what price:

1. Fundamental analysis maintains that markets may incorrectly price a security in the short run but that the "correct" price will eventually be reached. Profits can be made by purchasing the wrongly priced security and then waiting for the market to recognize its "mistake" and reprice the security.
2. Technical analysis maintains that all information is reflected already in the price of a security. Technical analysts look at trends and believe that sentiment changes predate and

predict trend changes. Investors' emotional responses to price movements lead to recognizable price chart patterns. Technical analysts also evaluate historical trends to predict future price movement.

Investors can use one or both of these complementary methods for stock picking. For example, many fundamental investors use technicals for deciding entry and exit points. Similarly, a large proportion of technical investors use fundamentals to limit their universe of possible stock to "good" companies.

The choice of stock analysis is determined by the investor's belief in the different paradigms for "how the stock market works".

Fundamental analysis includes:

1. Economic analysis
2. Industry analysis
3. Company analysis

The intrinsic value of the shares is determined based upon these three analyses. It is this value that is considered the true value of the share. If the intrinsic value is higher than the market price, buying the share is recommended. If it is equal to market price, it is recommended to hold the share; and if it is less than the market price, then one should sell the shares.

Use by Different Portfolio Styles

Investors may also use fundamental analysis within different portfolio management styles.

- Buy and hold investors believe that latching on to good businesses allows the investor's asset to grow with the business. Fundamental analysis lets them find "good" companies, so they lower their risk and the probability of wipe-out.
- Value investors restrict their attention to under-valued companies, believing that "it's hard to fall out of a ditch". The values they follow come from fundamental analysis.
- Managers may use fundamental analysis to correctly value "good" and "bad" companies. "Bad" companies' stock prices will eventually fluctuate, which can create opportunities for profit.
- Managers may also consider the economic cycle in determining whether conditions are "right" to buy fundamentally suitable companies.
- Contrarian investors hold that "in the short run, the market is a voting machine, not a weighing machine". Fundamental analysis allows a broker to make his or her own decision on value, while ignoring the opinions of the market.
- Managers may use fundamental analysis to determine future growth rates for buying high priced growth stocks.
- Managers may include fundamental factors along with technical factors in computer models (quantitative analysis).

Top-down and Bottom-up Approaches

Investors using fundamental analysis can use either a top-down or bottom-up approach.

- The top-down investor starts their analysis with global economics, including both international and national economic indicators. These may include GDP growth rates, inflation, interest rates, exchange rates, productivity, and energy prices. They subsequently narrow their search to regional/ industry analysis of total sales, price levels, the effects of competing products, foreign competition, and entry or exit from the industry. Only then do they refine their search to the best business in the area being studied.
- The bottom-up investor starts with specific businesses, regardless of their industry/region, and proceeds in reverse of the top-down approach.

Procedures

The analysis of a business's health starts with a financial statement analysis that includes financial ratios. It looks at dividends paid, operating cash flow, new equity issues and capital financing. The earnings estimates and growth rate projections published widely by Thomson Reuters and others can be considered either "fundamental" (they are facts) or "technical" (they are investor sentiment) based on perception of their validity.

Determined growth rates (of income and cash) and risk levels (to determine the discount rate) are used in various valuation models. The foremost is the discounted cash flow model, which calculates the present value of the future:

- dividends received by the investor, along with the eventual sale price; (Gordon model)
- earnings of the company;
- or cash flows of the company.

The amount of debt a company possesses is also a major consideration in determining its health. It can be quickly assessed using the debt-to-equity ratio and the *current ratio* (current assets/ current liabilities).

The simple model commonly used is the P/E ratio (price-to-earnings ratio). Implicit in this model of a perpetual annuity (time value of money) is that the "flip" of the P/E is the discount rate appropriate to the risk of the business. The multiple accepted is adjusted for expected growth (which is not built into the model).

Growth estimates are incorporated into the PEG ratio. Its validity depends on the length of time analysts believe the growth will continue. IGAR models can be used to impute expected changes in growth from current P/E and historical growth rates for the stocks relative to a comparison index.

Computer modelling of stock prices has now replaced much of the subjective interpretation of fundamental data (along with technical data) in the industry. Since about the year 2000, a new job role has been invented with computers now able to crunch vast amounts of data. At some funds (Quant Funds) managers' decisions have been replaced by proprietary mathematical models.

Automation

The process of fundamental analysis has significantly dropped in difficulty over the past 10 years. Ever since computers became a household product, people have built software designed to make the investor's life easier. Fundamental analysis is one of the most time consuming forms of analysis. Furthermore, with the fast paced trading style of the 21st century, where markets are dominated by HFT firms and day traders, it is difficult to keep up with the market in a timely fashion. One way to go about cutting down analysis time, is to subscribe to either free or paid screening services. Screening services will allow you to search the entire market for stocks that match the quantitative fields you are looking for. These types of software then automatically give you results, hence cutting down on time spent sifting through SEC filings.

Criticisms

- Economists such as Burton Malkiel suggest that neither fundamental analysis nor technical analysis is useful in outperforming the markets

Economic Analysis

A particular firm or company is a micro unit of the economy as a whole. Fluctuations in security markets are related to changes in expectations for the aggregate economy. Prospects of the firms are tied to those of the broader economy even that of international economy. For some firms, macroeconomic and industry circumstances might have a greater influence on profits and cash flows that the firm's relative performance within its industry.

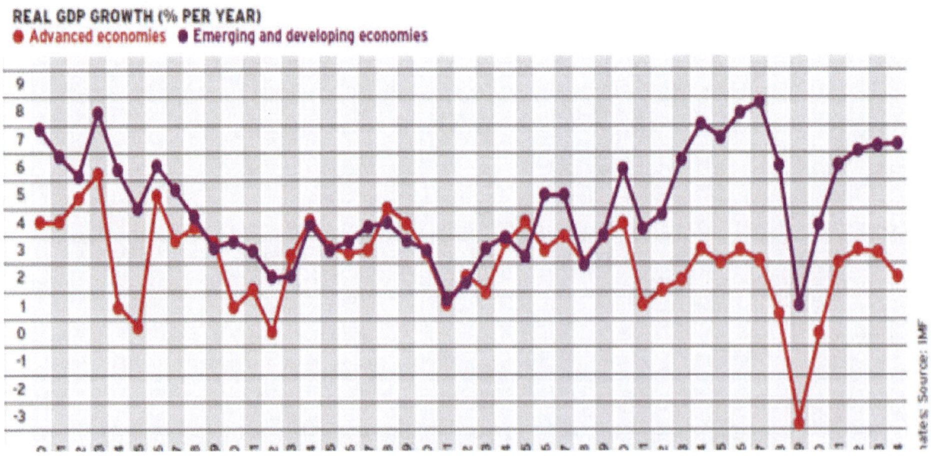

Real GDP Growth – Developed Vs. Emerging Economies

Global Economy: The economic analysis should start from the global economy. Since the economies are interrelated – thus the firms across economies, the international economy can affect a firm's prospects. It affects the price competition it faces from competitors, or the profits it makes on investments abroad. At a particular point of time, there can be variations in the economic performance across countries. Similarly, political risks can be of greater magnitude in other countries compared to domestic political environment. Fluctuations in currency exchange rate also affect the performance of companies. Figure depicts the real GDP growth of developed and emerging economies. One can see that trend is not always similar and the pattern in rate of growth is also different. The emerging economies show higher growth in comparison to developed economies. One need not be surprised about attraction of investors towards emerging economies. If explored further, different countries in a particular group [emerging or developed] would also show varied GDP growth and pattern.

Domestic Macro Economy: An analyst should be able to forecast about domestic macro economy better than other analysts. By this, the analyst [for that matter, a fund manager] can outsmart the peers in showing investment performance. The key macroeconomic variables that an analyst should look at are:

- Gross Domestic Product: Measure of the economy's total production of goods and services. Growth in GDP reflects opportunities for a firm to increase its revenue by selling more products or services.
- Industrial Growth Rate: Although part of GDP growth, industry growth rates indicates the activity in manufacturing sector of the economy.
- Monsoon and Agriculture: For agrarian economies these two factors are pertinent. Several industries also depend on agriculture for inputs. Level of monsoon indicates the likely performance of agriculture sector.
- Employment and Capacity Utilization: The employment of labour as well as other factors of production [like machine capacity] indicates the level of economic activity in the country.
- Price Level and Inflation: The general level of price rise is known as inflation. When demand for products and services are higher than the productive capacity, there can be high inflation. The governments and monetary regulators like Reserve Bank of India try to draw a balance between inflation, growth and unemployment.
- Interest Rates: Sectors like consumer durables, automobiles and housing are highly sensitive to interest rates. High interest rates also reduce the present value of investment.
- Budget Deficit: This is the difference between government spending and revenues. The shortfall is taken care by government borrowing. Government borrowing can impact interest rates as well as restrict the private sector borrowings from market.
- Sentiment: Depending upon the level of confidence of consumers in future income levels, they will like to spend more in future which in turn affects the confidence of producers. Accordingly producers plan their investment activity.

Figure shows the trend in GDP in India vs. BSE Sensex. One can see that from 2002-03 till 2007-08, BSE Sensex has moved in tandem with GDP.

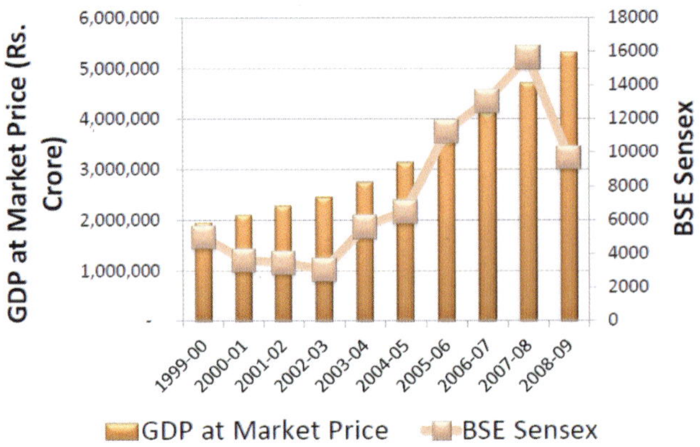

BSE Sensex and GDP of India

Demand Shock

In economics, a demand shock is a sudden event that increases or decreases demand for goods or services temporarily.

A positive demand shock increases demand and a negative demand shock decreases demand. Prices of goods and services are affected in both cases. When demand for a good or service increases, its price typically increases because of a shift in the demand curve to the right. When demand decreases, its price typically decreases because of a shift in the demand curve to the left. Demand shocks can originate from changes in things such as tax rates, money supply, and government spending. For example, taxpayers owe the government less money after a tax cut, thereby freeing up more money available for personal spending. When the taxpayers use the money to purchase goods and services, their prices go up.

In the midst of a poor economic situation in the United Kingdom in November 2002, the Bank of England's deputy governor, Mervyn King, warned that the domestic economy was sufficiently imbalanced that it ran the risk of causing a "large negative demand shock" in the near future. At the London School of Economics, he elaborated by saying, "Beneath the surface of overall stability in the UK economy lies a remarkable imbalance between a buoyant consumer and housing sector, on the one hand, and weak external demand on the other."

During the global financial crisis of 2008, a negative demand shock in the United States economy was caused by several factors that included falling house prices, the subprime mortgage crisis, and lost household wealth, which led to a drop in consumer spending. To counter this negative demand shock, the Federal Reserve System lowered interest rates. Before the crisis occurred, the world's economy experienced a positive global supply shock. Immediately afterward, however, a positive global demand shock led to global overheating and rising inflationary pressures.

Supply Shock

A supply shock is an event that suddenly increases or decreases the supply of a commodity or service, or of commodities and services in general. This sudden change affects the equilibrium price of the good or service or the economy's general price level.

In the short run, an economy-wide negative supply shock will shift the aggregate supply curve leftward, decreasing the output and increasing the price level. For example, the imposition of an embargo on trade in oil would cause an adverse supply shock, since oil is a key factor of production for a wide variety of goods. A supply shock can cause stagflation due to a combination of rising prices and falling output.

In the short run, an economy-wide positive supply shock will shift the aggregate supply curve rightward, increasing output and decreasing the price level. A positive supply shock could be an advance in technology (a technology shock) which makes production more efficient, thus increasing output.

Technical Analysis

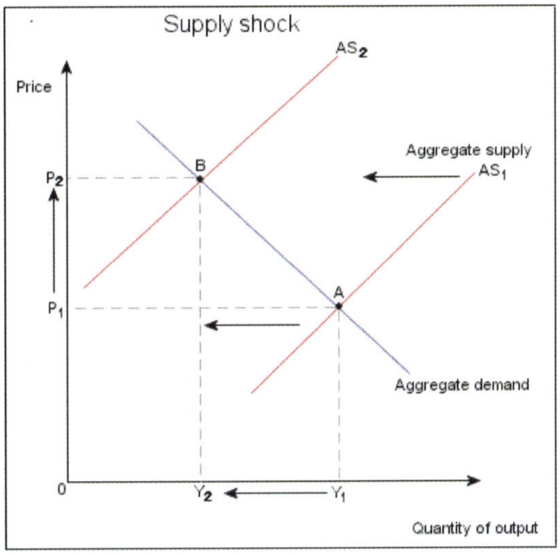

Negative supply shock

The diagram to the right demonstrates a negative supply shock; The initial position is at point A, producing output quantity Y_1 at price level P_1. When there is a supply shock, this has an adverse effect on aggregate supply: the supply curve shifts left (from AS_1 to AS_2), while the demand curve stays in the same position. The intersection of the supply and demand curves has now moved and the equilibrium is now point B; quantity has been reduced to Y_2, while the price level has been increased to P_2.

The slope of the demand curve determines how much the price level and output respond to the shock, with more inelastic demand (and hence a steeper demand curve) causing there to be a larger effect on the price level and a smaller effect on quantity.

Shock Therapy (Economics)

In economics, shock therapy refers to the sudden release of price and currency controls, withdrawal of state subsidies, and immediate trade liberalization within a country, usually also including large-scale privatization of previously public-owned assets.

As *shock policy*, the term was coined by economist Milton Friedman. In time, it became absorbed into the group of ideas about economics, that are sometimes referred to as economic liberalism.

The economist Jeffrey Sachs coined the expression of *shock therapy*. The alleged difference between the two *shock* expressions lies only in the degree of economic liberalisation. Sachs' ideas were based on studying historic periods of monetary and economic crisis and noting that a decisive stroke could end monetary chaos, often in a day.

The first instance of shock therapy were the neoliberal pro-market reforms of Chile in 1975, carried out after the military coup by Augusto Pinochet. The reforms, dubbed a *shock policy* at the time by Milton Friedman, were based on the liberal economic ideas centered on the University of Chicago.

The term was truly born after Bolivia successfully tackled hyperinflation in 1985 under Gonzalo Sánchez de Lozada, using Sachs' ideas. In particular, Sachs and Sanchez de Lozada cited West Germany as inspiration where, during a period over 1947–1948, price controls and government support were withdrawn over a very short period, kick-starting the German economy and completing its transition from an authoritarian post-War state.

Economic liberalism rose to prominence after the 1970s and liberal shock therapy became increasingly used as a response to economic crises, for example by the International Monetary Fund (IMF) in the 1997 Asian Financial Crisis. Liberal shock therapy became very controversial, with its proponents arguing that it helped to end economic crises, stabilise economies and pave the way for economic growth, while its critics (like Joseph Stiglitz) believed that it helped deepen them unnecessarily and created unnecessary social suffering.

Sachs' ideas were applied to the post-communist states in their transition to capitalist systems with very mixed results. Some countries that used shock therapy (e.g., Poland, Czech Republic) did better than those that did not. To further cloud understanding, China made its highly successful transition in a gradualist fashion. One opinion is that successful market economies rest on a framework of law, regulation, and established practice that cannot be instantaneously created in a society that was formerly authoritarian, heavily centralised, and subject to state ownership of assets.

History

West Germany 1948

Though the term *shock therapy* only came into existence after Bolivia's actions in 1985, both Gonzalo Sánchez de Lozada (the architect of the policy in Bolivia) and Jeffrey Sachs (its economic architect) were heavily influenced by West Germany's reforms in 1948.

Background

Germany ended the European Theatre of World War II with its unconditional surrender on the 8 May 1945. It faced war damage to its economy and the problems of mass migration due to the expulsion of ethnic Germans from areas east of the Oder-Neisse Line.

April 1945 to July 1947 saw the Allied occupation of Germany implement Joint Chiefs of Staff directive 1067 (JCS 1067). This directive aimed to transfer Germany's economy from one centred on heavy industry to a pastoral one to prevent Germany from having the capacity for war. Civilian industries that might have military potential, which in the modern era of "total war" included virtually all, were severely restricted. The restriction of the latter was set to Germany's *approved peacetime needs*, which were set on the average European standard. To achieve this, each type of industry was subsequently reviewed to see how many factories Germany required under these minimum level of industry requirements. In May 1946, the first plan stated that German heavy industry must be lowered to 50% of its 1938 levels by the destruction of 1,500 listed manufacturing plants. Restrictions on steel followed.

It soon became obvious that this policy was not sustainable. Germany could not grow enough food for itself and malnutrition was becoming increasingly common. The European post-war economic recovery did not materialise and it became increasingly obvious that the European economy had depended on German industry.

In July 1947, President Harry S. Truman rescinded on "national security grounds" the punitive JCS 1067, which had directed the U.S. forces of occupation in Germany to "take no steps looking toward the economic rehabilitation of Germany." It was replaced by JCS 1779, which instead stressed that "an orderly, prosperous Europe requires the economic contributions of a stable and productive Germany."

By 1948, Germany suffered from rampant hyperinflation. The currency of the time (the Reichsmark) had no public confidence, and thanks to that and price controls, black market trading boomed and bartering proliferated. Banks were over their heads in debt and surplus currency abounded.

However, thanks to the introduction of JCS 1779 and the first Allied attempts to set up German governance, something could be done about this. Ludwig Erhard, an economist, who had spent much time working on the problem of post war recovery, had worked his way up the administration created by the occupying American forces until he became the Director of Economics in the Bizonal Economic Council in the joint British and American occupied zones (which later, with the addition of the French occupied territory, became the basis for West Germany). He was placed in charge of currency reform and became a central figure in events that were to follow.

Economic Reforms

In spring of 1948, the Allies decided to reform the currency. In preparation for this, a new central bank system was established in West Germany with independent Land Central Banks and the Bank deutscher Lander with headquarters in Frankfurt am Main.

Currency reform took effect on June 20, 1948, through the introduction of the Deutsche Mark to replace the Reichsmark and by transferring to the Bank deutscher Lander the sole right to print money. Each person received a per capita allowance of 60 DM, payable in two installments (40 DM and 20 DM) and business quota of 60 DM per employee.

Under the German Currency Conversion Law on 27 June, private non-bank credit balances were converted at a rate of 10 RM to 1 DM, with half remaining in a frozen bank account. Although the money stock was very small in terms of national product, the adjustment in the price structure immediately led to sharp price increases, fuelled by the high velocity of money through the system. As a result, on 4 October, the military governments wiped out 70% of the remaining frozen balances, resulting in an effective exchange of 10:0.65. Holders of financial assets (including many small-time savers) were dispossessed and the banks' debt in Reichsmarks was eliminated, transferred instead into claims on the Lander and later the Federal Government. Wages, rents, pensions and other recurring liabilities were transferred at 1:1.

On the day of the currency reform, Ludwig Erhard announced, despite the reservations of the Allies, that rationing would be considerably relaxed and price controls abolished.

Results

In the short term, the currency reforms and abolition of price controls helped end hyperinflation. The new currency enjoyed considerable confidence and was accepted by the public as a medium of payment. The currency reforms had ensured that money was once more scarce, and the relaxation of price controls created incentives for production, sales and earning this money. The removal of price controls also meant shops filled up with goods again, which was a huge psychological factor in the adoption of the new currency.

In the long term, these reforms helped set the stage for the Wirtschaftswunder (German for economic miracle) in the 1950s.

Chile 1975

Chile's reforms under the government of Augusto Pinochet are held as the origin of neoliberal shock therapy.

Background

In September 1970, Salvador Allende, the UP candidate, was elected president of Chile. Over the next three years, a unique political and economic experience followed. The UP was a coalition of left and center-left parties dominated by the Socialist Party of Chile and the Communist Party of Chile, both of which sought to implement deep institutional, political, and economic reforms. The UP's program called for a democratic "Chilean road to [socialism]." When Allende took office in November 1970, his UP government faced a stagnant economy weakened by inflation, which hit a rate of 35 percent in 1970. Between 1967 and 1970, real GDP per capita had grown only 1.2 percent per annum, a rate significantly below the Latin American average.

The UP had a number of short-run economic objectives: initiating structural economic transformations, including a program of nationalization; increasing real wages; reducing inflation; spurring economic growth; increasing consumption, especially by poorer people; and reducing the economy's dependence on the rest of the world. The UP wanted to achieve their nationalization program through a combination of new legislation, requisitions, and stock purchases from small shareholders. The other goals—output and increased consumption, with rising salaries and declining inflation—were to be accomplished by a boost in aggregate demand, mainly generated by higher government expenditures, accompanied by strict price controls and measures to redistribute income.

The UP's macroeconomic program was based on several key assumptions, the most important being that the manufacturing sector had ample underutilized capacity. This provided the theoretical basis for the belief that large fiscal deficits were not necessarily inflationary. The lack of full utilization was, in turn, attributed to two fundamental factors: the monopolistic nature of the manufacturing industry and the structure of income distribution. Based on this diagnosis, it was thought that if income were redistributed toward the poorer groups through wage increases and if prices were properly controlled, demand and output would expand significantly.

During 1972, macroeconomic problems continued to mount. Inflation surpassed 200 percent, and the fiscal deficit surpassed 13 percent of GDP. Domestic credit to the public sector grew at almost 300 percent, and international reserves dipped below US$77 million. Real wages fell 25 percent in 1972. The underground economy grew as more and more activities moved out of the official economy. As a result, more and more sources of tax revenues disappeared. A vicious cycle began: repressed inflation encouraged the informal economy, thus reducing tax revenues and leading to higher deficits and even higher inflation. In 1972 two stabilization programs were implemented, both unsuccessfully.

During the first quarter of 1973, Chile's economic problems became extremely serious. Inflation reached an annual rate of more than 120 percent, industrial output declined by almost 6 percent, and foreign-exchange reserves held by the Central Bank were barely above US$40 million. The black market by then covered a widening range of transactions in foreign exchange. The fiscal deficit continued to climb as a result of spiralling expenditures and of rapidly disappearing sources of taxation. For that year, the fiscal deficit ended up exceeding 23% of GDP.

The depth of the economic crisis seriously affected the middle class, and relations between the UP government and the political opposition became increasingly confrontational. On September 11, 1973, the UP regime came to a sudden and shocking end with a violent military coup and President Allende's death.

When the military took over in September 1973, the country was divided politically, and the economy was a shambles. Inflation was galloping, and relative price distortions, stemming mainly from massive price controls, were endemic. In addition, black-market activities were rampant, real wages had dropped drastically, the economic prospects of the middle class had darkened, the external sector was facing a serious crisis, production and investment were falling steeply, and government finances were completely out of hand. After the military took over the government, there was a year and a half of benign neglect of the economy as the regime consolidated its power.

Economic Reforms

The government welcomed foreign investment and eliminated protectionist trade barriers, forcing Chilean businesses to compete with imports on an equal footing, or else go out of business. The main copper company, Codelco, remained in government hands due the nationalization of copper completed by Salvador Allende, however, private companies were allowed to explore and develop new mines. Copper resources were, however, declared "inalienable" by the 1980 Constitution.

In the short term, the reforms stabilised the economy.

In the long term, Chile has had higher GDP growth than its neighbouring countries, but also high gini index, expressed in a noticeable inequality.

Bolivia 1985

The term *shock therapy* originates from Bolivia's tackling of hyper-inflation in 1985, and was thought to have been coined by the media. On 29 August, just three weeks after the election of Víctor Paz Estenssoro as President, and the appointment of Gonzalo Sánchez de Lozada, the architect of shock therapy, as Planning Minister, Decree 21060 was passed. This decree tackled all aspects of the Bolivian economy and ended the hyper-inflation.

Background

Between 1979 and 1982, Bolivia was ruled by a series of coups, counter-coups, and caretaker governments, including the notorious dictatorship of Luis García Meza Tejada. This period of political instability set the stage for the hyperinflation that later crippled the country. In October 1982, the military convened a Congress elected in 1980 to lead choose a new Chief Executive. The country elected Hernán Siles Zuazo, under whose term the galloping hyperinflationary process started. Zuazo received scant support from the political parties or members of congress, most of whom were eager to flex their newly acquired political muscles after so many years of authoritarianism. Zuazo refused to take extra-constitutional powers (as previous military governments had done in similar crises) and concentrated on preserving the democracy instead, shortening his term by one year in response to his unpopularity and the crisis racking his country. On 6 August 1985, President Víctor Paz Estenssoro was elected. He appointed his President of the Senate, Gonzalo Sánchez de Lozada, as Planning Minister with a mandate to fix the economy.

Prelude to Decree 21060

Decree 21060 was the famous decree that covered all aspects of the Bolivian economy, later referred to as shock therapy. In the run-up to the decree, Gonzalo Sánchez de Lozada recalls what the new government set out to do:

> People felt you couldn't stop hyperinflation in a democracy; that you had to have a military government, an authoritarian government to take all these tough steps that had to be taken. Bolivia was the first country to stop hyperinflation in a democracy without depriving people of their civil rights and without violating human rights.

In the three weeks between the inauguration of the President and decree 21060, he notes:

> We spent one week saying, "Do we really need to do something? Do we really need radical change?" and then another week debating shock treatment versus gradualism. Finally, we took one week to write it all up.

Once they had decided to act, de Lozada recalls that

> There was a big discussion whether you could stop hyperinflation or inflation, period, by taking gradual steps. Many people said you had to take it slowly. You have to cure the patient. Shock treatment means you have a very sick patient [and] you have to operate before the patient dies. You have to get the cancer out, or you have to stop the infection. That's why we coined the phrase that inflation is like a tiger and you have only one shot; if you don't get it with that one shot, it'll get you. You have a credibility that you have to achieve. If you keep to gradualism, people don't believe you, and the hyperinflation just keeps roaring stronger. So shock therapy is get it over, get it done, stop hyperinflation, and then start rebuilding your economy so you achieve growth.

It is notable that de Lozada viewed shock therapy as an issue of political credibility, and less an economic issue as Sachs, its economic pioneer, did. Like Sachs, he was strongly influenced by the German government in 1947, but noted that they, like the new Bolivian government of Victor Paz, were a new government that acted decisively in the first 100 days, resolving the economic situation.

Decree 21060

Decree 21060 included the following measures:

- Allowing the peso to float against the dollar.
- Ending price controls and eliminating subsidies to the public sector.
- Cutting two thirds of the employees of the state oil and tin companies. Freezing the pay of the remaining employees and public sector workers.
- Liberalising import tariffs by imposing a uniform 20% tariff.
- Stopping the payment of foreign debt under a deal negotiated with the IMF.

Results

In the short term, the decree smothered hyperinflation. Within a few months, inflation had dropped to between 10–20 percent. The crash of the tin market in October of the same year and the reforms led to an estimated unemployment rate of 21.5 percent by 1987 (the unemployment rate had risen steadily from 5.5 percent in 1978 to 10.9 percent in 1982, 15.5 percent in 1984, and 20 percent in 1986).

Post-Communist States

The next important chapter in the history of shock therapy was the collapse of communism in Europe in 1989. This left many post-communist states in central and eastern Europe with centralised authoritarian economies that had to transition to decentralised, market-orientated capitalist economies.

Inspired by Bolivia's example, and advised by institutions like the International Monetary Fund and individuals like Jeffrey Sachs, many countries chose shock therapy to shake off the economic lethargy of the communist era and transition to the capitalist systems they wanted to be. These transitions provide an interesting and important view into shock therapy and its consequences, especially when contrasted with China, which began a gradualist transition (the opposite of the shock therapy approach) in 1978 under Deng Xiaoping.

Advocates of shock therapy view Poland as the success story of shock therapy in the post-communist states and point out that shock therapy was not applied appropriately in Russia, while critics point out that Poland's reforms were the most gradualist of all the countries and compare China's reforms with those of Russia and their vastly different effects.

Poland

Poland is viewed both as the success story of shock therapy by its supporters and as a vindication of its failures by its critics.

Background

After the failure of the Communist government in the elections of June 4, 1989, it became clear that the previous regime was no longer legitimate. The unofficial talks at Magdalenka and then the Polish Round Table talks of 1989 allowed for a peaceful transition of power to the democratically elected government.

The economic situation was that inflation was high, peaking at around 600%, and the majority of state-owned monopolies and holdings were largely ineffective and completely obsolete in terms of technology. Although there was practically no unemployment in Poland, wages were low and the shortage economy led to a lack of even the most basic foodstuffs in the shops. Unlike the other post-communist countries, however, Poland did have some experience with a capitalist economy, as there was still private property in agriculture and food was still sold in farmers' markets.

In September 1989 a commission of experts was formed under the presidency of Leszek Balcerowicz, Poland's leading economist, Minister of Finance and deputy Premier of Poland. Among the members of the commission were Jeffrey Sachs, Stanisław Gomułka, Stefan Kawalec and Wojciech Misiąg. The commission prepared a plan of extensive reforms that were to enable fast transformation of Poland's economy from obsolete and ineffective central planning to advanced capitalism, as adopted by the states of Western Europe and America.

Balcerowicz Plan

On October 6 the program was presented on public television and in December the Sejm passed a packet of 11 acts, all of which were signed by the president on December 31, 1989. These were:

1. *Act on Financial Economy Within State-owned Companies*, which allowed for state-owned businesses to declare bankruptcy and ended the fiction by which companies were able to exist even if their effectiveness and accountability was close to none.
2. *Act on Banking Law*, which forbade financing the state budget deficit by the national central bank and forbade the issue of new currency.
3. *Act on Credits*, which abolished the preferential laws on credits for state-owned companies and tied interest rates to inflation.
4. *Act on Taxation of Excessive Wage Rise*, introducing the so-called popiwek tax limiting the wage increase in state-owned companies in order to limit hyperinflation.
5. *Act on New Rules of Taxation*, introducing common taxation for all companies and abolishing special taxes that could previously have been applied to private companies through means of administrative decision.
6. *Act on Economic Activity of Foreign Investors*, allowing foreign companies and private people to invest in Poland and export their profits abroad.
7. *Act on Foreign Currencies*, introducing internal exchangeability of the złoty and abolishing the state monopoly in international trade.
8. *Act on Customs Law*, creating a uniform customs rate for all companies.

9. *Act on Employment*, regulating the duties of unemployment agencies.
10. *Act on Special Circumstances Under Which a Worker Could be Laid Off*, protecting the workers of state firms from being fired in large numbers and guaranteeing unemployment grants and severance pay.

Privatization of companies was left until later.

Results

In the short term, the reforms smothered the building hyperinflation before it reached high levels, ended food shortages, restored goods on the shelves of shops and halved the absence of employees in the work place. However, the reforms also caused many state companies to close at once, leaving their workers unemployed, and government statistics show this change as unemployment rose from 0.3% in January 1990 (just after the reforms) to 6.5% by the end of that year, and a shrinking in the GDP for the next two consecutive years by 9.78% in the first and 7.02%.

In the long term, the reforms paved the way for economic recovery, with the GDP growing steadily to about 6–7% between 1995–7, falling to a low of 1.2% in 2001 before rising back up to the 6–7% region by 2007, often led by small service businesses, long suppressed by the Communist government. However, despite GDP indicating prosperity for Poland, the unemployment rate continued to rise steadily, peaking at 16.9% in July 1994 before steadily falling down to a low of 9.5% in August 1998 before rising once more to a high of 20.7% in February 2003, from which it had fallen until the year 2008. During the early years, the unemployment rate is thought to have been lower due to many of those claiming unemployment working in the grey (informal) economy, although this can account for no more than 5% of the unemployment rate.

The long-term results of shock therapy point to both a rise and a fall in living standards. Ownership of consumables (cars, TVs, VCRs, washing machines, refrigerators, personal computers, etc.) boomed, as did consumption of fruit and vegetables, meat and fish. However, the huge economic adjustment Poland underwent created massive anxiety.

New Zealand

The economic reforms of New Zealand's 1984 Labour government, collectively known as Rogernomics (after New Zealand Finance Minister Roger Douglas), constitute an example of shock therapy. In this case, the previous economic direction and management of Rob Muldoon was portrayed as leading the country into a desperate fiscal crisis, and this crisis was the continued reason given for the necessity of economic shock policies. The 'shock' element of the New Zealand experiment, can be considered as such, because the Labour Party initially complied with its policies, not withdrawing its support until later in Roger's term.

Post-Soviet

Since the USSR's collapse, the post-Soviet states faced many problems. Poverty in the region had increased more than tenfold. The economic crisis that struck all post-Soviet countries in the 1990s was twice as intense as the Great Depression in the countries of Western Europe and the United States in the 1930s.

However, it has not been established whether these adverse outcomes were due to the general collapse of the Soviet economy (which began before 1989) or the policies subsequently implemented or a combination of both. Some research suggests that the very fast pace of 'shock therapy' privatization mattered, and had a particularly harsh effect on the death rate in Russia. Sachs himself resigned from his post as advisor, after stating that he felt his advice was unheeded and his policy recommendations were not actually put into practice.

Poland

Poland has been cited by some as an example of the successful use of shock therapy, though this is disputed. When economic liberalism came to this nation, the government took Sachs' advice and immediately withdrew regulations, price controls and subsidies to state-owned industries. However, with respect to the privatization of the state sector (which may or may not be considered as part of shock therapy depending on the definition being used) the change was much more gradualist. Whereas many economic factors were immediately applied, privatization of state-owned enterprises was delayed until society could safely handle the divestiture, as contrasted with the 'robber baron' state of affairs in Russia.

Productivity increased although at the same time unemployment rates rose as well. As of 2008, the GNP was 77% higher than in 1989. Moreover, inequality in Poland actually decreased right after the economic reforms were implemented, although it rose back up again in later years. Today, although Poland is confronted with a variety of economic problems, it still has a higher GDP than during communist times, and a gradually developing economy. Poland was converging towards the EU as regards the income level in 1993–2004.

Theory

Hyperinflation

Jeffrey Sachs first proposed shock therapy when he noticed that most periods of hyperinflation had been ended in a decisive stroke, often in a day. Therefore, it is important to look at the theoretical basis for hyperinflation to understand why Sachs noticed shock therapy proved so successful in fighting it.

There are two main models used to explain hyperinflation, the *confidence model* and the *monetary model*. Hyperinflations see a rapid increase in the money supply and the velocity of money. Either one, or both of these together, is the root cause of hyperinflation and in both models, one follows from the other.

In the *confidence model*, some event, or series of events, such as defeats in battle, or a run on stocks of the specie that back a currency, removes the belief that the authority issuing the money will remain solvent—whether a bank or a government. Because people do not want to hold notes that may become valueless, they want to spend them in preference to holding notes that will lose value. Sellers, realizing that there is a higher risk for the currency, demand a greater and greater premium over the original value. War is one commonly cited cause of crisis of confidence, particularly losing in a war, as occurred during Napoleonic Vienna, and capital flight, sometimes because of "contagion" is another. In this view, the increase in the circulating medium is the result of the government attempting to buy time without coming to terms with the root cause of the lack of confidence itself. A crisis of confidence is particularly damaging to a fiat currency (i.e. most modern currencies), a currency whose value is unrelated to any physical quantity, as fiat money is typically backed by future tax revenues and its (typically exclusive) acceptability to the government for payment of taxes and charges.

In the *monetary model*, hyperinflation is a positive feedback cycle of rapid monetary expansion. It has the same cause as all other inflation: money-issuing bodies, central or otherwise, produce currency to pay spiralling costs, often from lax fiscal policy, or the mounting costs of warfare. When businesspeople perceive that the issuer is committed to a policy of rapid currency expansion, they mark up prices to cover the expected decay in the currency's value. The issuer must then accelerate its expansion to cover these prices, which pushes the currency value down even faster than before. According to this model the issuer cannot "win" and the only solution is to abruptly stop expanding the currency. Unfortunately, the end of expansion can cause a severe financial shock to those using the currency as expectations are suddenly adjusted. This policy, combined with reductions of pensions, wages, and government outlays, formed part of the Washington consensus of the 1990s.

Ending hyperinflation depends on which model is the main cause. In the confidence model, the method of ending hyperinflation is to change the backing of the currency—often by issuing a completely new one. Also, if possible, any action that restores confidence in the government can help end the hyperinflation (e.g. the psychological effect of food in the shops after shortages in most hyperinflations, the election of a new government both capable of and dedicated to tackling the problem). In the monetary model, the issuer of the currency must stop expanding the currency.

Shock Therapy as an Artificial Economic Shock

A shock in economics is defined as an unexpected or unpredictable event that affects an economy, either positively or negatively. Recessions are often modelled as negative economic shocks in which the current state of the economy is untenable and the economy tries to restore itself to a new equilibrium position. In the short-run, as the economy adjusts to the shock but before it reaches the new equilibrium, the shock often causes productivity to fall, unemployment rise, and closure of firms that are now non-viable in the new environment. The new environment enables new kinds of businesses and people must learn new skills and exploit new opportunities to achieve long-run equilibrium.

Shock therapy can be largely understood by thinking of it as an artificial shock imposed by government policies. Neoclassical theory provides a very useful tool in trying to describe an artificial shock theoretically, in that neoclassical theory provides an idealised view of an economy based on certain assumptions, most of which are made true through market institutions (often but not necessarily provided by the government), law, culture or historical practise, and is very useful in explaining most situations (especially in modern Westernised economies). Even when some of the assumptions required for neoclassical theory are not in place resulting in an imperfect market and the results of neoclassical theory becoming distorted or failing, comparing the result with neoclassical theory can prove useful. Other, slightly different formulations of economic thought strive to describe shocks, the most important of which is economic liberalism.

Neoclassical Shocks

In neoclassical theory, large negative shocks cause unemployment in the short run, and the larger the shock, the larger the unemployment. As a result, large shocks can lead to grave social problems, political unrest and, in the worst cases revolution. However, the market is already adjusting itself to return to the new equilibrium, causing job creation and opportunities. If there is no interference to prevent the markets adjusting to the new equilibrium, the markets immediately correct themselves with new firms and full employment, providing workers can acquire the new skills to exploit these new jobs, or are able to move to areas where they can find new employment.

In response to a shock created by bad government policies, sudden market liberalisation can allow the free markets to reach the equilibrium that the bad government policies prevented them reaching. If the response originates in the markets or other external factors, government intervention slows the free market's path to optimal recovery and liberalisation of the economy speed recovery. However, if the shock is large—causing social and political conditions that destroy or prevent the recovery (e.g., revolution)—government intervention to slow the recovery using gradualist policies and spreading the pain is justifiable.

Imperfect Market Shocks

The most important type of nearly neoclassical shock is due to market failure and imperfect markets. Sudden free market liberalisation in the absence of free market institutions (as was the case in post-Communist states) or in which a Western-style economy is unnecessarily liberalised (e.g. cutting police budgets, removing regulation) are both examples of imperfect market shocks.

The nature of the imperfect market shock depends on what assumption of the perfect market is voided. The most important assumption for all markets is the idea of property rights. The free market doesn't just depend on the exchange of commodities, but on the rights to use them in particular ways for particular amounts of time. Markets are institutions that organize the exchange of control of commodities, where the nature of the control is defined by the property rights attached to the commodities. Property rights are the most important because they can have the most dramatic effect on the results, and are thought to be behind the most important causes of market failure.

Another important assumption is perfect competition, which has many smaller assumptions tied to it. These include perfect information, no barriers to entry and many competitors. Again, there are different imperfect markets depending on what assumption is relaxed.

Many competitors assumes that there is more than one firm producing any commodity. In the event of large-scale privatisation of a state-owned company as part of shock therapy, privatising such a company without waiting for a competitor creates a monopoly where the company can use its pre-eminent position to create barriers to entry, control prices and maintain its monopoly. Also, in post-authoritarian systems with fragile legal and democratic systems, such pre-eminent companies can also influence the government and the legal system to help maintain its monopoly.

Perfect information assumes that prices and product quality is known to all consumers and producers. The idea of *imperfect information* (most commonly called *information asymmetry)* has many ramifications for markets. The most important one concerning shock therapy is international trade and financial liberalisation. Because international banks possess better information about other international firms than they do about local firms in a country (and local banks possess better information about other local firms), liberalisation of trade and finance never leads to an even playing field for local firms if international investment is high. Hernando de Soto Polar also notes that in conjunction with imperfect property rights, local firms may not be able to access foreign capital when borrowing against their own capital, which may have imperfect property rights (his so-called *dead capital*), while local lenders know more about the conditions under which something is owned and can be borrowed against.

Imperfect Market Failure in Russia

Prominent economist Joseph Stiglitz ties all these ideas together to explain the reason why shock therapy failed in Russia.

Through the idea of property rights, Stiglitz uses the idea of Adam Smith's invisible hand to explain that, in the presence of severe corruption, a lack of institutionalized law and order and artificially depressed exchange rates, the free market created by shock therapy in Russia created a race to the bottom to asset strip the country and remove the capital abroad, rather than the mutually beneficial race to control the market in commodities that would otherwise happen. Competition meant that if the nominal owner of the capital didn't asset strip the capital first, someone else would.

Likewise, with the previously large Soviet nationalised industries being privatised quickly created a situation where major markets operated in a monopoly owned by a few individuals (the Russian oligarchs) who had links with the government of Boris Yeltsin.

Miscellaneous other Shocks

Neoclassical models of the economy tend not to incorporate the idea of feedback. Feedback is important as it can cause economies that are doing well or badly to undergo positive feedback, making downturns worse and recoveries into bubbles that then burst into recessions. In the presence of positive feedback, shocks become amplified, becoming much more serious than they are. As a result, shock therapy is never the answer to economic recovery, and there is often wisdom to initial government intervention to break the vicious cycle.

Illusionary Shock

Illusion Therapy refers to the imposition of shock economic policies on economy in a way that the society doesn't feel the shock or assumes that the dramatic change in policies is not as shocking or radical as it is in the real world. The situation of "Illusion" can be created using a wide range of sociopolitical tools and techniques including information blackout on national statistics, imposing repeated false news shocks before the final shock (to decrease the social sensitivity or to habituate the people to the future shock), spreading misinformation, rewarding the society with interim exogenous rents and promoting them as the benefits of the shock, etc. Illusion Therapy is used to soften or elude the potential social backlash during the shock. The first experience of illusion therapy has been documented after the implementation of Iran's subsidy reform project.

People

- Ludwig Erhard, architect of the West German post-War recovery
- Gonzalo Sánchez de Lozada, architect of shock therapy in Bolivia
- Jeffrey Sachs, chief economic proponent of shock therapy
- Leszek Balcerowicz, architect of Balcerowicz Plan for shock therapy in Poland
- Yegor Gaidar, architect of shock therapy in Russia

Economic Plans

- Bolivian Decree 21060, the original shock therapy reforms in Bolivia
- Economy and Free Market reforms in Chile under Pinochet, a.k.a. the Miracle of Chile
- Balcerowicz Plan
- Russia under Yeltsin and the History of post-Soviet Russia
- Reaganomics
- Rogernomics

Analysing Macro Economy - Demand and Supply Shocks

Analysing Macro Economy - Demand and Supply Shocks: The different factors that affect the macro economy can broadly be considered as demand and supply shocks. Demand shocks are the events that affect the demand for goods and services in the economy. Demand shocks are characterized by aggregate output moving in the same direction as interest rates and inflation. For example, reduction in tax rates can increase the disposable income of the consumers. This is expected to increase the demand for products and services, which in turn can lead to increase in inflation. The events that influence production capacity and costs are known as supply shocks. Supply shocks are usually characterized by aggregate output moving in the opposite direction of inflation and interest rates. Natural calamity can adversely affect the production in the economy, thus reducing the aggregate output and increase in the cost of production and output. Consumers will not be willing to purchase the outputs at higher prices. Overall GDP is likely to fall. Some of the examples of demand and supply shocks are given below. Analysts need to identify industries based on the demand and supply conditions and devise the switching strategy [from one industry to another].

Demand Shocks	Supply Shocks
• Reduction in Tax rates	• Natural calamity
• Increase in money supply	• Changes in educational level of workforce
• Increases in government spending	• Changes in the wage rates
	• Changes in the price of imported oil

Public Policy

Public policy is the principled guide to action taken by the administrative executive branches of the state with regard to a class of issues, in a manner consistent with law and institutional customs. The foundation of public policy is composed of national constitutional laws and regulations. Further substrates include both judicial interpretations and regulations which are generally authorized by legislation. Public policy is considered strong when it solves problems efficiently and effectively, serves justice, supports governmental institutions and policies, and encourages active citizenship.

Other scholars define public policy as a system of "courses of action, regulatory measures, laws, and funding priorities concerning a given topic promulgated by a governmental entity or its representatives." Public policy is commonly embodied in "constitutions, legislative acts, and judicial decisions."

In the United States, this concept refers not only to the result of policies, but more broadly to the decision-making and analysis of governmental decisions. As an academic discipline, public policy is studied by professors and students at public policy schools of major universities throughout the country. The U.S. professional association of public policy practitioners, researchers, scholars, and students is the Association for Public Policy Analysis and Management.

Government Actions and Process

Public policy making can be characterized as a dynamic, complex, and interactive system through which public problems are identified and countered by creating new public policy or by reforming existing public policy. Public problems can originate in endless ways and require different policy responses (such as regulations, subsidies, quotas, and laws) on the local, national, or international level.

Public policy making is a continuous process that has many feedback loops. Verification and program evaluation are essential to the functioning of this system. The public problems that influence public policy making can be of economic, social, or political nature. Each system is influenced by different public problems and issues, and has different stakeholders; as such, each requires different public policy.

In public policy making, numerous individuals, corporations, non-profit organizations and interest groups compete and collaborate to influence policymakers to act in a particular way. The large set of actors in the public policy process, such as politicians, civil servants, lobbyists, domain experts, and industry or sector representatives, use a variety of tactics and tools to advance their aims, including advocating their positions publicly, attempting to educate supporters and opponents, and mobilizing allies on a particular issue. Many actors can be important in the public policy process, but government officials ultimately choose public policy in response to the public issue or problem at hand. In doing so, government officials are expected to meet public sector ethics and take the needs of all stakeholders into account.

Since societies have changed in the past decades, the public policy making system changed too. In the 2010s, public policy making is increasingly goal-oriented, aiming for measurable results and goals, and decision-centric, focusing on decisions that must be taken immediately. Furthermore, mass communications and technological changes such as the widespread availability of the Internet have caused the public policy system to become more complex and interconnected. The changes pose new challenges to the current public policy systems and pressures leaders to evolve to remain effective and efficient.

Academic Discipline

As an academic discipline, public policy brings in elements of many social science fields and concepts, including economics, sociology, political economy, program evaluation, policy analysis, and public management, all as applied to problems of governmental administration, management, and operations. At the same time, the study of public policy is distinct from political science or economics, in its focus on the application of theory to practice. While the majority of public policy degrees are master's and doctoral degrees, there are several universities also offer undergraduate education in public policy.

Traditionally, the academic field of public policy focused on domestic policy. However, the wave of economic globalization which occurred in the late 20th and early 21st centuries created a need for a subset of public policy that focuses on global governance, especially as it relates to issues that transcend national borders such as climate change, terrorism, nuclear proliferation, and economic development. Consequently, many traditional public policy schools had to tweak their curricula to adjust to this new policy landscape, as well as developed whole new ones.

Government Policy: Governments and monetary authorities devise policies affecting both demand and supply conditions in the economy.

Demand-side Policies are expected to stimulate the total demand for goods and services. The two major demand-side policies are fiscal and monetary policies. Fiscal policy denotes the spending and tax actions of the government and is part of demand-side management. Government has to strike the delicate balance between political condition and economic stability. Government may hesitate in curtailing the spending in social sector because of electoral compulsion. Increase in tax rates can decrease the disposable income of the consumers. But the increased tax collection can facilitate greater spending by the government for the economy. Without appropriate tax collection, the deficit will increase thus leading to borrowing by the government. Monetary policy intends to regulate the money supply to affect the macroeconomy. Primarily the effect of monetary policy is seen in terms of change in interest rate. Expansionary monetary policy lowers the interest rate and stimulates investment and consumption demand in short run. But it can also lead to higher prices, thus inflation in long run. Fiscal policy is designed by the government while monetary policy is designed and implemented by the monetary authority i.e. the central bank of the country.

Economic Indicator

An economic indicator is a statistic about an economic activity. Economic indicators allow analysis of economic performance and predictions of future performance. One application of economic indicators is the study of business cycles. Economic indicators include various indices, earnings reports, and economic summaries. Examples: unemployment rate, quits rate (quit rate in U.S. English), housing starts, consumer price index (a measure for inflation), consumer leverage ratio, industrial production, bankruptcies, gross domestic product, broadband internet penetration, retail sales, stock market prices, money supply changes.

The leading business cycle dating committee in the United States of America is the National Bureau of Economic Research (private). The Bureau of Labor Statistics is the principal fact-finding agency for the U.S. government in the field of labor economics and statistics. Other producers of economic indicators includes the United States Census Bureau and United States Bureau of Economic Analysis.

Classification by Timing

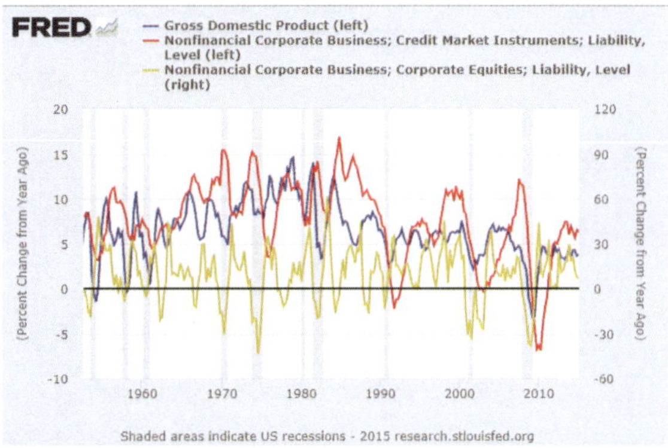

Equities as leading, GDP as coincident, and business credit as lagging indicator.

Economic indicators can be classified into three categories according to their usual timing in relation to the business cycle: leading indicators, lagging indicators, and coincident indicators.

Leading Indicators

Leading indicators are indicators that usually, but not always, change before the economy as a whole changes. They are therefore useful as short-term predictors of the economy. Stock market returns are a leading indicator: the stock market usually begins to decline before the economy as a whole declines and usually begins to improve before the general economy begins to recover from a slump. Other leading indicators include the index of consumer expectations, building permits, and the money supply. The Conference Board publishes a composite Leading Economic Index consisting of ten indicators designed to predict activity in the U. S. economy six to nine months in future.

Components of the Conference Board's Leading Economic Indicators Index

1. Average weekly hours (manufacturing) — Adjustments to the working hours of existing employees are usually made in advance of new hires or layoffs, which is why the measure of average weekly hours is a leading indicator for changes in unemployment.

2. Average weekly jobless claims for unemployment insurance — The CB reverses the value of this component from positive to negative because a positive reading indicates a loss in jobs. The initial jobless-claims data is more sensitive to business conditions than other measures of unemployment, and as such leads the monthly unemployment data released by the U.S. Department of Labor.

3. Manufacturers' new orders for consumer goods/materials — This component is considered a leading indicator because increases in new orders for consumer goods and materials usually mean positive changes in actual production. The new orders decrease inventory and contribute to unfilled orders, a precursor to future revenue.

4. Vendor performance (slower deliveries diffusion index) — This component measures the time it takes to deliver orders to industrial companies. Vendor performance leads the business cycle because an increase in delivery time can indicate rising demand for manufacturing supplies. Vendor performance is measured by a monthly survey from the National Association of Purchasing Managers (NAPM). This diffusion index measures one-half of the respondents reporting no change and all respondents reporting slower deliveries.

5. Manufacturers' new orders for non-defense capital goods — As stated above, new orders lead the business cycle because increases in orders usually mean positive changes in actual production and perhaps rising demand. This measure is the producer's counterpart of new orders for consumer goods/materials component.

6. Building permits for new private housing units.

7. The Standard & Poor's 500 stock index — The S&P 500 is considered a leading indicator because changes in stock prices reflect investor's expectations for the future of the economy and interest rates.

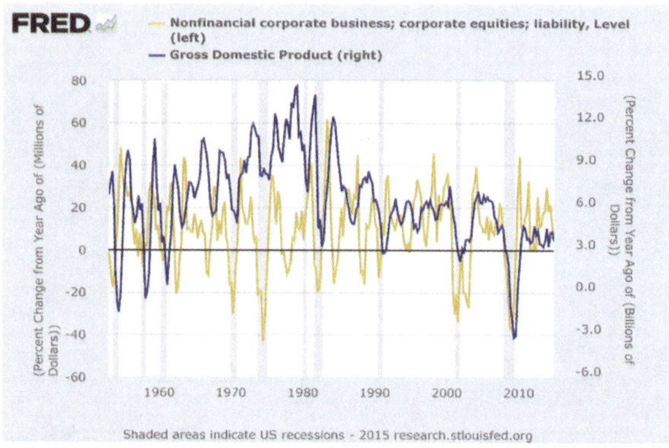

Corporate equities as leading indicator with respect to GDP.

8. Money Supply (M2) — The money supply measures demand deposits, traveler's checks, savings deposits, currency, money market accounts, and small-denomination time deposits. Here, M2 is adjusted for inflation by means of the deflator published by the federal government in the GDP report. Bank lending, a factor contributing to account deposits, usually declines when inflation increases faster than the money supply, which can make economic expansion more difficult. Thus, an increase in demand deposits will indicate expectations that inflation will rise, resulting in a decrease in bank lending and an increase in savings.

9. Interest rate spread (10-year Treasury vs. Federal Funds target) — The interest rate spread is often referred to as the yield curve and implies the expected direction of short-, medium- and long-term interest rates. Changes in the yield curve have been the most accurate predictors of downturns in the economic cycle. This is particularly true when the curve becomes inverted, that is, when the longer-term returns are expected to be less than the short rates.

10. Index of consumer expectations — This is the only component of the leading indicators that is based solely on expectations. This component leads the business cycle because consumer expectations can indicate future consumer spending or tightening. The data for this component comes from the University of Michigan's Survey Research Center, and is released once a month.

Lagging Indicators

Lagging indicators are indicators that usually change after the economy as a whole does. Typically the lag is a few quarters of a year. The unemployment rate is a lagging indicator: employment tends to increase two or three quarters after an upturn in the general economy. In finance, Bollinger bands are one of various lagging indicators in frequent use. In a performance measuring system, profit earned by a business is a lagging indicator as it reflects a historical performance; similarly, improved customer satisfaction is the result of initiatives taken in the past.

The Index of Lagging Indicators is published monthly by The Conference Board, a non-governmental organization, which determines the value of the index from seven components.

The Index tends to *follow* changes in the overall economy.

The components on the Conference Board's index are:

- The average duration of unemployment (inverted)
- The value of outstanding commercial and industrial loans
- The change in the Consumer Price Index for services
- The change in labour cost per unit of output
- The ratio of manufacturing and trade inventories to sales
- The ratio of consumer credit outstanding to personal income
- The average prime rate charged by banks

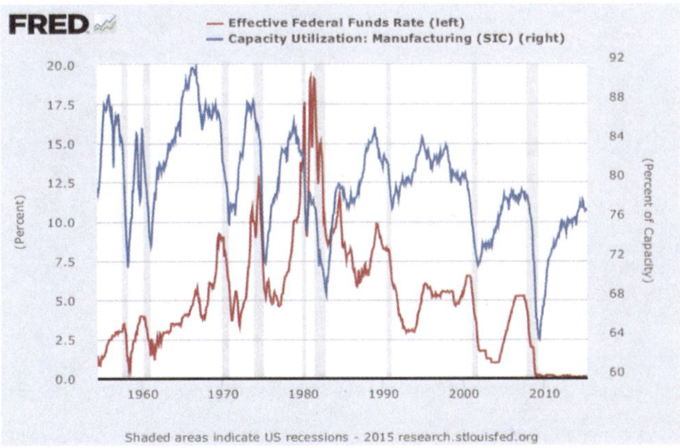

Federal Funds Rate in the USA lagging behind capacity utilization in manufacturing.

Coincident Indicators

Coincident indicators change at approximately the same time as the whole economy, thereby providing information about the current state of the economy. There are many coincident economic indicators, such as Gross Domestic Product, industrial production, personal income and retail sales. A coincident index may be used to identify, after the fact, the dates of peaks and troughs in the business cycle.

There are four economic statistics comprising the Index of Coincident Economic Indicators:

- Number of employees on non-agricultural payrolls
- Personal income less transfer payments
- Industrial production
- Manufacturing and trade sale

The Philadelphia Federal Reserve produces state-level coincident indexes based on 4 state-level variables:

- Nonfarm payroll employment
- Average hours worked in manufacturing
- Unemployment rate
- Wage and salary disbursements deflated by the consumer price index (U.S. city average)

By Direction

There are also three terms that describe an economic indicator's *direction* relative to the direction of the general economy:

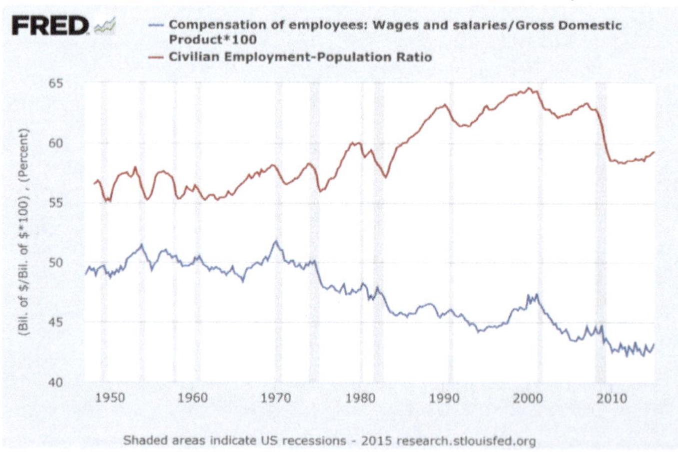

The wage share (arguably) as countercyclical, but also as a lagging indicator with respect to the employment rate as procyclical indicator in the USA

Procyclical indicators

move in the same direction as the general economy: they increase when the economy is doing well; decrease when it is doing badly. Gross domestic product (GDP) is a procyclic indicator.

Countercyclical indicators

move in the opposite direction to the general economy. The unemployment rate and the wage share are countercyclic: in the short run they rise when the economy is deteriorating.

Acyclical indicators

are those with little or no correlation to the business cycle: they may rise or fall when the general economy is doing well, and may rise or fall when it is not doing well.

Local Indicators

Local governments often need to project future tax revenues. The city of San Francisco, for example, uses the price of a one-bedroom apartment on Craigslist, weekend subway ridership numbers, parking garage usage, and monthly reports on passenger landings at the city's airport.

Economic environment goes through different stages or phases. These sequential stages together are known as business cycle. The business cycle can be explained as a pattern of changing economic output and growth: an initial period of rapid growth followed by a period of slow growth or even stagnation after which the economy contracts (Mayo, 2006).

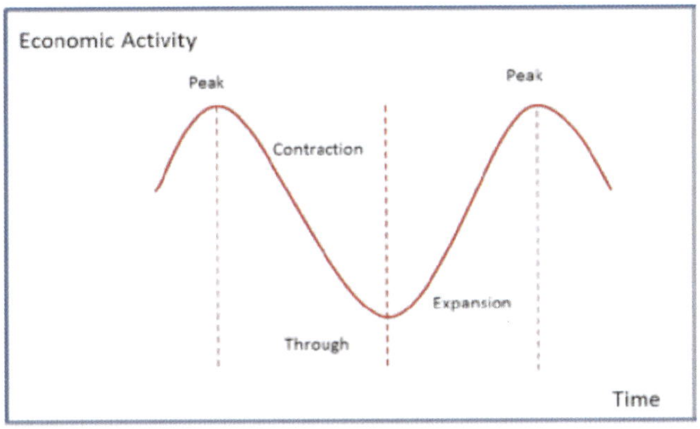

Business Cycle

Different industries show varied performance as the economy moves from one stage to another stage. Cyclical industries like producers of capital goods takes the hit when economy goes through slow down but outperform other industries during expansion. Defensive industries like food producers and pharmaceutical firms are less sensitive to business cycle and do better compared to other industries during recession.

Cyclical Indicators: Because of cyclical nature of the business cycle, the different phases of business cycle can be predicted. The Conference Board provides a set of cyclical indicators that helps forecast, measure and interpret short-term fluctuations in economic activity. The Conference Board is a worldwide, not-for-profit and nonpartisan business membership organization that provides timely research on management practices and economic trends. The cyclical indicators are classified as below:

- Leading Indicators: Economic series that usually reach peaks or troughs before corresponding peaks or troughs in aggregate economy activity.
- Coincidence Indicators: Economic series that have peaks and troughs that roughly coincide with the peaks and troughs in the business cycle.
- Lagging Indicators: Economic series that experience their peaks and troughs after those of the aggregate economy.

Table: List of Cyclical Indicators

Leading Indicators	**Coincidence Indicators**
Average weekly hours, manufacturing	Employees on nonagricultural payrolls
Average weekly initial claims for unemployment insurance	Personal income less transfer payments
Manufacturers' new orders, consumer goods and materials	Index of industrial production
Vendor performance, slower deliveries diffusion index	Manufacturing and trade sales
Manufacturers' new orders, nondefense capital goods	**Lagging Indicators**
Building permits, new private housing units	Average duration of unemployment
Stock prices, 500 common stocks	Inventories to sales ratio, manufacturing and trade
Money supply, M2	Change in labor cost per unit of output, manufacturing (%)
Interest rate spread, 10-year Treasury bonds less Federal funds (%)	Average prime rate charged by banks (%)
Index of consumer expectations	Commercial and industrial loans outstanding
	Consumer installment credit outstanding to personal income ratio
	Change in consumer price index for services (%)

Trend in few Leading Indicators with reference to Indian Market: Select charts of cyclical indicators in Indian context are given below.

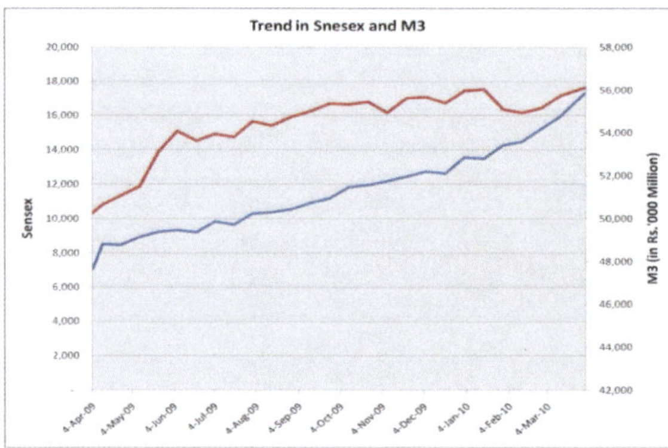

Leading Indicators

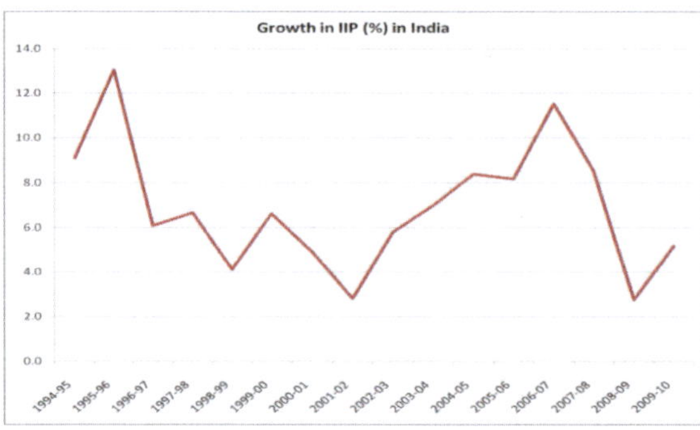

Coincidence Indicator

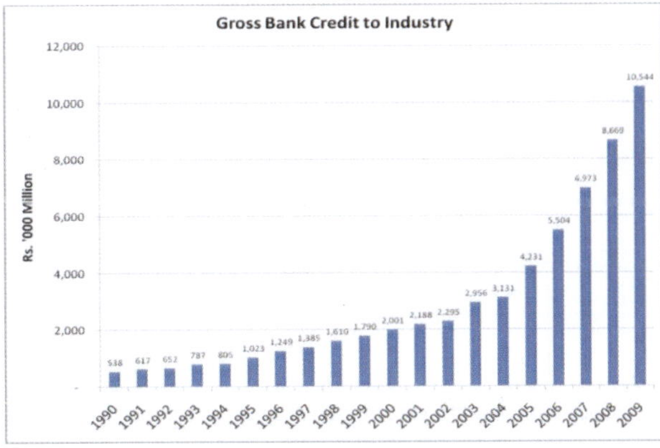

Lagging Indicator

Analysts are expected to look at trends in individual indicators in a particular category [leading, lagging or coincidence] and a composite time series that combines the indicators in terms of an index for a particular category. This would indicate the overall trend in economic condition.

Analyzing the Indicators: One simple way of analyzing the economic indicators is to find out the rate of change over previous period. While a positive rate of change indicates a growth, one has to look for the trend in such rate of change i.e. increasing or decreasing. The rate of change reaches peaks before the just before the peak in the series itself. Another important tool is to find out the diffusion index. It is a measure of how widespread a phenomenon and is based on the trends, direction of change, rate of change and comparison of previous business cycles. One can set of a diffusion index of leading indicators by counting the number of indicators that rise during a particular period and expressing it as a percentage of total. This can indicate the probable length of a particular phenomenon in the economy. The movements of individual series during the current business cycle can be compared with that in the previous cycles.

Monetary variables, Inflation and Securities Market: Rsearchers have found close relationship between security prices and monetary variables that are dictated by monetary policy of a country. The monetary policy instruments affect money supply, interest rates, inflation etc. among other things. The central banks engage in open market operations like buying and selling government securities and control liquidity in market. This can lead to change in interest rates thus affecting the prices of debt instruments like bonds and in turn stock prices. Hence it is imperative to forecast the growth in money supply as an important task while forecasting the stock prices. There is also a strong relationship between inflation and interest rates. An anticipated increase in inflation rate can lead to rise in expected rate of return for investors. This in turn leads to decrease in bond prices. But the relationship between inflation and stock prices is not direct. It all depends upon how the cash flows of the companies are affected by inflation.

Financial Conditions Index: Goldman Sachs has created a composite financial condsiotns series (the Goldman Sachs Financial Conditions Index – GSFCI) that can show the overall trend in financial market. This index consists of four variables with respective weights as below:

- Real three-month LIBOR (0.35)
- Real A-rated corporate bond yield (0.55)

- Real Goldman Sachs Trade-Weighted Dollar Index (0.05)
- The equity market capitalization / GDP ratio (0.05)

An increase in GSFCI reflects a tightening of the monetary environment. Goldman Sachs has also designed a Financial Conditions Index for India (GS India FCI) with following variables and respective weights:

- interest rates (0.55)
- money supply (0.29)
- exchange rate (0.125)
- stock market (0.035).

Procyclical and Countercyclical

Procyclical and countercyclical are terms used to describe how an economic quantity is related to economic fluctuations. Their meanings may vary with regard to business cycle theory and economic policy making.

The terms are often used loosely to describe a government's approach to spending and taxation. A 'procyclical fiscal policy' can be summarised simply as governments choosing to increase public spending and reduce taxes during an economic boom, but reduce spending and increase taxes during a recession. A 'countercyclical' fiscal policy refers to the opposite approach: reducing spending and raising taxes during a boom period, and increasing spending/cutting taxes during a recession.

Business Cycle Theory

Procyclical

In business cycle theory and finance, any economic quantity that is positively correlated with the overall state of the economy is said to be procyclical. That is, any quantity that tends to increase in expansion and tend to decrease in recession is classified as procyclical. Gross Domestic Product (GDP) is an example of a procyclical economic indicator. Many stock prices are also procyclical, because they tend to increase when the economy is growing quickly.

Countercyclical

Conversely, any economic quantity that is negatively correlated with the overall state of the economy is said to be countercyclical. That is, quantities that tend to increase when the overall economy is slowing down are classified as 'countercyclical'. Unemployment is an example of a countercyclical variable. Similarly, business failures and stock market prices tend to be countercyclical. In finance, an asset that tends to do well while the economy as a whole is doing poorly is referred to as countercyclical, and could be for example a business or a financial instrument whose value is derived from sales of an inferior good.

Economic Policy Making

Procyclical

Procyclical has a different meaning in the context of economic policy. In this context, it refers to any aspect of economic policy that could magnify economic or financial fluctuations. Of course, since effects of particular policies are often uncertain or disputed, a policy will be often procyclical, counter cyclical or acyclical according to the view of the one judging it.

Thus the financial regulations of the Basel II Accord have been criticized for their possible procyclicality. The accord requires banks to increase their capital ratios when they face greater risks. Unfortunately, this may require them to lend less during a recession or a credit crunch, which could aggravate the downturn. A similar criticism has been directed at fair value accounting rules. The effect of the single Eurozone interest rate on the relatively high-inflation countries in the Eurozone periphery is also pro-cyclical, leading to very low or even negative real interest rates during an upturn which magnifies the boom (e.g. 'Celtic Tiger' upturn in Ireland) and property and asset price bubbles whose subsequent bust magnifies the downturns.

Countercyclical

Conversely, an economic or financial policy is called countercyclical if it works against the cyclical tendencies in the economy. That is, countercyclical policies are ones that cool down the economy when it is in an upswing, and stimulate the economy when it is in a downturn.

Keynesian economics advocates the use of automatic and discretionary countercyclical policies to lessen the impact of the business cycle. One example of an automatically countercyclical fiscal policy is progressive taxation. By taxing a larger proportion of income when the economy expands, a progressive tax tends to decrease demand when the economy is booming, thus reining in the boom. Other schools of economic thought, such new classical macroeconomics, hold that countercyclical policies may be counterproductive or destabilizing, and therefore favor a laissez-faire fiscal policy as a better method for maintaining an overall robust economy. When the government adopts a countercyclical fiscal policy in response to a threat of recession the government might increase infrastructure spending.

Economic Forecasting

Economic forecasting is the process of making predictions about the economy. Forecasts can be carried out at a high level of aggregation—for example for GDP, inflation, unemployment or the fiscal deficit—or at a more disaggregated level, for specific sectors of the economy or even specific firms.

Overview

Many institutions engage in economic forecasting, including international organisations such as the International Monetary Fund, World Bank and the OECD, national governments and central banks, and private sector entities, including think-tanks, banks, consultants and companies. Some forecasts are produced annually, but many are updated more frequently.

Economists select which variables are important to the subject material under discussion. Economists may use statistical analysis of historical data to determine the apparent relationships between particular independent variables and their relationship to the dependent variable under study. For example, to what extent did changes in housing prices affect the net worth of the population overall in the past? This relationship can then be used to forecast the future. That is, if housing prices are expected to change in a particular way, what effect would that have on the future net worth of the population? Forecasts are generally based on sample data rather than a complete population, which introduces uncertainty. The economist conducts statistical tests and develops statistical models (often using regression analysis) to determine which relationships best describe or predict the behavior of the variables under study. Historical data and assumptions about the future are applied to the model in arriving at a forecast for particular variables.

The economist typically considers risks (i.e., events or conditions that can cause the result to vary from their initial estimates). These risks help illustrate the reasoning process used in arriving at the final forecast numbers. Economists typically use commentary along with data visualization tools such as tables and charts to communicate their forecast.

Purpose

Forecasts are used for a variety of purposes. Governments and businesses use economic forecasts to help them determine their strategy, multi-year plans, and budgets for the upcoming year. Stock market analysts use forecasts to help them estimate the valuation of a company and its stock.

Sources of Forecasts

Global Scope

The Economic Outlook is the OECD's twice-yearly analysis of the major economic trends and prospects for the next two years. The IMF publishes the World Economic Outlook report twice annually, which provides comprehensive global coverage.

U.S. Forecasts

The U.S. Congressional Budget Office (CBO) publishes a report titled "The Budget and Economic Outlook" annually, which primarily covers the following ten-year period. The U.S. Federal Reserve Board of Governors members also give speeches, provide testimony, and issue reports throughout the year that cover the economic outlook.

Large banks such as Wells Fargo and JP Morgan Chase provide economics reports and newsletters.

Combining Forecasts

Forecasts from multiple sources may be combined and published by some entities. *Consensus Economics*, among others, compiles the macroeconomic forecasts prepared by a variety of forecasters, and publishes them every month. *The Economist* magazine regularly provides such a snapshot as well, for a narrower range of countries and variables.

Forecast Methods

The process of economic forecasting is similar to data analysis and results in estimated values for key economic variables in the future. An economist applies the techniques of econometrics in their forecasting process. Typical steps may include:

1. Scope: Key economic variables and topics for forecast commentary are determined based on the needs of the forecast audience.
2. Literature review: Commentary from sources with summary-level perspective, such as the IMF, OECD, U.S. Federal Reserve, and CBO helps with identifying key economic trends, issues and risks. Such commentary can also help the forecaster with their own assumptions while also giving them other forecasts to compare against.
3. Obtain data inputs: Historical data is gathered on key economic variables. This data is contained in print as well as electronic sources such as the FRED database or Eurostat, which allow users to query historical values for variables of interest.
4. Determine historical relationships: Historical data is used to determine the relationships between one or more independent variables and the dependent variable under study, often by using regression analysis.
5. Model: Historical data inputs and assumptions are used to develop an econometric model. Models typically apply a computation to a series of inputs to generate an economic forecast for one or more variables.
6. Report: The outputs of the model are included in reports that typically include information graphics and commentary to help the reader understand the forecast.

Forecasters may use computational general equilibrium models or dynamic stochastic general equilibrium models. The latter are often used by central banks.

Methods of forecasting include Econometric models, Economic base analysis, Shift-share analysis, Input-output model and the Grinold and Kroner Model.Reference class forecasting, Transportation planning, Calculating Demand Forecast Accuracy and Consensus forecasts.

The World Bank provides a means for individuals and organizations to run their own simulations and forecasts using its *iSimulate platform*.

Issues in Forecasting

Forecast Accuracy

"Prediction is very difficult, especially about the future."

Niels Bohr

There are many studies on the subject of forecast accuracy. Accuracy is one of the main, if not the main criteria, used to judge forecast quality. Some of the references below relate to academic studies of forecast accuracy.

In early 2014 the OECD carried out a self-analysis of its projections. "The OECD also found that it was too optimistic for countries that were most open to trade and foreign finance, that had the most tightly regulated markets and weak banking systems" according to the Financial Times.

Forecasts and the Great Recession

The financial and economic crisis that erupted in 2007—arguably the worst since the Great Depression of the 1930s—was not foreseen by most of the forecasters, even if a few lone analysts had been predicting it for some time (for example, Nouriel Roubini and Robert Shiller). The failure to forecast the "Great Recession" has caused a lot of soul searching in the profession. The Queen of England herself asked why had nobody noticed that the credit crunch was on its way, and a group of economists—experts from business, the City, its regulators, academia, and government—tried to explain in a letter.

Business Cycle

The business cycle or economic cycle is the downward and upward movement of gross domestic product (GDP) around its long-term growth trend. The length of a business cycle is the period of time containing a single boom and contraction in sequence. These fluctuations typically involve shifts over time between periods of relatively rapid economic growth (expansions or booms), and periods of relative stagnation or decline (contractions or recessions).

Business cycles are usually measured by considering the growth rate of real gross domestic product. Despite the often-applied term cycles, these fluctuations in economic activity do not exhibit uniform or predictable periodicity.

The common or popular usage boom-and-bust cycle refers to fluctuations in which the expansion is rapid and the contraction severe.

History

Theory

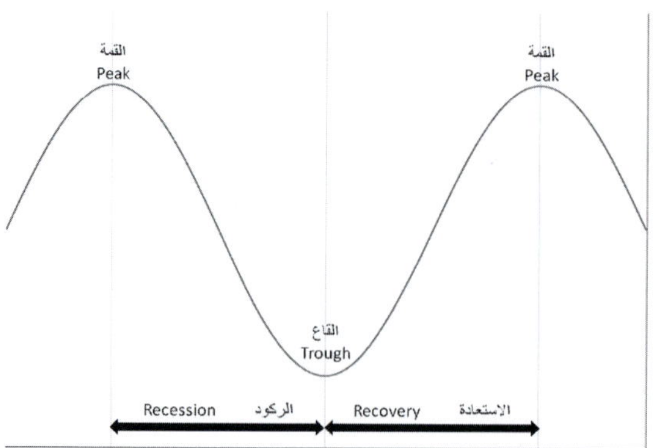

Phases of the business cycle

The first systematic exposition of periodic economic crises, in opposition to the existing theory of economic equilibrium, was the 1819 *Nouveaux Principes d'économie politique* by Jean Charles

Léonard de Sismondi. Prior to that point classical economics had either denied the existence of business cycles, blamed them on external factors, notably war, or only studied the long term. Sismondi found vindication in the Panic of 1825, which was the first unarguably international economic crisis, occurring in peacetime.

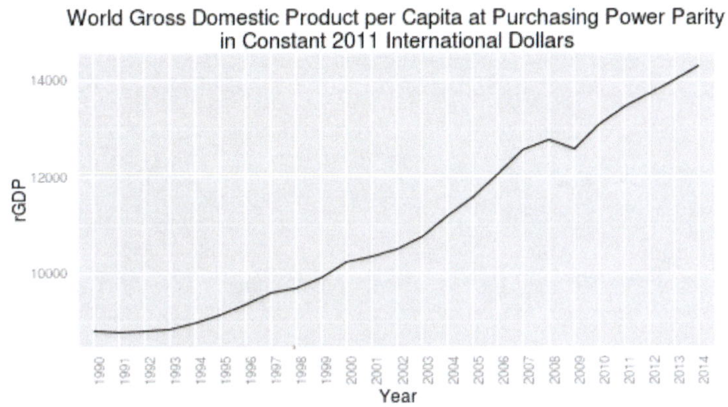

Long Term Growth of GDP

Sismondi and his contemporary Robert Owen, who expressed similar but less systematic thoughts in 1817 *Report to the Committee of the Association for the Relief of the Manufacturing Poor,* both identified the cause of economic cycles as overproduction and underconsumption, caused in particular by wealth inequality. They advocated government intervention and socialism, respectively, as the solution. This work did not generate interest among classical economists, though underconsumption theory developed as a heterodox branch in economics until being systematized in Keynesian economics in the 1930s.

Sismondi's theory of periodic crises was developed into a theory of alternating *cycles* by Charles Dunoyer, and similar theories, showing signs of influence by Sismondi, were developed by Johann Karl Rodbertus. Periodic crises in capitalism formed the basis of the theory of Karl Marx, who further claimed that these crises were increasing in severity and, on the basis of which, he predicted a communist revolution. He devoted hundreds of pages of *Das Kapital* (1867) to crises. In *Progress and Poverty* (1879), Henry George focused on land's role in crises – particularly land speculation – and proposed a single tax on land as a solution.

Classification by Periods

In 1860 French economist Clement Juglar first identified economic cycles 7 to 11 years long, although he cautiously did not claim any rigid regularity. Later, economist Joseph Schumpeter (1883–1950) argued that a Juglar Cycle has four stages:

1. expansion (increase in production and prices, low interest-rates)
2. crisis (stock exchanges crash and multiple bankruptcies of firms occur)
3. recession (drops in prices and in output, high interest-rates)
4. recovery (stocks recover because of the fall in prices and incomes)

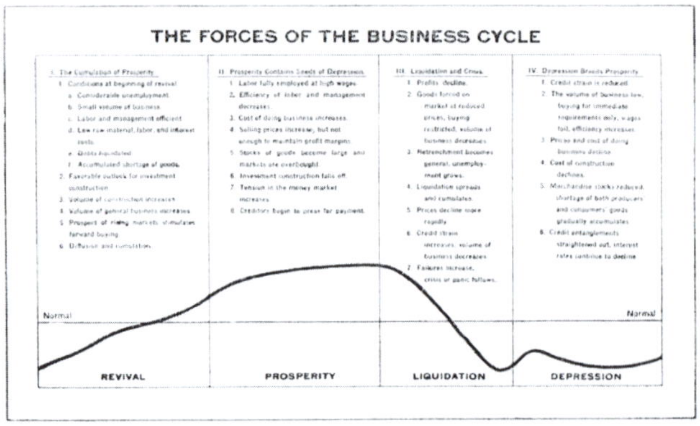

Business cycle with it specific forces in four stages according to Malcolm C. Rorty, 1922

Schumpeter's Juglar model associates recovery and prosperity with increases in productivity, consumer confidence, aggregate demand, and prices.

In the mid-20th century, Schumpeter and others proposed a typology of business cycles according to their periodicity, so that a number of particular cycles were named after their discoverers or proposers:

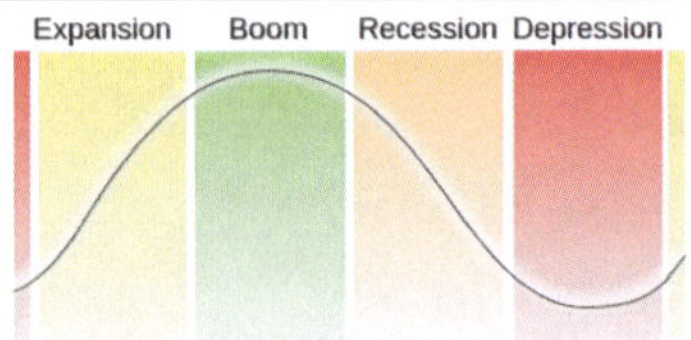

Proposed Economic Waves

Cycle/Wave Name	Period (years)
Kitchin cycle (inventory, e.g. pork cycle)	3–5
Juglar cycle (fixed investment)	7–11
Kuznets swing (infrastructural investment)	15–25
Kondratiev wave (technological basis)	45–60

- the Kitchin inventory cycle of 3 to 5 years (after Joseph Kitchin).
- the Juglar fixed-investment cycle of 7 to 11 years (often identified as "the" business cycle).
- the Kuznets infrastructural investment cycle of 15 to 25 years (after Simon Kuznets – also called "building cycle").
- the Kondratiev wave or long technological cycle of 45 to 60 years (after the Soviet economist Nikolai Kondratiev).

Interest in the different typologies of cycles has waned since the development of modern macroeconomics, which gives little support to the idea of regular periodic cycles.

Occurrence

There were great increases in productivity, industrial production and real per capita product throughout the period from 1870 to 1890 that included the Long Depression and two other recessions. There were also significant increases in productivity in the years leading up to the Great Depression. Both the Long and Great Depressions were characterized by overcapacity and market saturation.

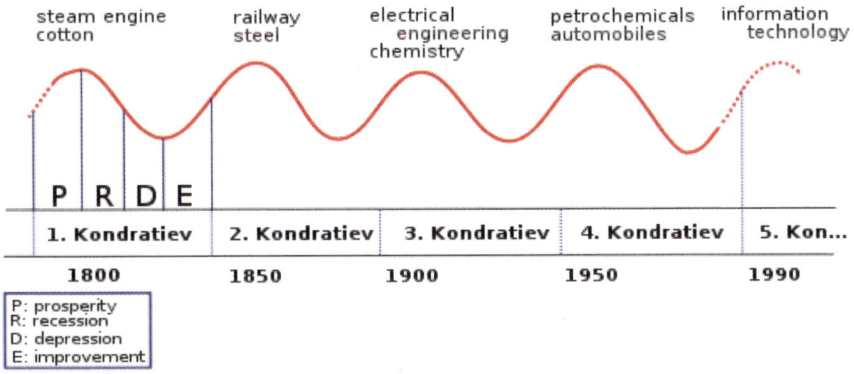

A simplified Kondratiev wave, with the theory that productivity enhancing innovations drive waves of economic growth.

Over the period since the Industrial Revolution, technological progress has had a much larger effect on the economy than any fluctuations in credit or debt, the primary exception being the Great Depression, which caused a multi-year steep economic decline. The effect of technological progress can be seen by the purchasing power of an average hour's work, which has grown from $3 in 1900 to $22 in 1990, measured in 2010 dollars. There were similar increases in real wages during the 19th century.

There were frequent crises in Europe and America in the 19th and first half of the 20th century, specifically the period 1815–1939. This period started from the end of the Napoleonic wars in 1815, which was immediately followed by the Post-Napoleonic depression in the United Kingdom (1815–30), and culminated in the Great Depression of 1929–39, which led into World War II. The first of these crises not associated with a war was the Panic of 1825.

Business cycles in OECD countries after World War II were generally more restrained than the earlier business cycles. This was particularly true during the Golden Age of Capitalism (1945/50–1970s), and the period 1945–2008 did not experience a global downturn until the Late-2000s recession. Economic stabilization policy using fiscal policy and monetary policy appeared to have dampened the worst excesses of business cycles, and automatic stabilization due to the aspects of the government's budget also helped mitigate the cycle even without conscious action by policy-makers.

In this period, the economic cycle – at least the problem of depressions – was twice declared dead. The first declaration was in the late 1960s, when the Phillips curve was seen as being able to steer the economy. However, this was followed by stagflation in the 1970s, which discredited the theory. The second declaration was in the early 2000s, following the stability and growth in the 1980s and 1990s in what came to be known as The Great Moderation. Notably, in 2003, Robert Lucas, in his presidential address to the American Economic Association, declared that the "central problem of depression-prevention [has] been solved, for all practical purposes." Unfortunately, this was followed by the 2008–2012 global recession.

Various regions have experienced prolonged depressions, most dramatically the economic crisis in former Eastern Bloc countries following the end of the Soviet Union in 1991. For several of these countries the period 1989–2010 has been an ongoing depression, with real income still lower than in 1989. This has been attributed not to a cyclical pattern, but to a mismanaged transition from command economies to market economies.

Identifying

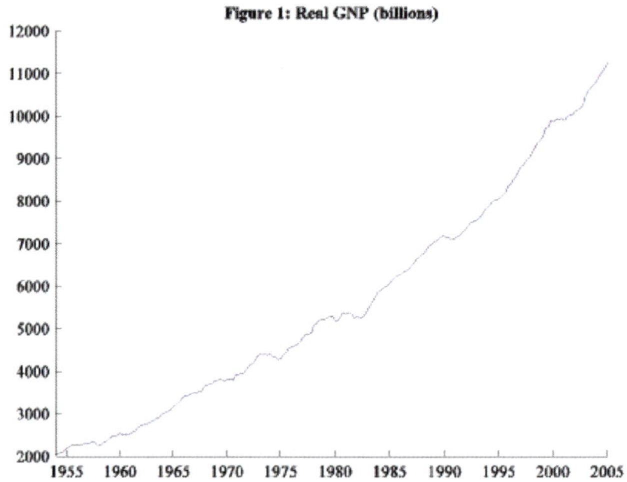

Economic activity in the US, 1954–2005.

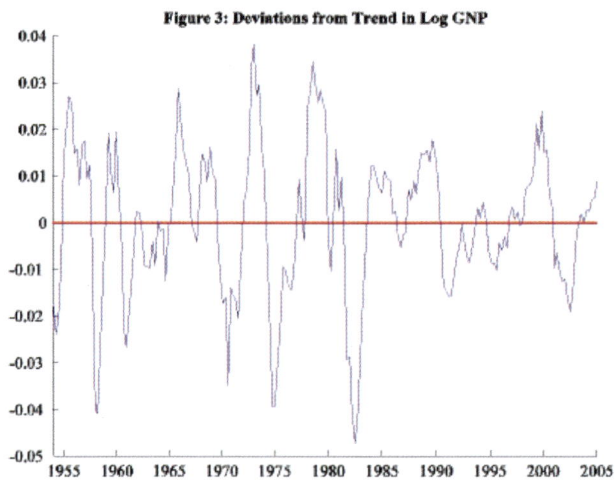

Deviations from the long-term US growth trend, 1954–2005.

In 1946, economists Arthur F. Burns and Wesley C. Mitchell provided the now standard definition of business cycles in their book *Measuring Business Cycles*:

> Business cycles are a type of fluctuation found in the aggregate economic activity of nations that organize their work mainly in business enterprises: a cycle consists of expansions occurring at about the same time in many economic activities, followed by similarly general recessions, contractions, and revivals which merge into the expansin phase of the next cycle; in duration, business cycles vary from more than one year to ten or twelve years; they are not divisible into shorter cycles of similar characteristics with amplitudes approximating their own.

According to A. F. Burns:

> Business cycles are not merely fluctuations in aggregate economic activity. The critical feature that distinguishes them from the commercial convulsions of earlier centuries or from the seasonal and other short term variations of our own age is that the fluctuations are widely diffused over the economy – its industry, its commercial dealings, and its tangles of finance. The economy of the western world is a system of closely interrelated parts. He who would understand business cycles must master the workings of an economic system organized largely in a network of free enterprises searching for profit. The problem of how business cycles come about is therefore inseparable from the problem of how a capitalist economy functions.

In the United States, it is generally accepted that the National Bureau of Economic Research (NBER) is the final arbiter of the dates of the peaks and troughs of the business cycle. An expansion is the period from a trough to a peak, and a recession as the period from a peak to a trough. The NBER identifies a recession as "a significant decline in economic activity spread across the economy, lasting more than a few months, normally visible in real GDP, real income, employment, industrial production".

Upper Turning Points of Business Cycle, Commodity Prices and Freight Rates

There is often a close timing relationship between the upper turning points of the business cycle, commodity prices and freight rates, which is shown to be particularly tight in the grand peak years of 1873, 1889, 1900 and 1912.

Spectral Analysis of Business Cycles

Recent research employing spectral analysis has confirmed the presence of Kondratiev waves in the world GDP dynamics at an acceptable level of statistical significance. Korotayev & Tsirel also detected shorter business cycles, dating the Kuznets to about 17 years and calling it the third sub-harmonic of the Kondratiev, meaning that there are three Kuznets cycles per Kondratiev.

Cycles or Fluctuations?

In recent years economic theory has moved towards the study of *economic fluctuation* rather than a 'business cycle' – though some economists use the phrase 'business cycle' as a convenient shorthand. For Milton Friedman calling the business cycle a "cycle" is a misnomer, because of its non-cyclical nature. Friedman believed that for the most part, excluding very large supply shocks, business declines are more of a monetary phenomenon.

Proposed Explanations

The explanation of fluctuations in aggregate economic activity is one of the primary concerns of macroeconomics. The main framework for explaining such fluctuations is Keynesian economics. In the Keynesian view, business cycles reflect the possibility that the economy may reach short-run equilibrium at levels below or above full employment. If the economy is operating with less than full employment, i.e., with high unemployment, Keynesian theory states that monetary policy and fiscal policy can have a positive role to play in smoothing the fluctuations of the business cycle.

Beside the Keynesian explanation there are a number of alternative theories of business cycles, largely associated with particular schools or theorists in heterodox economics. A common alternative within mainstream economics is real business cycle theory. Nowadays other notable theories are credit-based explanations such as debt deflation and the financial instability hypothesis. The latter two gained interest for being able to explain the subprime mortgage crisis and financial crises.

Exogenous vs. Endogenous

Within mainstream economics, the debate over external (exogenous) versus internal (endogenous) being the causes of the economic cycles, with the classical school (now neo-classical) arguing for exogenous causes and the underconsumptionist (now Keynesian) school arguing for endogenous causes. These may also broadly be classed as "supply-side" and "demand-side" explanations: supply-side explanations may be styled, following Say's law, as arguing that "supply creates its own demand", while demand-side explanations argue that effective demand may fall short of supply, yielding a recession or depression.

This debate has important policy consequences: proponents of exogenous causes of crises such as neoclassicals largely argue for minimal government policy or regulation (laissez faire), as absent these external shocks, the market functions, while proponents of endogenous causes of crises such as Keynesians largely argue for larger government policy and regulation, as absent regulation, the market will move from crisis to crisis. This division is not absolute – some classicals (including Say) argued for government policy to mitigate the damage of economic cycles, despite believing in external causes, while Austrian School economists argue against government involvement as only worsening crises, despite believing in internal causes.

The view of the economic cycle as caused exogenously dates to Say's law, and much debate on endogeneity or exogeneity of causes of the economic cycle is framed in terms of refuting or supporting Say's law; this is also referred to as the "general glut" debate.

Until the Keynesian revolution in mainstream economics in the wake of the Great Depression, classical and neoclassical explanations (exogenous causes) were the mainstream explanation of economic cycles; following the Keynesian revolution, neoclassical macroeconomics was largely rejected. There has been some resurgence of neoclassical approaches in the form of real business cycle (RBC) theory. The debate between Keynesians and neo-classical advocates was reawakened following the recession of 2007.

Mainstream economists working in the neoclassical tradition, as opposed to the Keynesian tradition, have usually viewed the departures of the harmonic working of the market economy as due to exogenous influences, such as the State or its regulations, labor unions, business monopolies, or shocks due to technology or natural causes.

Contrarily, in the heterodox tradition of Jean Charles Léonard de Sismondi, Clement Juglar, and Marx the recurrent upturns and downturns of the market system are an endogenous characteristic of it.

The 19th-century school of underconsumptionism also posited endogenous causes for the business cycle, notably the paradox of thrift, and today this previously heterodox school has entered the mainstream in the form of Keynesian economics via the Keynesian revolution.

Keynesian

According to Keynesian economics, fluctuations in aggregate demand cause the economy to come to short run equilibrium at levels that are different from the full employment rate of output. These fluctuations express themselves as the observed business cycles. Keynesian models do not necessarily imply periodic business cycles. However, simple Keynesian models involving the interaction of the Keynesian multiplier and accelerator give rise to cyclical responses to initial shocks. Paul Samuelson's "oscillator model" is supposed to account for business cycles thanks to the multiplier and the accelerator. The amplitude of the variations in economic output depends on the level of the investment, for investment determines the level of aggregate output (multiplier), and is determined by aggregate demand (accelerator).

In the Keynesian tradition, Richard Goodwin accounts for cycles in output by the distribution of income between business profits and workers' wages. The fluctuations in wages are almost the same as in the level of employment (wage cycle lags one period behind the employment cycle), for when the economy is at high employment, workers are able to demand rises in wages, whereas in periods of high unemployment, wages tend to fall. According to Goodwin, when unemployment and business profits rise, the output rises.

Credit/Debt Cycle

One alternative theory is that the primary cause of economic cycles is due to the credit cycle: the net expansion of credit (increase in private credit, equivalently debt, as a percentage of GDP) yields economic expansions, while the net contraction causes recessions, and if it persists, depressions. In particular, the bursting of speculative bubbles is seen as the proximate cause of depressions, and this theory places finance and banks at the center of the business cycle.

A primary theory in this vein is the debt deflation theory of Irving Fisher, which he proposed to explain the Great Depression. A more recent complementary theory is the Financial Instability Hypothesis of Hyman Minsky, and the credit theory of economic cycles is often associated with Post-Keynesian economics such as Steve Keen.

Post-Keynesian economist Hyman Minsky has proposed an explanation of cycles founded on fluctuations in credit, interest rates and financial frailty, called the Financial Instability Hypothesis. In an expansion period, interest rates are low and companies easily borrow money from banks to invest. Banks are not reluctant to grant them loans, because expanding economic activity allows business increasing cash flows and therefore they will be able to easily pay back the loans. This process leads to firms becoming excessively indebted, so that they stop investing, and the economy goes into recession.

While credit causes have not been a primary theory of the economic cycle within the mainstream, they have gained occasional mention, such as (Eckstein & Sinai 1986), cited approvingly by (Summers 1986).

Carlota Perez blames "financial capital" for excess speculation, which she claims is likely to occur in the "frenzy" stage of a new technology, such as the 1998–2000 computer, internet, dot.com mania and bust. Perez also says excess speculation is likely to occur in the mature phase of a technological age.

Real Business Cycle Theory

Within mainstream economics, Keynesian views have been challenged by real business cycle models in which fluctuations are due to technology shocks. This theory is most associated with Finn E. Kydland and Edward C. Prescott, and more generally the Chicago school of economics (freshwater economics). They consider that economic crisis and fluctuations cannot stem from a monetary shock, only from an external shock, such as an innovation.

RBC theory has been categorically rejected by a number of mainstream economists in the Keynesian tradition, such as (Summers 1986) and Paul Krugman.

Politically Based Business Cycle

Another set of models tries to derive the business cycle from political decisions. The *partisan business cycle* suggests that cycles result from the successive elections of administrations with different policy regimes. Regime A adopts expansionary policies, resulting in growth and inflation, but is voted out of office when inflation becomes unacceptably high. The replacement, Regime B, adopts contractionary policies reducing inflation and growth, and the downwards swing of the cycle. It is voted out of office when unemployment is too high, being replaced by Party A.

The political business cycle is an alternative theory stating that when an administration of any hue is elected, it initially adopts a contractionary policy to reduce inflation and gain a reputation for economic competence. It then adopts an expansionary policy in the lead up to the next election, hoping to achieve simultaneously low inflation and unemployment on election day.

The political business cycle theory is strongly linked to the name of Michał Kalecki who discussed "the reluctance of the 'captains of industry' to accept government intervention in the matter of employment." Persistent full employment would mean increasing workers' bargaining power to raise wages and to avoid doing unpaid labor, potentially hurting profitability. (He did not see this theory as applying under fascism, which would use direct force to destroy labor's power.) In recent years, proponents of the "electoral business cycle" theory have argued that incumbent politicians encourage prosperity before elections in order to ensure re-election – and make the citizens pay for it with recessions afterwards.

Marxian Economics

For Marx the economy based on production of commodities to be sold in the market is intrinsically prone to crisis. In the heterodox Marxian view profit is the major engine of the market economy, but business (capital) profitability has a tendency to fall that recurrently creates crises, in which mass unemployment occurs, businesses fail, remaining capital is centralized and concentrated and profitability is recovered. In the long run these crises tend to be more severe and the system will eventually fail.

Some Marxist authors such as Rosa Luxemburg viewed the lack of purchasing power of workers as a cause of a tendency of supply to be larger than demand, creating crisis, in a model that has similarities with the Keynesian one. Indeed, a number of modern authors have tried to combine Marx's and Keynes's views. Henryk Grossman reviewed the debates and the counteracting tendencies and Paul Mattick subsequently emphasized the basic differences between the Marxian and the

Keynesian perspective: while Keynes saw capitalism as a system worth maintaining and susceptible to efficient regulation, Marx viewed capitalism as a historically doomed system that cannot be put under societal control.

The American mathematician and economist, Richard M. Goodwin formalised a Marxist model of business cycles, known as the Goodwin Model in which recession was caused by increased bargaining power of workers (a result of high employment in boom periods) pushing up the wage share of national income, suppressing profits and leading to a breakdown in capital accumulation. Later theorists applying variants of the Goodwin model have identified both short and long period profit-led growth and distribution cycles in the United States, and elsewhere. David Gordon provided a Marxist model of long period institutional growth cycles, in an attempt to explain the Kondratiev wave. This cycle is due to the periodic breakdown of the 'social structure of accumulation' – a set of institutions which secure and stabilise capital accumulation.

Austrian School

Economists of the Austrian School argue that business cycles are caused by excessive issuance of credit by banks in fractional reserve banking systems. According to Austrian economists, excessive issuance of bank credit may be exacerbated if central bank monetary policy sets interest rates too low, and the resulting expansion of the money supply causes a "boom" in which resources are misallocated or "malinvested" because of artificially low interest rates. Eventually, the boom cannot be sustained and is followed by a "bust" in which the malinvestments are liquidated (sold for less than their original cost) and the money supply contracts.

One of the criticisms of the Austrian business cycle theory is based on the observation that the United States suffered recurrent economic crises in the 19th century, notably the Panic of 1873, which occurred prior to the establishment of a U.S. central bank in 1913. Adherents of the Austrian School, such as the historian Thomas Woods, argue that these earlier financial crises were prompted by government and bankers' efforts to expand credit despite restraints imposed by the prevailing gold standard, and are thus consistent with Austrian Business Cycle Theory.

The Austrian explanation of the business cycle differs significantly from the mainstream understanding of business cycles and is generally rejected by mainstream economists. Mainstream economists generally do not support Austrian school explanations for business cycles, on both theoretical as well as real-world empirical grounds.

Yield Curve

The slope of the yield curve is one of the most powerful predictors of future economic growth, inflation, and recessions. One measure of the yield curve slope (i.e. the difference between 10-year Treasury bond rate and the 3-month Treasury bond rate) is included in the Financial Stress Index published by the St. Louis Fed. A different measure of the slope (i.e. the difference between 10-year Treasury bond rates and the federal funds rate) is incorporated into the Index of Leading Economic Indicators.

An inverted yield curve is often a harbinger of recession. A positively sloped yield curve is often a harbinger of inflationary growth. Work by Dr. Arturo Estrella & Dr. Tobias Adrian has established the predictive power of an inverted yield curve to signal a recession. Their models show that when the difference between short-term interest rates (he uses 3-month T-bills) and long-term interest rates (10-year Treasury bonds) at the end of a federal reserve tightening cycle is negative or less than 93 basis points positive that a rise in unemployment usually occurs. The New York Fed publishes a monthly recession probability prediction derived from the yield curve and based on Dr. Estrella's work.

All the recessions in the US since 1970 (up through 2016) have been preceded by an inverted yield curve (10-year vs 3-month). Over the same time frame, every occurrence of an inverted yield curve has been followed by recession as declared by the NBER business cycle dating committee.

Event	**Date of Inversion Start**	**Date of the Recession Start**	**Time from Inversion to Recession Start**	**Duration of Inversion**	**Time from Recession Start to NBER Announcement**	**Time from Disinversion to Recession End**	**Duration of Recession**	**Time from Recession End to NBER Announcement**	**Max Inversion**
			Months	**Months**	**Months**	**Months**	**Months**	**Months**	**Basis Points**
1970 Recession	Dec-68	Jan-70	13	15	NA	8	11	NA	−52
1974 Recession	Jun-73	Dec-73	6	18	NA	3	16	NA	−159
1980 Recession	Nov-78	Feb-80	15	18	4	2	6	12	−328
1981–1982 Recession	Oct-80	Aug-81	10	12	5	13	16	8	−351
1990 Recession	Jun-89	Aug-90	14	7	8	14	8	21	−16
2001 Recession	Jul-00	Apr-01	9	7	7	9	8	20	−70
2008–2009 Recession	Aug-06	Jan-08	17	10	11	24	18	15	−51
Average since 1969			12	12	7	10	12	15	−147
Std Dev since 1969			3.83	4.72	2.74	7.50	4.78	5.45	138.96

Dr. Estrella has postulated that the yield curve affects the business cycle via the balance sheet of banks (or bank-like financial institutions). When the yield curve is inverted banks are often caught paying more on short-term deposits than they are making on long-term loans leading to a loss of profitability and reluctance to lend resulting in a credit crunch. When the yield curve is upward sloping, banks can profitably take-in short term deposits and make long-term loans so they are eager to supply credit to borrowers. This eventually leads to a credit bubble.

Georgism

Henry George claimed land price fluctuations were the primary cause of most business cycles. The theory is generally ignored in most of today's discussions of the subject despite two of the greatest economic contractions of the last 100 years (1929–1933 and 2008–2009) involving speculative real estate bubbles.

George observed that one necessary factor in production – land – has an inherent tendency to rise in price on an exponential basis as the economy grows. The reason for this is that the quantity of land (the stock of locations and natural resources) is fixed, while its quality is improved due to improvements such as transportation infrastructures and economic development of the surroundings. Investors see this tendency as the economy grows and they buy land ahead of the boom areas, withholding it from use in order to take advantage of its increased value in the future. Because housing and commercial real estate provide collateral for a large portion of lending, there is a tendency for real estate prices to rise faster than the rate of inflation in business cycle upswings. Speculation in land concentrates profits in landholders and diverts economic resources to speculation in land, squeezing profits away from production that has to occur on this land.

In effect, land speculation creates a built-in supply shock, that squeezes the economy just as economic output increases. This is a systemic retardation of the economy, placing a sharp brake on further economic expansion. This shock to the economy occurs as long as there is land speculation, creating an underlying tendency toward inflation and recession late in the growth phase of the business cycle. Land speculation, according to George, is always the cause of economic downturns. There are any number of contributing causes; things like oil price shocks, consumer confidence crises, international trade fluctuations, natural disasters – but none of these things creates the underlying weakness.

Land speculation slows the economy in two ways. It increases production costs by making land in general more expensive (shifting the Aggregate supply (AS) curve upward) as well as decreasing productivity by denying access to the best locations, shifting the AS curve to the left and lowering "potential output".

Mitigating an Economic Downturn

Many social indicators, such as mental health, crimes, and suicides, worsen during economic recessions (though general mortality tends to fall, and it is in expansions when it tends to increase). As periods of economic stagnation are painful for the many who lose their jobs, there is often political pressure for governments to mitigate recessions. Since the 1940s, following the Keynesian revolution, most governments of developed nations have seen the mitigation of the business cycle as part of the responsibility of government, under the rubric of stabilization policy.

Since in the Keynesian view, recessions are caused by inadequate aggregate demand, when a recession occurs the government should increase the amount of aggregate demand and bring the economy back into equilibrium. This the government can do in two ways, firstly by increasing the money supply (expansionary monetary policy) and secondly by increasing government spending or cutting taxes (expansionary fiscal policy).

By contrast, some economists, notably New classical economist Robert Lucas, argue that the welfare cost of business cycles are very small to negligible, and that governments should focus on long-term growth instead of stabilization.

However, even according to Keynesian theory, managing economic policy to smooth out the cycle is a difficult task in a society with a complex economy. Some theorists, notably those who believe in Marxian economics, believe that this difficulty is insurmountable. Karl Marx claimed that recurrent business cycle crises were an inevitable result of the operations of the capitalistic system. In this view, all that the government can do is to change the *timing* of economic crises. The crisis could also show up in a different *form*, for example as severe inflation or a steadily increasing government deficit. Worse, by delaying a crisis, government policy is seen as making it *more dramatic* and thus more painful.

Additionally, since the 1960s neoclassical economists have played down the ability of Keynesian policies to manage an economy. Since the 1960s, economists like Nobel Laureates Milton Friedman and Edmund Phelps have made ground in their arguments that inflationary expectations negate the Phillips curve in the long run. The stagflation of the 1970s provided striking support for their theories while proving a dilemma for Keynesian policies, which appeared to necessitate both expansionary policies to mitigate recession and contractionary policies to reduce inflation. Friedman has gone so far as to argue that all the central bank of a country should do is to avoid making large mistakes, as he believes they did by contracting the money supply very rapidly in the face of the Wall Street Crash of 1929, in which they made what would have been a recession into the Great Depression.

References

- Holmes, J. W (1995). Toward Better Governance - Public Service Reform in New Zealand (1984-94) and its Relevance to Canada. Office of the Auditor General of Canada. ISBN 978-0662231677
- Matkowski, Z., Prochniak, M. "Real Economic Convergence in the EU Accession Countries". International Journal of Applied Econometrics and Quantitative Studies. Euro-American Association of Economic Development (3): 5–38
- Eckstein, Otto; Sinai, Allen (1990). "1. The Mechanisms of the Business Cycle in the Postwar Period". In Robert J. Gordon. The American Business Cycle: Continuity and Change. University of Chicago Press. ISBN 978-0-226-30453-3
- "UK could be in for demand shock". Television New Zealand. 2002-11-20. Archived from the original on 2011-05-20. Retrieved 2008-11-02
- Robert Hall, Marc Lieberman (2012), Economics: Principles and Applications, Cengage Learning, p. 849, ISBN 1-111-82234-4
- Pierella Pacia Marcin J. Sasinb and Jos Verbeek. "Economic growth, income distribution and poverty in Poland during transition" (PDF). Retrieved December 23, 2006
- Atashbar, T. (2012). "Illusion therapy: How to impose an economic shock without social pain". Journal of Policy Modeling. 34: 99. doi:10.1016/j.jpolmod.2011.09.005
- Murphy, John J. (1999). Technical analysis of the financial markets : a comprehensive guide to trading methods and applications (2nd ed.). New York [u.a.]: New York Institute of Finance. ISBN 0735200661

3

Industry Analysis and its Techniques

Industry analysis is a tool that helps a company in developing an understanding of its position in the market. The processes involved in this are market analysis, balanced scorecard, growth-share matrix, Porter's five forces analysis and market environment. Industry analysis techniques are best understood in confluence with the major topics listed in the following chapter.

Industry Analysis

Although overall economy has got its own cycle of ups and downs, all industries in the economy need not necessarily move in tandem with the economy. Some industries lag the economy, some might lead. At the same time, the performance of different industries varies. Hence it is important to analyse the industry – the second stage of E-I-C analysis.

Different industries have got different risk-return characteristics during a particular time period. The stages of the industries can also be different. Some might be mature while some industries might be at a nascent stage of development. In a particular industry also, different companies vary in their performance and stage of development. Hence for the analyst it might be opportune to make buy or sell recommendation based on industry.

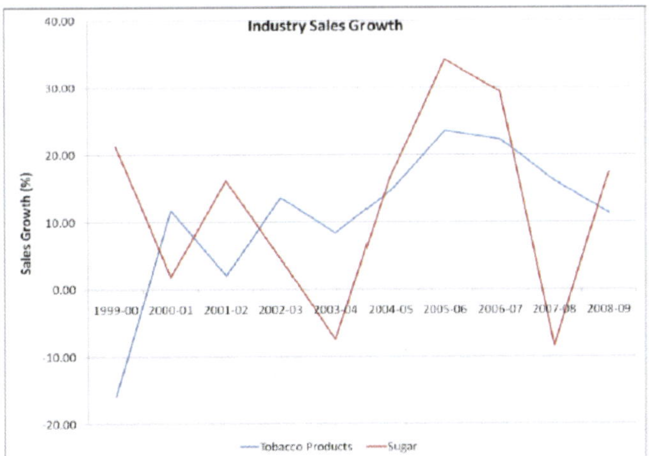

Sales Growth in Sample Industries

Figure above shows the sales growth of two different industries over a 10 year period of time. One can see that the two industries have shown considerable difference in sales growth. Similarly next Figure shows the average return on net worth (RoNW in %) of companies in of different industries vis-à-vis S&P CNX Nifty and BSE Sensex for 2008-09. While the RoNW is around 15 to 16% for the two indices, the same varies from -6.6% for textile industry to 22% for IT industry. Figure provides the annual index return of S&P CNX Nifty, BSE Sensex and different sector indices. One can observe a wide variation in the return shown by different sector specific indices. These provides ample justification for analyzing the industry performance while doing security analysis. While industry analysis is essential, it is not enough only to do so. Firms in a particular industry perform differently from each other. Hence analysis of firm/ company is also essential.

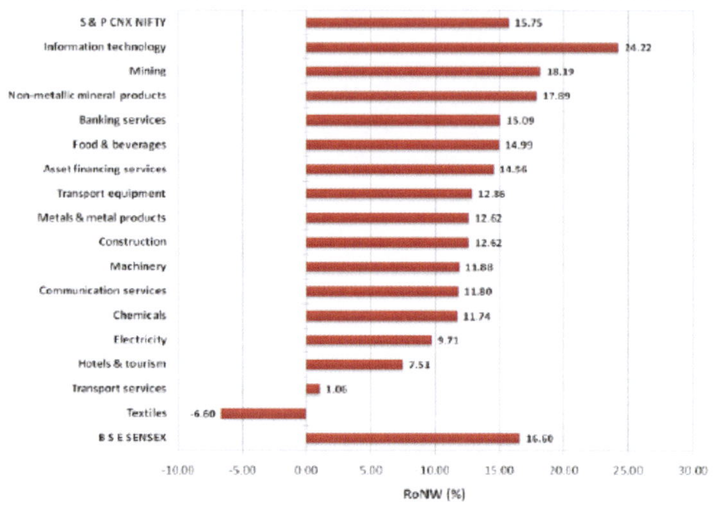

Return on Net Worth (RoNW in %), 2008-09 of different industries and indices

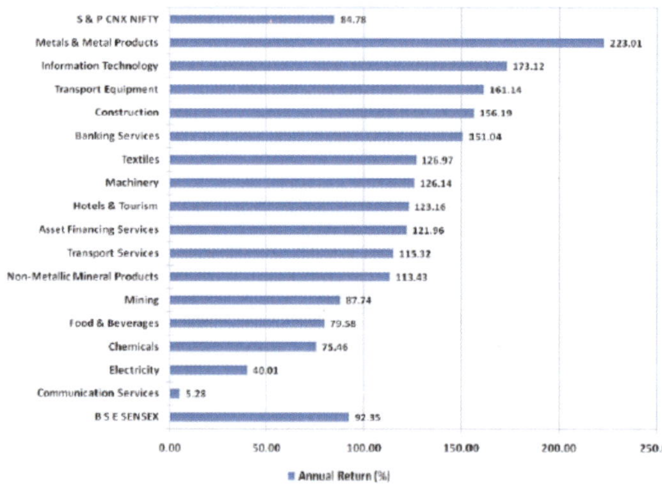

Annual Index Return, 2009-10

Industry Analysis Process

The first thing one has to find out is the industry classification. Because of continuous development in product and process technologies, innovation and technological changes, the structure of different industries change from time to time. Hence it is difficult to categorize the economy into different industries for all the time at once. This keeps changing, if not frequently. There are different ways in which industry classification is done. One such way is two digit/ three digit standard industry codes (SIC). The examples of such codes are as below:

Table: Sample two digit and three digit SIC Codes in India

SIC Code	**Name of the industry**	**SIC Code**	**Name of the industry**
01	AGRICULTURAL PRODUCTION-CROPS	29	PETROLEUM AND COAL PRODUCTS
011	Cash Grains	291	Petroleum Refining
013	Field Crops, Except Cash Grains	295	Asphalt Paving and Roofing Materials
016	Vegetables and Melons	299	Misc. Petroleum and Coal Products
017	Fruits and Tree Nuts	49	ELECTRIC, GAS, AND SANITARY SERVICES
018	Horticultural Specialties	491	Electric Services
019	General Farms, Primarily Crop	492	Gas Production And Distribution
		493	Combination Electric And Gas, And Other Utility

Another alternate industry classification which is accepted worldwide is the industry group given by North American Industry Classification System (NAICS Codes). NAICS assigns two digit '11' for major industry: Agriculture, Forestry, Fishing and Hunting. Further in this category sub industries are identified with six digit codes. For example, 111110 is assigned to Soybean Farming, 111422 is assigned to Floriculture Production1. Different stock exchanges and other agencies also classify industries and develop sector specific indices to track the market performance of different industry sectors. The industry classification by different agencies might not be the perfect one, but it serves the purpose to a considerable extent for security analysis.

Industry analysis process comprises of different elements viz. business cycle vs. industry sectors, structural economic changes vs. alternate industries, industry life cycle and industry competition analysis.

The business cycle and industrial sectors: Business cycle denotes the ups and downs in the economy. Industry performance is related to these movements in the economy. However all the industries do not move in tandem with the economy – where lies the challenge for the analyst to choose an industry for investment. The investors should be prudent to switch from one industry to another at opportune time. This is known as industry or sector rotation. Investors should be able to identify the industry that is likely to do better than others in a particular stage of the business cycle. This can be done by monitoring relevant economic trends and industry characteristics.

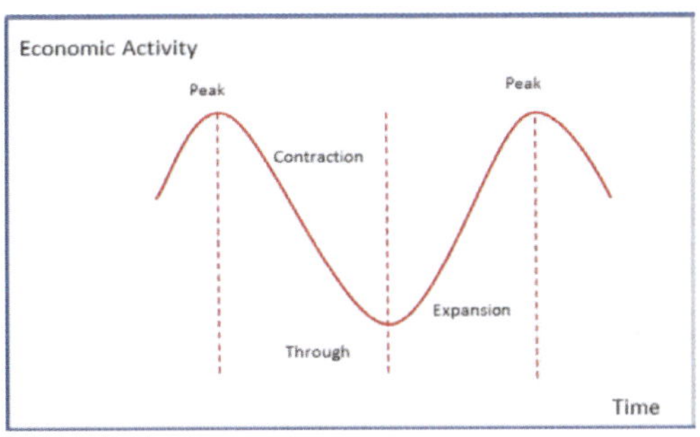

Business Cycle

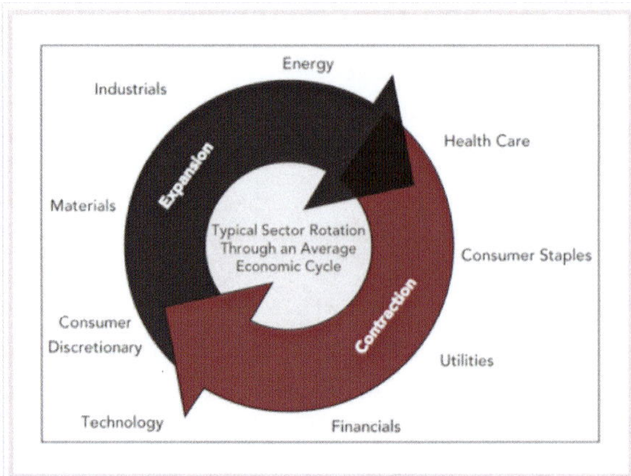

Rotation Strategy

Figure of business cycle and figure of rotation strategy suggests which industry is likely to do better at a particular stage of business cycle, so that one can rotate the investment from one industry to another. When the business cycle is at its peak, the basic materials industries like oil, metals etc. [source of raw materials] should become investor favorites. Inflation, which is high at the time of peak have little effect on these industries and these industries can increase prices thus showing higher profit margins. During recession, some industries perform better than others. Although the aggregate spending of people decline during recession, the spending on necessities remain almost intact. Hence consumer staples like pharmaceuticals, food and beverages outperform other sectors during a recession. Cyclical industries like consumer durables, luxury items benefit the most at the time of expansion. The firms with high financial or operating leverage show higher growth in profit in relation to growth in sales. Banking industry also performs better during expansion. Since cyclical industries behave the way the business cycle behaves, the investor should switch from this sector when contraction sets in. Investors need to forecast important economic variables and switch to industries accordingly just before the opportune time.

Structural Economic Changes vs. Alternate Industries: besides cyclical changes, the structural changes like those in demographics, technology, lifestyles and regulatory environment also affect different industries differently. Demographics includes growth in population, age distribution, geographic distribution of people, income distribution and changes in all such attributes over time. Looking at India, the population in the young group is quite high. Hence industries like retail, lifestyle products, fashion etc. are likely to do better. The industries like information technology (IT) and IT enabled services also do better because of availability brainpower. Lifestyles the set of living standard, consumption pattern, education level etc. keep changing from time to time. At present, in India, one can see a lot of consumer interest in entertainment like multiplexes, restaurants, travel and leisure, automobiles. People also would like to spend in high-end consumer products, gadgets etc. Technology affects how products are produced and delivered. This makes some industries redundant and new industries come into vogue. Developments in information technology added with that in mobiles, have changed the banking service delivery. People need not visit banks for a host of banking services. Cloud computing is likely to make the local serves and computer data storage redundant. Ready-mix concrete does away with the retailing of building materials and reduces time to construct for buildings. With technology like bar coding, radio-frequency identification (RFID) the tracking of inventory is on real time basis for retailers and suppliers also come to know the stock level on real time basis so that the replenishment can take place before stock-out occurs. Regulatory and political changes also affect the industries in a great way. With proper regulatory mechanism, one can see investor interest in telecom, insurance, pension fund etc. in India. Retail sector is expected to see foreign players since foreign direct investment is recently [November – December, 2012] allowed in multi brand retail.

Besides the above, the life cycle of industry and level of competition in a particular industry also affect the industry performance. These are discussed in the subsequent session.

Market Analysis

A market analysis studies the attractiveness and the dynamics of a special market within a special industry. It is part of the industry analysis and thus in turn of the global environmental analysis. Through all of these analyses, the strengths, weaknesses, opportunities and threats (SWOT) of a company can be identified. Finally, with the help of a SWOT analysis, adequate business strategies of a company will be defined. The market analysis is also known as a documented investigation of a market that is used to inform a firm's planning activities, particularly around decisions of inventory, purchase, work force expansion/contraction, facility expansion, purchases of capital equipment, promotional activities, and many other aspects of a company.

Market Segmentation

Market segmentation is the basis for a differentiated market analysis. Differentiation is important. One main reason is the saturation of consumption, which exists due to the increasing competition in offered products. Consumers ask for more individual products and services and are better informed about the range of products than before. As a consequence, market segmentation is necessary. Segmentation includes a lot of market research, since a lot of market knowledge is required to segment the market. Market research about market structures and processes must be done to define the "relevant market". The relevant market is an integral part of the whole market, on which the company focuses its activities. To identify and classify the relevant market, a market classification or segmentation has to be done.

Market segmentation is an important way to find competitive advantage with its differentiation in market analysis. Market segmentation concentrates on market energy and power to gain competitive advantage. In other words, market segmentation is the concept tool to get the force (Thomas, 2007). In market analysis, market knowledge is required to analyze market structure and process. Since segmentation requires a lot of market research, various information can be extracted from it. Market segmentation can identify customer needs and wants and develop products to their satisfaction. Market segmentation can identify different products for different groups, better match customer wants and product benefits, maximize the use of available resources and focus marketing expenditures and competitive advantages (Karlsson,2012).

There is no specific way to segment market. However, businesses can follow generalized rules like geographic, demographic, psychographic, and behavioral. A good market segmentation should be sustainable, accessible, actionable, measurable, and differentiable (Karlsson,2012).

Dimensions of Market Analysis

David A. Aaker outlined the following dimensions of a market analysis:

- Market size (current and future)
- Market trends
- Market growth rate
- Market profitability
- Industry cost structure
- Distribution channels
- Key success factors
- Key success details

Market analysis strives to determine the attractiveness of a market, currently and in the future. Organizations evaluate future attractiveness of a market by understanding evolving opportunities, and threats as they relate to that organization's own strengths and weaknesses.

Organizations use these findings to guide the investment decisions they make to advance their success. The findings of a market analysis may motivate an organization to change various aspects of its investment strategy. Affected areas may include inventory levels, a work force expansion/contraction, facility expansion, purchases of capital equipment, and promotional activities.

Elements

Market Size

The market size is defined through the market volume and the market potential. The market volume exhibits the totality of all realized sales volume of a special market. The volume is therefore dependent on the quantity of consumers and their ordinary demand. Furthermore, the market volume is either measured in quantities or qualities. The quantities can be given in technical terms, like GW for power capacities, or in numbers of items. Qualitative measuring mostly uses the sales turnover as an indicator. That means that the market price and the quantity are taken into account. Besides the market volume, the market potential is of equal importance. It defines the upper limit of the total demand and takes potential clients into consideration. Although the market potential is rather fictitious, it offers good values of orientation. The relation of market volume to market potential provides information about the chances of market growth. The following are examples of information sources for determining market size:

- Government data
- Trade association data
- Financial data from major players
- Customer surveys

Market Trends

Market trends are the upward or downward movement of a market, during a period of time. The market size is more difficult to estimate if one is starting with something completely new. In this case, you will have to derive the figures from the number of potential customers, or customer segments.

Besides information about the target market, one also needs information about one's competitors, customers, products, etc. Lastly, you need to measure marketing effectiveness. A few techniques are:

- Customer analysis
- Choice modelling
- Competitor analysis
- Risk analysis
- Product research
- Advertising the research
- Marketing mix modeling
- Simulated Test Marketing

Changes in the market are important because they often are the source of new opportunities and threats. Moreover, they have the potential to dramatically affect the market size.

Examples include changes in economic, social, regulatory, legal, and political conditions and in available technology, price sensitivity, demand for variety, and level of emphasis on service and support.

Market Growth Rate

A simple means of forecasting the market growth rate is to extrapolate historical data into the future. While this method may provide a first-order estimate, it does not predict important turning points. A better method is to study market trends and sales growth in complementary products. Such drivers serve as leading indicators that are more accurate than simply extrapolating historical data.

Important inflection points in the market growth rate sometimes can be predicted by constructing a product diffusion curve. The shape of the curve can be estimated by studying the characteristics of the adoption rate of a similar product in the past.

Ultimately, many markets mature and decline. Some leading indicators of a market's decline include market saturation, the emergence of substitute products, and/or the absence of growth drivers.

Market Opportunity

A market opportunity product or a service, based on either one technology or several, fulfills the need(s) of a (preferably increasing) market better than the competition and better than substitution-technologies within the given environmental frame (e.g. society, politics, legislation, etc.).

Market Profitability

While different organizations in a market will have different levels of profitability, they are all similar to different market conditions. Michael Porter devised a useful framework for evaluating the attractiveness of an industry or market. This framework, known as Porter five forces analysis, identifies five factors that influence the market profitability:

- Buyer power
- Supplier power
- Barriers to entry
- Threat of substitute products
- Rivalry among firms in the industry

Industry Cost Structure

The cost structure is important for identifying key factors for success. To this end, Porter's value chain model is useful for determining where value is added and for isolating the costs.

The cost structure also is helpful for formulating strategies to develop a competitive advantage. For example, in some environments the experience curve effect can be used to develop a cost advantage over competitors.

Distribution Channels

Examining the following aspects of the distribution system may help with a market analysis:

- Existing distribution channels - can be described by how direct they are to the customer.
- Trends and emerging channels - new channels can offer the opportunity to develop a competitive advantage.
- Channel power structure - for example, in the case of a product having little brand equity, retailers have negotiating power over manufacturers and can capture more margin.

Success Factors

The key success factors are those elements that are necessary in order for the firm to achieve its marketing objectives. A few examples of such factors include:

- Access to essential unique resources
- Ability to achieve economies of scale
- Access to distribution channels
- Technological progress

It is important to consider that key success factors may change over time, especially as the product progresses through its life cycle.

Environmental Analysis

The environmental analysis can be divided into two parts which are external and internal factors. External factors. Political issues, social potential force, and local economy called external environmental factors. Internal environmental factors belongs to company's internal position such as employees, department structure, budget and so forth (Christina, n.d.). How environmental effect markets. According to the Parry, the government limit pollution emission, they mention environmental taxes to prevent company which produce pollution substance. In other words, the government drives the organization. On the contrary, the cost of products increase due to the environmental taxes. It means that company may take measure of reducing production which may grow unemployment rate by emission tax. Therefore, the environmental taxes leads a income equality. It is not an excuse ignore our serious environmental problem. Even though the higher income group also can benefit from windfall gains(Parry, 2002).

Competitive Analysis

According to the Christina, competitive analysis is that company must know their competitors which have the same common services and products. The business can use like product cost, operational efficiency, brand recognition and market Dimensions of market analysis.

Except for David A. Aaker's 7 main dimension of a market analysis including market size, market growth rate, market profitability, industry cost structure, distribution channel, market trends, and key success factor, there is another analysis of dimension market analysis. Based on Christina Callaway, dimension of market analysis can be divided into four parts which is environmental analysis, competitive analysis, target audience analysis, and SWOT analysis. The market analysis is to help company to illustrate current trend in the market and may affect the profitability (Christina, n.d.). At the same time, market analysis is also to determine the attractiveness in the market. A good marketing analysis can improve organization investment decision accurately, they can based on the attractiveness to change investment tactical.

The market analysis is to help company to illustrate current trend in the market and may affect the profitability for the business(Thomas,2007). It can be seen as a part of industry analysis with using global environmental analysis. Company can identify strengths, weakness, opportunities and threats so that the business can define the business strategy. The market analysis is also reference for company's activity, like decisions of inventory, purchase, work force, facility expansion and many aspects of company.

penetration to find the difference or competitive advantages between two similarly companies(Christina, n.d). How can we find the competitive advantage? Kevin (2016) says that "Anticipating and reading market needs can help business leaders take significant steps towards changing the game and obtaining competitive advantage."(p. 70). How can we sustain competitive advantages? In terms of Richard research, The company should focus on sustaining competitive advantage due to the swift growth global competition. Therefore, Business practice management is the follow principle to maintain competitive advantage(Richard,2006).

Target Audience Analysis

In the Christina contribution, target audience is for company to target their customer group who most likely to buy their products(Christina, n.d.). The group can be classified with location, age, gender, income, ethnicity, and behaviors. And people who make a decision of purchase can also be divided in the target audience. How identify market in accordance with Women's enterprise centre the market can be classified in three types which are consumer market, industrial market, and reseller market. The company segment their market, research market, and identify why customer would like to buy their products (women's enterprise centre, 2011).

SWOT Analysis

SWOT is strengths, weakness, opportunities, and threats. It matches internal strengths and weaknesses up against opportunities and threats (Christina, n.d.). Strengths and weakness are internal factors which we can control. And opportunities and threats are external factors that businesses can't control, but can however impact on. When using strengths and weakness, businesses need to collect raw data to get information. Businesses can get information by customer feedback, employee surveys. Furthermore, businesses also can identify the capability if it is weakness or strengths, resources and process. Opportunities and threats are the external factors. Business can get information from secondary data like environmental information, industry information and competitive data. The purpose of the business use the SWOT analysis is to get the information from it and match each other to develop the ideas and get into goal statement to form strategic development (Olsen, 2008).

Market communication has significant impact on building and maintaining the relationship of stakeholders. Market analysis elements is to form a strategic planning and the information is responsiveness, intelligence generation, and dissemination(Mike, Sandra& Felix, 2005). Besides, market communication provide the information focus on the customer needs and competitive advantage. At the same time, these information spread to customers means the company spread its brand value so that customer can make awareness of the company's products. It is the communication channel between business and customers(Mike, Sandra& Felix, 2005).

Market Segmentation

Market segmentation is one of the important way to find competitive advantage with its differentiation in market analysis. Market segmentation concentrate on market energy and power to gain competitive advantage. In other words, market segmentation is the concept tool to get the force(Thomas,2007). In the market analysis, we need a lot of market knowledge to analysis market structure and process. Since segmentation need to do a lot of market research so that we can get the information from it. Market segmentation recommend the market strategy. Market segmentation can identity customer needs and wants and develop products to satisfied with them. Market segmentation can identity different products for different groups, better match between customer wants and product benefits, maximize the use of available resources, focused marketing expenditures and competitive advantages (karlsson,2012).

There is no only way to segment market but business can follow some rules like geographic, demographic, psychographic, and behavioral. A good market segmentation should be sustainable, accessible, actionable, measurable, and differentiable (karlsson,2012).

Global Market Segmentation

Since the globalization more and more developed, the global market become indispensability part of the business thinking. In order to explore global market, how market segmentation can be used in the global market. There are some aspects of defining the global market so which is more efficient to segment global market. Some researchers mention about Cross-National and Cross-Cultural Approach to segment global market. To differentiate country and culture, the company have to identify two areas which is vertical market segment existing internal area. Another area is external market segments which a group of countries has relationship of each other and share their characteristics. Compared with cross- cultural approach and cross-national approach, cross-cultural approach has its cultural stability of traditional values. cultural stability has a wide range of shared national-cultural values features, due to group solidarity, interpersonal harmony and so forth(Agarwal, Malhotra & Bolto, 2010). However, cross-cultural approach has challenge of environmental changes, cultural change and some other unstable factors(Agarwal, Malhotra & Bolto, 2010). Therefore, the main principle of looking at cross-cultural approach and cross- national approach base on perceive service quality. In the global service marketing, the marketing manager face a challenge of international services on account of the intangibility of services, unification standardizing services across national borders and difference of preference for customized services in different countries and culture. Therefore, it is significance for business to have a deep understanding service quality in facing across different countries, regions and cultures(Agarwal, Malhotra & Bolto, 2010).

In the software market, the trend of software is the price is high and coverage is low. In order to improve the trend, there is some problems of software market. Zhang (2014) mention that" (1) What possibly discourages product differentiation in such a competitive market? (2) Why is versioning absent here? (3) How does the presence of free alternatives in this market impact its structure?"(p. 589). In order to improve these problems, Zhang mention that quality competition and market segmentation apply to the software market. In Zhang's research, the software company lack of developed the method of quality competition, market segmentation, and versioning. In terms of market segmentation, software company think segmentation consumer market is not useful. Therefore, even though versioning is the least costless way of spread product information, the company still ignore it (Zhang, 2014).

The relationship between market segmentation and communication in marketing is interaction. For example, market segmentation is important in the social media. There is three perspectives supplier perspectives, interaction perspectives, and buyer perspectives. In order to balance these three relationships, business must do segment well. Otherwise, the buyer perspective and supplier perspective cannot interact very well may lead loss of promotion (Oxfordlearninglab, 2009). Therefore, social media is important method of communication in the market and market segmentation also unnecessary before the business use social media channel.

Applications

The literature defines several areas in which market analysis is important. These include: sales forecasting, market research, and marketing strategy. Not all managers will need to conduct a market analysis. Nevertheless, it would be important for managers that use market analysis data to know how analysts derive their conclusions and what techniques they use to do so.

Porter's Five Forces Analysis

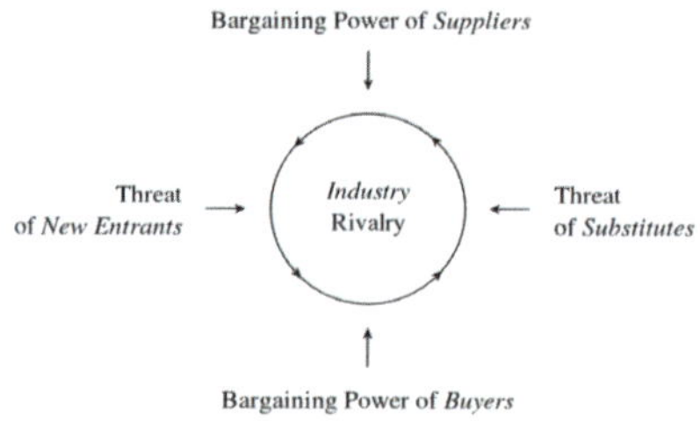

A graphical representation of Porter's five forces

Porter's five forces analysis is a framework for analyzing the level of competition within an industry and business strategy development. It draws upon industrial organization (IO) economics to derive five forces that determine the competitive intensity and therefore the attractiveness of an industry. Attractiveness in this context refers to the overall industry profitability. An "unattractive" industry is one in which the combination of these five forces acts to drive down overall profitability. A very unattractive industry would be one approaching "pure competition", in which available profits for all firms are driven to normal profit. This analysis is associated with its principal innovator Michael E. Porter of Harvard University.

Porter refers to these forces as the micro environment, to contrast it with the more general term macro environment. They consist of those forces close to a company that affect its ability to serve its customers and make a profit. A change in any of the forces normally requires a business unit to re-assess the marketplace given the overall change in industry information. The overall industry attractiveness does not imply that every firm in the industry will return the same profitability. Firms are able to apply their core competencies, business model or network to achieve a profit above the industry average. A clear example of this is the airline industry. As an industry, profitability is low and yet individual companies, by applying unique business models, have been able to make a return in excess of the industry average.

Porter's five forces include three forces from 'horizontal' competition: the threat of substitute products or services, the threat of established rivals, and the threat of new entrants; and two forces from 'vertical' competition: the bargaining power of suppliers and the bargaining power of customers.

Porter developed his five forces analysis in reaction to the then-popular SWOT analysis, which he found unrigorous and *ad hoc*. Porter's five forces is based on the structure–conduct–performance paradigm in industrial organizational economics. It has been applied to a diverse range of problems, from helping businesses become more profitable to helping governments stabilize industries. Other Porter strategic frameworks include the value chain and the generic strategies.

Five Forces

Threat of New Entrants

Profitable markets that yield high returns will attract new firms. This results in many new entrants, which eventually will decrease profitability for all firms in the industry. Unless the entry of new firms can be blocked by incumbents (which in business refers to the largest company in a certain industry, for instance, in telecommunications, the traditional phone company, typically called the "incumbent operator"), the abnormal profit rate will trend towards zero (perfect competition).

The following factors can have an effect on how much of a threat new entrants may pose:

- The existence of barriers to entry (patents, rights, etc.). The most attractive segment is one in which entry barriers are high and exit barriers are low. Few new firms can enter and non-performing firms can exit easily.
- Government policy
- Capital requirements
- Absolute cost
- Cost disadvantages independent of size
- Economies of scale
- Economies of product differences
- Product differentiation
- Brand equity
- Switching costs or sunk costs
- Expected retaliation
- Access to distribution
- Customer loyalty to established brands
- Industry profitability (the more profitable the industry the more attractive it will be to new competitors)
- Network effect

Threat of Substitutes

The existence of products outside of the realm of the common product boundaries increases the propensity of customers to switch to alternatives. For example, tap water might be considered a substitute for Coke, whereas Pepsi is a competitor's similar product. Increased marketing for drinking tap water might "shrink the pie" for both Coke and Pepsi, whereas increased Pepsi advertising would likely "grow the pie" (increase consumption of all soft drinks), albeit while giving Pepsi a larger slice at Coke's expense. Another example is the substitute of a landline phone with a cellular phone.

Potential factors:

- Buyer propensity to substitute
- Relative price performance of substitute

- Buyer switching costs
- Perceived level of product differentiation
- Number of substitute products available in the market
- Ease of substitution
- Substandard product
- Quality depreciation
- Availability of close substitute

Bargaining Power of Customers

The bargaining power of customers is also described as the market of outputs: the ability of customers to put the firm under pressure, which also affects the customer's sensitivity to price changes. Firms can take measures to reduce buyer power, such as implementing a loyalty program. The buyer power is high if the buyer has many alternatives. The buyer power is low if they act independently e.g. If a large number of customers will act with each other and ask to make prices low the company will have no other choice because of large number of customers pressure.

Potential factors:

- Buyer concentration to firm concentration ratio
- Degree of dependency upon existing channels of distribution
- Bargaining leverage, particularly in industries with high fixed costs
- Buyer switching costs relative to firm switching costs
- Buyer information availability
- Force down prices
- Availability of existing substitute products
- Buyer price sensitivity
- Differential advantage (uniqueness) of industry products
- RFM (customer value) Analysis
- The total amount of trading

Bargaining Power of Suppliers

The bargaining power of suppliers is also described as the market of inputs. Suppliers of raw materials, components, labor, and services (such as expertise) to the firm can be a source of power over the firm when there are few substitutes. If you are making biscuits and there is only one person who sells flour, you have no alternative but to buy it from them. Suppliers may refuse to work with the firm or charge excessively high prices for unique resources.

Potential factors are:

- Supplier switching costs relative to firm switching costs
- Degree of differentiation of inputs
- Impact of inputs on cost and differentiation
- Presence of substitute inputs
- Strength of distribution channel
- Supplier concentration to firm concentration ratio
- Employee solidarity (e.g. labor unions)
- Supplier competition: the ability to forward vertically integrate and cut out the buyer.

Industry Rivalry

For most industries the intensity of competitive rivalry is the major determinant of the competitiveness of the industry.

Potential factors:

- Sustainable competitive advantage through innovation
- Competition between online and offline companies
- Level of advertising expense
- Powerful competitive strategy
- Firm concentration ratio
- Degree of transparency

Usage

Strategy consultants occasionally use Porter's five forces framework when making a qualitative evaluation of a firm's strategic position. However, for most consultants, the framework is only a starting point or "checklist". They might use value chain or another type of analysis in conjunction. Like all general frameworks, an analysis that uses it to the exclusion of specifics about a particular situation is considered naive.

According to Porter, the five forces model should be used at the line-of-business industry level; it is not designed to be used at the industry group or industry sector level. An industry is defined at a lower, more basic level: a market in which similar or closely related products and/or services are sold to buyers A firm that competes in a single industry should develop, at a minimum, one five forces analysis for its industry. Porter makes clear that for diversified companies, the first fundamental issue in corporate strategy is the selection of industries (lines of business) in which the company should compete; and each line of business should develop its own, industry-specific, five forces analysis. The average Global 1,000 company competes in approximately 52 industries (lines of business).

Criticisms

Porter's framework has been challenged by other academics and strategists such as Stewart Neill. Similarly, Kevin P. Coyne and Somu Subramaniam have claimed that three dubious assumptions underlie the five forces:

- That buyers, competitors, and suppliers are unrelated and do not interact and collude.
- That the source of value is structural advantage (creating barriers to entry).
- That uncertainty is low, allowing participants in a market to plan for and respond to competitive behavior.

An important extension to Porter was found in the work of Adam Brandenburger and Barry Nalebuff of Yale School of Management in the mid-1990s. Using game theory, they added the concept of complementors (also called "the 6th force"), helping to explain the reasoning behind strategic alliances. Complementors are known as the impact of related products and services already in the market. The idea that complementors are the sixth force has often been credited to Andrew Grove, former CEO of Intel Corporation. According to most references, the sixth force is government or the public. Martyn Richard Jones, whilst consulting at Groupe Bull, developed an augmented 5 forces model in Scotland in 1993. It is based on Porter's model and includes Government (national and regional) as well as Pressure Groups as the notional 6th force. This model was the result of work carried out as part of Groupe Bull's Knowledge Asset Management Organisation initiative.

Porter indirectly rebutted the assertions of other forces, by referring to innovation, government, and complementary products and services as "factors" that affect the five forces.

It is also perhaps not feasible to evaluate the attractiveness of an industry independent of the resources a firm brings to that industry. It is thus argued (Wernerfelt 1984) that this theory be coupled with the Resource-Based View (RBV) in order for the firm to develop a much more sound strategy. It provides a simple perspective for accessing and analyzing the competitive strength and position of a corporation, business or organization.

Balanced Scorecard

The balanced scorecard (BSC) is a strategy performance management tool – a semi-standard structured report, supported by design methods and automation tools, that can be used by managers to keep track of the execution of activities by the staff within their control and to monitor the consequences arising from these actions.

The phrase 'balanced scorecard' is commonly used in two broad forms:

1. As individual scorecards that contain measures to manage performance, those scorecards may be operational or have a more strategic intent; and

2. As a Strategic Management System, as originally defined by Kaplan & Norton.

The critical characteristics that define a balanced scorecard are:

- its focus on the strategic agenda of the organization concerned
- the selection of a small number of data items to monitor
- a mix of financial and non-financial data items.

Use

Balanced scorecard is an example of a closed-loop controller or cybernetic control applied to the management of the implementation of a strategy. Closed-loop or cybernetic control is where actual performance is measured, the measured value is compared to a reference value and based on the difference between the two corrective interventions are made as required. Such control requires three things to be effective:

- a choice of data to measure,
- the setting of a reference value for the data,
- the ability to make a corrective intervention.

Within the strategy management context, all three of these characteristic closed-loop control elements need to be derived from the organisation's strategy and also need to reflect the ability of the observer to both monitor performance and subsequently intervene – both of which may be constrained. Initially, Balanced Scorecard emerged as a performance management system, over a period of time it has come to be known as a strategy management system, with its ultimate aim being the achievement of long term financial performance. Balanced scorecard is seen as a strategic management system enabling business leaders to meet the challenge of strategy execution.

Two of the ideas that underpin modern balanced scorecard designs concern facilitating the creation of such a control – through making it easier to select which data to observe, and ensuring that the choice of data is consistent with the ability of the observer to intervene.

History

Organizations have used systems consisting of a mix of financial and non-financial measures to track progress for quite some time. One such system was created by Art Schneiderman in 1987 at Analog Devices, a mid-sized semi-conductor company; the Analog Devices Balanced Scorecard. Schneiderman's design was similar to what is now recognised as a "First Generation" Balanced Scorecard design.

In 1990 Art Schneiderman participated in an unrelated research study led by Robert S. Kaplan in conjunction with US management consultancy Nolan-Norton, and during this study described his work on performance measurement. Subsequently, Kaplan and David P. Norton included anonymous details of this balanced scorecard design in a 1992 article. Kaplan and Norton's article wasn't the only paper on the topic published in early 1992 but the 1992 Kaplan and Norton paper was a popular success, and was quickly followed by a second in 1993. In 1996, the two authors published a book *The Balanced Scorecard*. These articles and the first book spread knowledge of the concept of balanced scorecard widely, and has led to Kaplan and Norton being seen as the creators of the concept.

While the "corporate scorecard" terminology was coined by Art Schneiderman, the roots of performance management as an activity run deep in management literature and practice. Management historians such as Alfred Chandler suggest the origins of performance management can be seen in the emergence of the complex organisation – most notably during the 19th Century in the USA. More recent influences may include the pioneering work of General Electric on performance measurement reporting in the 1950s and the work of French process engineers (who created the *tableau de bord* – literally, a "dashboard" of performance measures) in the early part of the 20th century. The tool also draws strongly on the ideas of the 'resource based view of the firm' proposed by Edith Penrose. However it should be noted that none of these influences is explicitly linked to original descriptions of balanced scorecard by Schneiderman, Maisel, or Kaplan & Norton.

Kaplan and Norton's first book remains their most popular. The book reflects the earliest incarnations of balanced scorecards – effectively restating the concept as described in the second Harvard Business Review article. Their second book, *The Strategy Focused Organization*, echoed work by others (particularly a book published the year before by Olve et al. in Scandinavia) on the value of visually documenting the links between measures by proposing the "Strategic Linkage Model" or strategy map.

As the title of Kaplan and Norton's second book highlights, even by 2000 the focus of attention among thought-leaders was moving from the design of Balanced Scorecards themselves, towards the use of Balanced Scorecard as a focal point within a more comprehensive strategic management system. Subsequent writing on Balanced Scorecard by Kaplan & Norton has focused on uses of Balanced Scorecard rather than its design (e.g. "The Execution Premium" in 2008), however many others have continued to refine the device itself (e.g. Abernethy et al.).

Characteristics

The characteristics of the balanced scorecard and its derivatives is the presentation of a mixture of financial and non-financial measures each compared to a 'target' value within a single concise report. The report is not meant to be a replacement for traditional financial or operational reports but a succinct summary that captures the information most relevant to those reading it. It is the method by which this 'most relevant' information is determined (i.e., the design processes used to select the content) that most differentiates the various versions of the tool in circulation. The balanced scorecard indirectly also provides a useful insight into an organisation's strategy – by requiring general strategic statements (e.g. mission, vision) to be precipitated into more specific/ tangible forms.

The first versions of balanced scorecard asserted that relevance should derive from the corporate strategy, and proposed design methods that focused on choosing measures and targets associated with the main activities required to implement the strategy. As the initial audience for this were the readers of the Harvard Business Review, the proposal was translated into a form that made sense to a typical reader of that journal – managers of US commercial businesses. Accordingly, initial designs were encouraged to measure three categories of non-financial measure in addition to financial outputs – those of "customer," "internal business processes" and "learning and growth." These categories were not so relevant to non-profits or units within complex organizations (which might have high degrees of internal specialization), and much of the early literature on balanced scorecard focused on suggestions of alternative 'perspectives' that might have more relevance to these groups.

Modern balanced scorecards have evolved since the initial ideas proposed in the late 1980s and early 1990s, and the modern performance management tools including Balanced Scorecard are significantly improved – being more flexible (to suit a wider range of organisational types) and more effective (as design methods have evolved to make them easier to design, and use).

Design

Design of a balanced scorecard is about the identification of a small number of financial and non-financial measures and attaching targets to them, so that when they are reviewed it is possible to determine whether current performance 'meets expectations'. By alerting managers to areas where performance deviates from expectations, they can be encouraged to focus their attention on these areas, and hopefully as a result trigger improved performance within the part of the organization they lead.

The original thinking behind a balanced scorecard was for it to be focused on information relating to the implementation of a strategy, and over time there has been a blurring of the boundaries between conventional strategic planning and control activities and those required to design a balanced scorecard. This is illustrated well by the four steps required to design a balanced scorecard included in Kaplan & Norton's writing on the subject in the late 1990s:

1. Translating the vision into operational goals.
2. Communicating the vision and link it to individual performance.
3. Business planning; index setting.
4. Feedback and learning, and adjusting the strategy accordingly.

These steps go far beyond the simple task of identifying a small number of financial and non-financial measures, but illustrate the requirement for whatever design process is used to fit within broader thinking about how the resulting balanced scorecard will integrate with the wider business management process.

Although it helps focus managers' attention on strategic issues and the management of the implementation of strategy, it is important to remember that the balanced scorecard itself has no role in the formation of strategy. In fact, balanced scorecards can co-exist with strategic planning systems and other tools.

First Generation

The first generation of balanced scorecard designs used a "4 perspective" approach to identify what measures to use to track the implementation of strategy. `The original four "perspectives" proposed were:

- Financial: encourages the identification of a few relevant high-level financial measures. In particular, designers were encouraged to choose measures that helped inform the answer to the question "How do we look to shareholders?" Examples: cash flow, sales growth, operating income, return on equity.
- Customer: encourages the identification of measures that answer the question "What is important to our customers and stakeholders?" Examples: percent of sales from new products, on time delivery, share of important customers' purchases, ranking by important customers.
- Internal business processes: encourages the identification of measures that answer the question "What must we excel at?"Examples: cycle time, unit cost, yield, new product introductions.
- Learning and growth: encourages the identification of measures that answer the question "How can we continue to improve, create value and innovate?". Examples: time to develop new generation of products, life cycle to product maturity, time to market versus competition.

The idea was that managers used these perspective headings to prompt the selection of a small number of measures that informed on that aspect of the organisation's strategic performance. The perspective headings show that Kaplan and Norton were thinking about the needs of non-divisional commercial organisations in their initial design. These headings are not very helpful to other kinds of organisations (e.g. multi-divisional or multi-national commercial organisations, governmental organisations, non-profits, non-governmental organisations, government agencies etc.), and much of what has been written on balanced scorecard since has, in one way or another, focused on the identification of alternative headings more suited to a broader range of organisations, and also suggested using either additional or fewer perspectives (e.g. Butler et al. (1997), Ahn (2001), Elefalke (2001), Brignall (2002), Irwin (2002), Radnor et al. (2003)).

These suggestions were notably triggered by a recognition that different but equivalent headings would yield alternative sets of measures, and this represents the major design challenge faced with this type of balanced scorecard design: justifying the choice of measures made. "Of all the measures you could have chosen, why did you choose these?" These issues contribute to dis-satisfaction with early Balanced Scorecard designs, since if users are not confident that the measures within the Balanced Scorecard are well chosen, they will have less confidence in the information it provides.

Although less common, these early-style balanced scorecards are still designed and used today.

In short, first generation balanced scorecards are hard to design in a way that builds confidence that they are well designed. Because of this, many are abandoned soon after completion.

Second Generation

In the mid-1990s, an improved design method emerged. In the new method, measures are selected based on a set of "strategic objectives" plotted on a "strategic linkage model" or "strategy map". With this modified approach, the strategic objectives are distributed across the four measurement perspectives, so as to "connect the dots" to form a visual presentation of strategy and measures.

In this modified version of balanced scorecard design, managers select a few strategic objectives within each of the perspectives, and then define the cause-effect chain among these objectives by drawing links between them to create a "strategic linkage model". A balanced scorecard of strategic performance measures is then derived directly by selecting one or two measures for each strategic objective. This type of approach provides greater contextual justification for the measures chosen, and is generally easier for managers to work through. This style of balanced scorecard has been commonly used since 1996 or so: it is significantly different in approach to the methods originally proposed, and so can be thought of as representing the "2nd generation" of design approach adopted for balanced scorecard since its introduction.

Third Generation

In the late 1990s, the design approach had evolved yet again. One problem with the "second generation" design approach described above was that the plotting of causal links amongst twenty or so medium-term strategic goals was still a relatively abstract activity. In practice it ignored the fact that opportunities to intervene, to influence strategic goals are, and need to be, anchored in current and real management activity. Secondly, the need to "roll forward" and test the impact of these goals necessitated the creation of an additional design instrument: the Vision or Destination Statement. This device was a statement of what "strategic success", or the "strategic end-state", looked like. It was quickly realized that if a Destination Statement was created at the beginning of the design process, then it was easier to select strategic activity and outcome objectives to respond to it. Measures and targets could then be selected to track the achievement of these objectives. Design methods that incorporate a Destination Statement or equivalent (e.g. the results-based management method proposed by the UN in 2002) represent a tangibly different design approach to those that went before, and have been proposed as representing a "third generation" design method for balanced scorecards.

Design methods for balanced scorecards continue to evolve and adapt to reflect the deficiencies in the currently used methods, and the particular needs of communities of interest (e.g. NGO's and government departments have found the third generation methods embedded in results-based management more useful than first or second generation design methods).

This generation refined the second generation of balanced scorecards to give more relevance and functionality to strategic objectives. The major difference is the incorporation of Destination Statements. Other key components are strategic objectives, strategic linkage model and perspectives, measures and initiatives.

Popularity

In 1997, Kurtzman found that 64 percent of the companies questioned were measuring performance from a number of perspectives in a similar way to the balanced scorecard. Balanced scorecards have been implemented by government agencies, military units, business units and corporations as a whole, non-profit organizations, and schools.

Balanced scorecard has been widely adopted, and has been found to be the most popular performance management framework in a recent survey.

Many examples of balanced scorecards can be found via web searches. However, adapting one organization's balanced scorecard to another is generally not advised by theorists, who believe that much of the benefit of the balanced scorecard comes from the design process itself. Indeed, it could be argued that many failures in the early days of balanced scorecard could be attributed to this problem, in that early balanced scorecards were often designed remotely by consultants. Managers did not trust, and so failed to engage with and use, these measure suites created by people lacking knowledge of the organization and management responsibility.

Variants

Since the balanced scorecard was popularized in the early 1990s, a large number of alternatives to the original 'four box' balanced scorecard promoted by Kaplan and Norton in their various articles and books have emerged. Most have very limited application, and are typically proposed either by academics as vehicles for expanding the dialogue beyond the financial bottom line – e.g. Brignall (2002) or consultants as an attempt at differentiation to promote sales of books and / or consultancy (e.g. Bourne (2002); Niven (2002).

Many of the structural variations proposed are broadly similar, and a research paper published in 2004 attempted to identify a pattern in these variations – noting three distinct types of variation. The variations appeared to be part of an evolution of the balanced scorecard concept, and so the paper refers to these distinct types as "generations". Broadly, the original 'measures in boxes' type design (as proposed by Kaplan & Norton) constitutes the 1st generation balanced scorecard design; balanced scorecard designs that include a 'strategy map' or 'strategic linkage model' (e.g. the Performance Prism, later Kaplan & Norton designs the Performance Driver model of Olve, Roy & Wetter (English translation 1999, 1st published in Swedish 1997)) constitute the 2nd Generation of Balanced Scorecard design; and designs that augment the strategy map / strategic linkage model with a separate document describing the long-term outcomes sought from the strategy (the "destination statement" idea) comprise the 3rd generation balanced scorecard design.

Variants that feature adaptations of the structure of balanced scorecard to suit better a particular viewpoint or agenda are numerous. Examples of the focus of such adaptations include the triple bottom line, decision support, public sector management, and health care management. The performance management elements of the UN's Results Based Management system have strong design and structural similarities to those used in the 3rd Generation Balanced Scorecard design approach.

Balanced scorecard is also often linked to quality management tools and activities. Although there are clear areas of cross-over and association, the two sets of tools are complementary rather than duplicative.

A common use of balanced scorecard is to support the payments of incentives to individuals, even though it was not designed for this purpose and is not particularly suited to it.

Criticism

The balanced scorecard has attracted criticism from a variety of sources. Most have come from the academic community, who dislike the empirical nature of the framework: Kaplan and Norton notoriously failed to include any citation of earlier articles in their initial papers on the topic. Some of this criticism focuses on technical flaws in the methods and design of the original balanced scorecard proposed by Kaplan and Norton,. Other academics have simply focused on the lack of citation support.

A second kind of criticism is that the balanced scorecard does not provide a bottom line score or a unified view with clear recommendations: it is simply a list of metrics (e.g. Jensen 2001). These critics usually include in their criticism suggestions about how the 'unanswered' question postulated could be answered, but typically the unanswered question relate to things outside the scope of balanced scorecard itself (such as developing strategies) (e.g. Brignall).

A third kind of criticism is that the model fails to fully reflect the needs of stakeholders – putting bias on financial stakeholders over others. Early forms of Balanced Scorecard proposed by Kaplan & Norton focused on the needs of commercial organisations in the USA – where this focus on investment return was appropriate. This focus was maintained through subsequent revisions. Even now over 20 years after they were first proposed, the four most common perspectives in Balanced Scorecard designs mirror the four proposed in the original Kaplan & Norton paper. There have been many studies that suggest other perspectives might better reflect the priorities of organisations – particularly but not exclusively relating to the needs of organisations in the public and Non Governmental sectors. For instance, the balanced scorecard does not address important aspects of nonprofit strategy such as social dimensions, human resource elements, political issues and the distinctive nature of competition and collaboration in nonprofit settings. Thus, the model seems to be less effective in nonprofit organisations as the model's strategy, cause-and-effect relationships and its four linked perspectives are incompatible to the unique nonprofit environment. More modern design approaches such as 3rd Generation Balanced Scorecard and the UN's Results Based Management methods explicitly consider the interests of wider stakeholder groups, and perhaps address this issue in its entirety.

There are few empirical studies linking the use of balanced scorecards to better decision making or improved financial performance of companies, but some work has been done in these areas. However, broadcast surveys of usage have difficulties in this respect, due to the wide variations in definition of 'what a balanced scorecard is' noted above (making it hard to work out in a survey if you are comparing like with like). Single organization case studies suffer from the 'lack of a control' issue common to any study of organizational change – what the organization would have achieved if the change had not been made isn't known, so it is difficult to attribute changes observed over time to a single intervention (such as introducing a balanced scorecard). However, such studies as have been done have typically found balanced scorecard to be useful.

A few studies go further, trying to explain PMS size differences in terms of cause and effect. For example, Hvolby and Thorstenson (2000) and McAdam (2000) suggest that the Balanced Scorecard is completely unsuitable for SMEs because of their lack of a longer-term strategic focus. They also argue that the characteristics of SMEs make most, if not all, PM models inappropriate although they do not develop the argument in terms of causality. Similarly, Rompho's (2011) study of a failed implementation of the Balanced Scorecard in an SME attributed the cause to too many changes to the organisation's strategy. Others have suggested that SMEs have limited knowledge about performance measurement in general (Rantanen and Holtari 2000) and do not understand the benefits of PMS implementation (McAdam 2000; Bourne 2001), but none of these studies attempts to theorise the reasons behind their findings.

Software Tools

It is important to recognize that the balanced scorecard by definition is not a complex thing – typically no more than about 20 measures spread across a mix of financial and non-financial topics, and easily reported manually (on paper, or using simple office software).

The processes of collecting, reporting, and distributing balanced scorecard information can be labor-intensive and prone to procedural problems (for example, getting all relevant people to return the information required by the required date). The simplest mechanism to use is to delegate these activities to an individual, and many Balanced Scorecards are reported via ad-hoc methods based around email, phone calls and office software.

In more complex organizations, where there are multiple balanced scorecards to report and/or a need for co-ordination of results between balanced scorecards (for example, if one level of reports relies on information collected and reported at a lower level) the use of individual reporters is problematic. Where these conditions apply, organizations use balanced scorecard reporting software to automate the production and distribution of these reports.

Recent surveys have consistently found that roughly one third of organizations used office software to report their balanced scorecard, one third used software developed specifically for their own use, and one third used one of the many commercial packages available.

Strategy Map

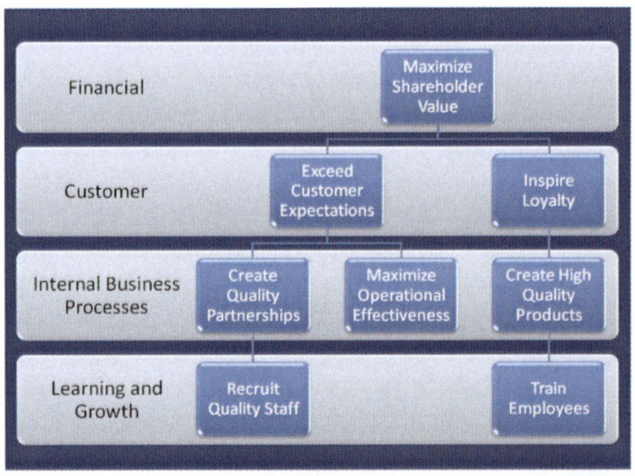

Generic Strategy Map

A strategy map is a diagram that is used to document the primary strategic goals being pursued by an organization or management team. It is an element of the documentation associated with the Balanced Scorecard, and in particular is characteristic of the second generation of Balanced Scorecard designs that first appeared during the mid-1990s. The first diagrams of this type appeared in the early 1990s, and the idea of using this type of diagram to help document Balanced Scorecard was discussed in a paper by Drs. Robert S. Kaplan and David P. Norton in 1996.

The strategy map idea featured in several books and articles during the late 1990s by Robert S. Kaplan and David P. Norton. Their original book in 1996, "The Balanced Scorecard, Translating strategy into action", contained diagrams which are later called strategy maps, but at this time they did nor refer to them as such. Kaplan & Norton's second book, The Strategy Focused Organization, explicitly refers to strategy maps and includes a chapter on how to build them. At this time, they said that "the relationship between the drivers and the desired outcomes constitute the hypotheses that define the strategy". Their Third book, Strategy Maps, goes into further detail about how to describe and visualise the strategy using strategy maps.

The Kaplan and Norton approach to strategy maps has:

- An underlying framework of horizontal perspectives arranged in a cause and effect relationship, typically Financial, Customer, Process and Learning & Growth.
- Objectives within those perspectives. Each objective as text appearing within a shape (usually an oval or rectangle). Relatively few objectives (usually fewer than 20).
- Vertical sets of linked objectives that span the perspectives. These are called strategic themes.
- Clear cause-and-effect relationships between these objectives, across the perspectives. The strategic themes represent hypotheses about how the strategy will bring about change to the outcomes of the organisation.

Across a broader range of published sources, a looser approach is sometimes used. In these approaches, there are only a few common attributes. Some approaches use a more broad causal relationships between objectives shown with arrows that either join objectives together, or placed in a way not linked with specific objectives but to provide general euphemistic indications of where causality lies. For instance, Olve and Wetter, in their 1999 book Performance Drivers, also describe early performance driver models, but do not refer to them as strategy maps.

The purpose of the strategy map in Balanced Scorecard design, and its emergence as a design aid, is discussed in some detail in a research paper on the evolution of Balanced Scorecard designs during the 1990s by Lawrie & Cobbold.

Origin of Strategy Maps

The Balanced Scorecard is a framework that is used to help in the design and implementation of strategic performance management tools within organizations. The Balanced Scorecard provides a simple structure for representing the strategy to be implemented, and has become associated with a wide selection of design tools that facilitate the identification of measures and targets that can inform on the progress the organization is making in implementing the strategy selected ("activities"), and also provide feedback on whether the strategy is having the kind of impact on organizational performance that was hoped for ("outcomes"). By providing managers with this direct feedback on whether the required actions are being carried out, and whether they are working, the Balanced Scorecard is thought to help managers focus their attention more closely on the interventions necessary to ensure the strategy is effectively and efficiently executed.

One of the big challenges faced in the design of Balanced Scorecard based performance management systems is deciding what activities and outcomes to monitor. By providing a simple visual representation of the strategic objectives to be focused on, along with additional visual cues in the form of the perspectives and causal arrows, the strategy map has been found useful in enabling discussion within a management team about what objectives to choose, and subsequently to support discussion of the actual performance achieved.

Perspectives

Very early Balanced Scorecard articles by Robert S. Kaplan and David P.Norton proposed a simple design method for choosing the content of the Balanced Scorecard based on answers to four generic questions about the strategy to be pursued by the organization. These four questions, one about finances, one about marketing, one about processes, and one about organizational development evolved quickly into a standard set of "perspectives" ("Financial", "Customer", "Internal Business Processes", "Learning & Growth").

Design of a Balanced Scorecard became a process of selecting a small number of objectives in each perspective, and then choosing measures and targets to inform on progress against this objective. But very quickly it was realized that the perspective headings chosen only worked for specific organisations (small to medium sized firms in North America - the target market of the Harvard Business Review), and during the mid to late 1990s papers began to be published arguing that other sets of headings would make more sense for specific organization types, and that some organisations would benefit from using more or less than four headings.

Despite these concerns, the 'standard' set of perspectives remains the most common, and traditionally is arrayed on the strategy map in the sequence (from bottom to top) "Learning & Growth", "Internal Business Processes", "Customer", "Financial" with causal arrows tending to flow "up" the page.

Links Between the Strategy Map and Strategy Development

The strategy map is a device that promotes three stages of conversation during the strategy development, implementation and learning process

- First to capture a strategy from a management team. To promote discussion amongst that team on the strategy, so they all leave the room telling the same story of their strategy.
- Secondly to communicate the strategy, focus organization efforts, and choose appropriate measures to report on an organisation's progress in implementing a strategy.
- Finally to provide a basis to review and potentially revise the strategy, (not simply the measures or targets) and support conversations and decision making, as the team learn from the strategy's implementation.

Over the years many have suggested that it can be used as, in part, a strategy development tool. Kaplan & Norton in their book "The Strategy Focused Organisation" argue that organisations could adopt 'industry standard' templates (basically a set of pre-determined strategic objectives).

Growth–share Matrix

The growth–share matrix (aka the product portfolio matrix, Boston Box, BCG-matrix, Boston matrix, Boston Consulting Group analysis, portfolio diagram) is a chart that was created by Bruce D. Henderson for the Boston Consulting Group in 1970 to help corporations to analyze their business units, that is, their product lines. This helps the company allocate resources and is used as an analytical tool in brand marketing, product management, strategic management, and portfolio analysis. Some analysis of market performance by firms using its principles has called its usefulness into question.

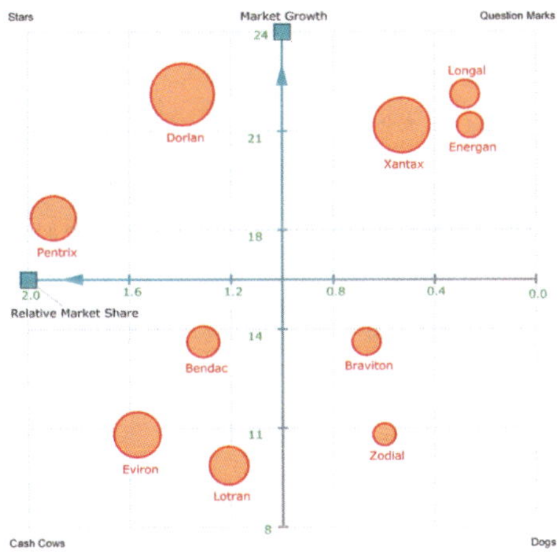

Portfolio growth–share matrix

Overview

To use the chart, analysts plot a scatter graph to rank the business units (or products) on the basis of their relative market shares and growth rates.

- *Cash cows* is where a company has high market share in a slow-growing industry. These units typically generate cash in excess of the amount of cash needed to maintain the business. They are regarded as staid and boring, in a "mature" market, yet corporations value owning them due to their cash-generating qualities. They are to be "milked" continuously with as little investment as possible, since such investment would be wasted in an industry with low growth.

- *Dogs*, more charitably called *pets*, are units with low market share in a mature, slow-growing industry. These units typically "break even", generating barely enough cash to maintain the business's market share. Though owning a break-even unit provides the social benefit of providing jobs and possible synergies that assist other business units, from an accounting point of view such a unit is worthless, not generating cash for the company. They depress a profitable company's return on assets ratio, used by many investors to judge how well a company is being managed. *Dogs*, it is thought, should be sold off.

- *Question marks* (also known as problem children) are businesses operating with a low market share in a high-growth market. They are a starting point for most businesses. Question marks have a potential to gain market share and become stars, and eventually cash cows when market growth slows. If question marks do not succeed in becoming a market leader, then after perhaps years of cash consumption, they will degenerate into dogs when market growth declines. Question marks must be analyzed carefully in order to determine whether they are worth the investment required to grow market share.

- *Stars* are units with a high market share in a fast-growing industry. They are graduated *question marks* with a market- or niche-leading trajectory, for example: amongst market share front-runners in a high-growth sector, and/or having a monopolistic or increasingly dominant unique selling proposition with burgeoning/fortuitous proposition drive(s) from: novelty (e.g. Last.FM upon CBS Interactive's due diligence), fashion/promotion (e.g.

newly prestigious celebrity-branded fragrances), customer loyalty (e.g. greenfield or military/gang enforcement backed, and/or innovative, grey-market/illicit retail of addictive drugs, for instance the British East India Company's, late-1700s opium-based Qianlong Emperor embargo-busting, Canton System), goodwill (e.g. monopsonies) and/or gearing (e.g. oligopolies, for instance Portland cement producers near boomtowns), etc. The hope is that stars become next cash cows.

Stars require high funding to fight competitors and maintain their growth rate. When industry growth slows, if they remain a niche leader or are amongst the market leaders, stars become cash cows; otherwise, they become dogs due to low relative market share.

As a particular industry matures and its growth slows, all business units become either *cash cows* or *dogs*. The natural cycle for most business units is that they start as *question marks*, then turn into *stars*. Eventually, the market stops growing; thus, the business unit becomes a *cash cow*. At the end of the cycle, the cash cow turns into a *dog*.

As BCG stated in 1970:

Only a diversified company with a balanced portfolio can use its strengths to truly capitalize on its growth opportunities. The balanced portfolio has:

- stars whose high share and high growth assure the future;
- cash cows that supply funds for that future growth; and
- question marks to be converted into stars with the added funds.

Practical Use

"*To be successful, a company should have a portfolio of products with different growth rates and different market shares. The portfolio composition is a function of the balance between cash flows. High growth products require cash inputs to grow. Low growth products should generate excess cash. Both kinds are needed simultaneously.*"—Bruce Henderson.

For each product or service, the 'area' of the circle represents the value of its sales. The growth–share matrix thus offers a "map" of the organization's product (or service) strengths and weaknesses, at least in terms of current profitability, as well as the likely cashflows.

The need which prompted this idea was, indeed, that of managing cash-flow. It was reasoned that one of the main indicators of cash generation was relative market share, and one which pointed to cash usage was that of market growth rate.

Relative Market Share

This indicates likely cash generation, because the higher the share the more cash will be generated. As a result of 'economies of scale' (a basic assumption of the BCG Matrix), it is assumed that these earnings will grow faster the higher the share. The exact measure is the brand's share relative to its largest competitor. Thus, if the brand had a share of 20 percent, and the largest competitor had the same, the ratio would be 1:1. If the largest competitor had a share of 60 percent, however, the ratio would be 1:3, implying that the organization's brand was in a relatively weak position. If the largest competitor only had a share of 5 percent, the ratio would be 4:1, implying that the brand owned was in a relatively strong position, which might be reflected in profits and cash flows. If this technique is used in practice, this scale is logarithmic, not linear.

On the other hand, exactly what is a high relative share is a matter of some debate. The best evidence is that the most stable position (at least in fast-moving consumer goods markets) is for the brand leader to have a share double that of the second brand, and triple that of the third. Brand leaders in this position tend to be very stable—and profitable; the Rule of 123.

The selection of the relative market share metric was based upon its relationship to the experience curve. The market leader would have greater experience curve benefits, which delivers a cost leadership advantage.

Another reason for choosing relative market share, rather than just profits, is that it carries more information than just cash flow. It shows where the brand is positioned against its main competitors, and indicates where it might be likely to go in the future. It can also show what type of marketing activities might be expected to be effective.

Market Growth Rate

Rapidly growing in rapidly growing markets, are what organizations strive for; but, as we have seen, the penalty is that they are usually net cash users – they require investment. The reason for this is often because the growth is being 'bought' by the high investment, in the reasonable expectation that a high market share will eventually turn into a sound investment in future profits. The theory behind the matrix assumes, therefore, that a higher growth rate is indicative of accompanying demands on investment. The cut-off point is usually chosen as 10 per cent per annum. Determining this cut-off point, the rate above which the growth is deemed to be significant (and likely to lead to extra demands on cash) is a critical requirement of the technique; and one that, again, makes the use of the growth–share matrix problematical in some product areas. What is more, the evidence, from fast-moving consumer goods markets at least, is that the most typical pattern is of very low growth, less than 1 per cent per annum. This is outside the range normally considered in BCG Matrix work, which may make application of this form of analysis unworkable in many markets. Where it can be applied, however, the market growth rate says more about the brand position than just its cash flow. It is a good indicator of that market's strength, of its future potential (of its 'maturity' in terms of the market life-cycle), and also of its attractiveness to future competitors. It can also be used in growth analysis.

Critical Evaluation

While theoretically useful, and widely used, several academic studies have called into question whether using the growth–share matrix actually helps businesses succeed, and the model has since been removed from some major marketing textbooks. One study (Slater and Zwirlein, 1992) which looked at 129 firms found that those who follow portfolio planning models like the BCG matrix had lower shareholder returns.

There are further criticisms to the B.C.G Matrix. The Matrix assumes that dogs have low market share and relatively low market growth rate. This can be challenged as there are several dogs on the market which are very profitable and retain significant market share. BIC razor blades are a modern day example. BIC Razor Blades cost the firm an average of £0.05 to produce and have a retail selling price of £2.43 . This market is to expand by 25% annually for the next 5 years. This demonstrates how the B.C.G Matrix contradicts itself as a dog with little cash usage has considerably high market share within the market.

Misuse

As originally practiced by the Boston Consulting Group, the matrix was used in situations where it could be applied for graphically illustrating a portfolio composition as a function of the balance between cash flows. If used with this degree of sophistication its use would still be valid. However, later practitioners have tended to over-simplify its messages. In particular, the later application of the names (problem children, stars, cash cows and dogs) has tended to overshadow all else—and is often what most students, and practitioners, remember.

This is unfortunate, since such simplistic use contains at least two major problems:

- 'Minority applicability'. The cashflow techniques are only applicable to a very limited number of markets (where growth is relatively high, and a definite pattern of product life-cycles can be observed, such as that of ethical pharmaceuticals). In the majority of markets, use may give misleading results.
- 'Milking cash cows'. Perhaps the worst implication of the later developments is that the (brand leader) cash cows should be milked to fund new brands. This is not what research into the fast-moving consumer goods markets has shown to be the case. The brand leader's position is the one, above all, to be defended, not least since brands in this position will probably outperform any number of newly launched brands. Such brand leaders will, of course, generate large cash flows; but they should not be 'milked' to such an extent that their position is jeopardized. In any case, the chance of the new brands achieving similar brand leadership may be slim—certainly far less than the popular perception of the Boston Matrix would imply.

Perhaps the most important danger is, however, that the apparent implication of its four-quadrant form is that there should be balance of products or services across all four quadrants; and that is, indeed, the main message that it is intended to convey. Thus, money must be diverted from 'cash cows' to fund the 'stars' of the future, since 'cash cows' will inevitably decline to become 'dogs'. There is an almost mesmeric inevitability about the whole process. It focuses attention, and funding, on to the 'stars'. It presumes, and almost demands, that 'cash cows' will turn into 'dogs'.

The reality is that it is only the 'cash cows' that are really important—all the other elements are supporting actors. It is a foolish vendor who diverts funds from a 'cash cow' when these are needed to extend the life of that 'product'. Although it is necessary to recognize a 'dog' when it appears (at least before it bites you) it would be foolish in the extreme to create one in order to balance up the picture. The vendor, who has most of his (or her) products in the 'cash cow' quadrant, should consider himself (or herself) fortunate indeed, and an excellent marketer, although he or she might also consider creating a few stars as an insurance policy against unexpected future developments and, perhaps, to add some extra growth. There is also a common misconception that 'dogs' are a waste of resources. In many markets 'dogs' can be considered loss-leaders that while not themselves profitable will lead to increased sales in other profitable areas.

Alternatives

As with most marketing techniques, there are a number of alternative offerings vying with the growth–share matrix although this appears to be the most widely used. The next most widely reported technique is that developed by McKinsey and General Electric, which is a three-cell by three-cell matrix—using the dimensions of 'industry attractiveness' and 'business strengths'. This approaches some of the same issues as the growth–share matrix but from a different direction and in a more complex way (which may be why it is used less, or is at least less widely taught). A more practical approach is that of the Boston Consulting Group's Advantage Matrix, which the consultancy reportedly used itself though it is little known amongst the wider population.

Other Uses

The initial intent of the growth–share matrix was to evaluate business units, but the same evaluation can be made for product lines or any other cash-generating entities. This should only be attempted for real lines that have a sufficient history to allow some prediction; if the corporation has made only a few products and called them a product line, the sample variance will be too high for this sort of analysis to be meaningful.

Market Environment

The business environment is a marketing term and refers to factors and forces that affect a firm's ability to build and maintain successful customer relationships. The three levels of the environment are:

1. Micro (internal) environment – small forces within the company that affect its ability to serve its customers.
2. Meso environment – the industry in which a company operates and the industry's market(s).
3. Macro (national) environment – larger societal forces that affect the microenvironment.

Micro-environment

Company aspect of micro-environment refers to the internal environment of the company. This includes all departments, such as management, finance, research and development, purchasing, operations and accounting. Each of these departments influences marketing decisions. For example, research and development have input as to the features a product can perform and accounting approves the financial side of marketing plans and budget in customer dissatisfaction. Marketing managers must watch supply availability and other trends dealing with suppliers to ensure that product will be delivered to customers in the time frame required in order to maintain a strong customer relationship.

Marketing intermediaries refers to resellers, physical distribution firms, marketing services agencies, and financial intermediaries. These are the people that help the company promote, sell, and distribute its products to final buyers. Resellers are those that hold and sell the company's product. They match the distribution to the customers and include places such as Wal-Mart, Target, and Best Buy. Physical distribution firms are places such as warehouses that store and transport the company's product from its origin to its destination. Marketing services agencies are companies that offer services such as conducting marketing research, advertising, and consulting. Financial intermediaries are institutions such as banks, credit companies and insurance companies.

Another aspect of micro-environment is the customer market. There are different types of customer markets including consumer markets, business markets, government markets, international markets, and reseller markets. The consumer market is made up of individuals who buy goods and services for their own personal use or use in their household. Business markets include those that buy goods and services for use in producing their own products to sell. This is different from the reseller market which includes businesses that purchase goods to resell as is for a profit. These are the same companies mentioned as market intermediaries. The government market consists of government agencies that buy goods to produce public services or transfer goods to others who need them. International markets include buyers in other countries and includes customers from the previous categories.

Competitors are also a factor in the micro-environment and include companies with similar offerings for goods and services. To remain competitive a company must consider who their biggest competitors are while considering its own size and position in the industry. The company should develop a strategic advantage over their competitors.

The final aspect of the micro environment is publics, which is any group that has an interest in or effect on the organization's ability to meet its goals. For example, financial publics can hinder a company's ability to obtain funds affecting the level of credit a company has. Media public include newspapers and magazines that can publish articles of interest regarding the company and editorials that may influence customers' opinions. Government public can affect the company by passing legislation and laws that put restrictions on the company's actions. Citizen-action publics include environmental groups and minority groups and can question the actions of a company and put them in the public spotlight. Local publics are neighborhood and community organizations and will also question a company's effect on the local area and the level of responsibility of their actions. The general public can affect the company as any change in their attitude, whether positive or negative, can cause sales to go up or down because the general public is often the company's customer base. And finally those who are employed within the company and deal with the organization and construction of the company's product.

Macro-environment

The macro-environment refers to all forces that are part of the larger society and affect the micro-environment. It includes concepts such as demography, economy, natural forces, technology, politics, and culture.

Factors affecting organization in Macro environment are known as PESTEL, that is: Political, Economical, Social, Technological, Environmental and Legal.

Demography refers to studying human populations in terms of size, density, location, age, gender, race, and occupation. This is a very important factor to study for marketers and helps to divide the population into market segments and target markets. An example of demography is classifying groups of people according to the year they were born. These classifications can be referred to as baby boomers, who are born between 1946 and 1964, generation X, who are born between 1965 and 1976, and generation Y, who are born between 1977 and 1994. Each classification has different characteristics and causes they find important. This can be beneficial to a marketer as they can decide who their product would benefit most and tailor their marketing plan to attract that segment. Demography covers many aspects that are important to marketers including family dynamics, geographic shifts, work force changes, and levels of diversity in any given area.

Another aspect of the macro-environment is the economic environment. This refers to the purchasing power of potential customers and the ways in which people spend their money. Within this area are two different economies, subsistence and industrialized. Subsistence economies are based more in agriculture and consume their own industrial output. Industrial economies have markets that are diverse and carry many different types of goods. Each is important to the marketer because each has a highly different spending pattern as well as different distribution of wealth.

The natural environment is another important factor of the macro-environment. This includes the natural resources that a company uses as inputs that affects their marketing activities. The concern in this area is the increased pollution, shortages of raw materials and increased governmental intervention. As raw materials become increasingly scarcer, the ability to create a company's product gets much harder. Also, pollution can go as far as negatively affecting a company's reputation if they are known for damaging the environment. The last concern, government intervention can make it increasingly harder for a company to fulfill their goals as requirements get more stringent.

The technological environment is perhaps one of the fastest changing factors in the macro-environment. This includes all developments from antibiotics and surgery to nuclear missiles and chemical weapons to automobiles and credit cards. As these markets develop it can create new markets and new uses for products. It also requires a company to stay ahead of others and update their own technology as it becomes outdated. They must stay informed of trends so they can be part of the next big thing, rather than becoming outdated and suffering the consequences financially.

The political environment includes all laws, government agencies, and groups that influence or limit other organizations and individuals within a society. It is important for marketers to be aware of these restrictions as they can be complex. Some products are regulated by both state and federal laws. There are even restrictions for some products as to who the target market may be, for example, cigarettes should not be marketed to younger children. There are also many restrictions on subliminal messages and monopolies. As laws and regulations change often, this is a very important aspect for a marketer to monitor.

The final aspect of the macro-environment is the cultural environment, which consists of institutions and basic values and beliefs of a group of people. The values can also be further categorized into core beliefs, which passed on from generation to generation and very difficult to change, and secondary beliefs, which tend to be easier to influence. As a marketer, it is important to know the difference between the two and to focus your marketing campaign to reflect the values of a target audience.

When dealing with the marketing environment it is important for a company to become proactive. By doing so, they can create the kind of environment that they will prosper in and can become more efficient by marketing in areas with the greatest customer potential. It is important to place equal emphasis on both the macro and micro environment and to react accordingly to changes within them.

Environmental Scanning

Environmental scanning is one of the essential components of the global environmental analysis. Environmental monitoring, environmental forecasting and environmental assessment complete the global environmental analysis. The global environment refers to the macro environment which comprises industries, markets, companies, clients and competitors. Consequently, there exist corresponding analyses on the micro-level. Suppliers, customers and competitors representing the micro environment of a company are analyzed within the industry analysis.

Environmental scanning can be defined as 'the study and interpretation of the political, economic, social and technological events and trends which influence a business, an industry or even a total market'. The factors which need to be considered for environmental scanning are events, trends, issues and expectations of the different interest groups. Issues are often forerunners of trend breaks. A trend break could be a value shift in society, a technological innovation that might be permanent or a paradigm change. Issues are less deep-seated and can be 'a temporary short-lived reaction to a social phenomenon'. A trend can be defined as an 'environmental phenomenon that has adopted a structural character'.

Environmental scanning is an ongoing process and organizations are always refining the way their particular company or business goes through the process. Environmental scanning reinforces productive strategic plans and policies that can be implemented to make the organization get the maximum use of the business environment they are in. Environmental scanning not only helps the business find its strengths in its current environment but it also finds the weakness of competitors, identifies new markets, potential customers and up and coming technological platforms and devices that can be best used to sell/market the product or service. Environmental scanning helps a business improve their decision-making process in times of risk to the external and internal environments the business is in.

Process

When scanning the environment, the organization need to look at all the influences of the company. The scanning process makes the organization aware of what the business environment is about. It allows the organization to adapt and learn from that environment. When the company responds to an environmental scanning process it allows them to easily respond and react to any changes to both the internal and external business environment. Environmental scanning is a useful tool for strategic management as it helps them to create and develop the aims and objectives of the company which assists with the production of the company or organization.

When looking at the weaknesses of the organization's placing in the current business environment a formal environmental scanning is used. A common formal environmental scanning process has five steps. The five steps are fundamental in the achievement of each step and may develop each other in some form:

1. The first step of the environmental scanning process requires the identification of the needs and the issues that have occurred that caused the organization to decide an environmental scanning is required. Before starting the process there are several factors that need to be considered which include the purpose of the scanning, who will be participating in the processes and the amount of time and the resources that will be allocated for the duration of the scanning process.
2. The second step of the scanning process is gathering the information. All the needs of the organization are translated into required pieces of information that will be useful in the process.
3. The third steps analyzing all the information that the business have collected. When analyzing the information organizations are made aware of the trends or issues that the organizations may be influenced by.
4. The step four of the environmental scanning process is all about the communication of the results obtained in step three. The appropriate decision makers analyze the translated information of the potential effects of the organization. All the information is presented in a simple and concise format.
5. With all the information obtained from steps three and four, step five is all about making informed decisions. Management creates appropriate steps that will position the organization in the current business environment.

Information Sources Used

The information sources used to gain knowledge and understanding of the current business environment the organization is in can be split into two categories. The external and internal information sources. The external sources aren't always those in a published form and can include verbal sources such as 'word of mouth'. The external information sources includes:

- Personal contacts
- Journals/magazines
- Books
- Newspapers
- Professional conferences/ meetings
- Radio, television and internet
- Professional colleagues
- Customers
- Commercial databases.

The internal information is all information that is specific to the organization. This information can be compared with the external sources to get the maximum use out of both types of sources for the organization, internal information includes:

- Personal contacts
- Internal reports
- Conference papers
- Internal memoranda
- Committees/ meetings
- Sales staff
- Other managers
- Other employees
- Internal databases.

Barriers

Environmental scanning isn't always as effective or useful in an organizational setting for several reasons. The volume of the information received through the scanning process can be disadvantageous when attempting to translate and make sense of the information as some information may get overlooked or just missed entirely. Because of the volume of information its hard to decipher what is important or not so management and key information may be missed. Another way vital information can be missed is if the information is unordered and unorganized. Due to ever changing environment all information runs under a time limit of validity. Another barrier to environment scanning is the interpretation of information that has been collected. Undetermined sources can cause confusion and irrelevance to the process.

Macro Environment

There are a number of common approaches how the external factors, which are mentioned in the definition of Kroon and which describe the macro environment, can be identified and examined. These factors indirectly affect the organization but cannot be controlled by it. One approach could be the PEST analysis. PEST stands for political, economic, social and technological. Two more factors, the environmental and legal factor, are defined within the PESTEL analysis (or PESTLE analysis).

The segmentation of the macro environment according to the six presented factors of the PESTEL analysis is the starting point of the global environmental analysis.

PESTEL Analysis

The six environmental factors of the PESTEL analysis are the following:

Political Factors

The company/organization needs to consider the political environment when creating business strategies. The entire political environment includes looking at government policies and the risk and instability of current political factors. Political risks can include an unexpected loss of ownership due to government takeover (nationalization), or changes in labour laws which might increase the cost of the company's workforce. However often business can anticipate issues by performing a political risk analysis. The political instability can influence the business and the duration of time that business/ organization is profitable.

- Taxation Policy
- Trade regulations
- Governmental stability
- Unemployment Policy, etc.
- political stability

Economical Factors

The economic factors of the business environment are all the variables that impact how the consumer spends their money and the power of that purchase. There are multiple factors that exist at any time. An example of an economic factor is the recent recession influenced people to spend less and save more which has impacted current consumer spending patterns. The economic development of a country Is an important element when scanning the economic environment. Countries are often categorized as either 'developing' or 'developed'. The exchange rate of a country can have an extensive impact on the profitability of a business. Relatively small changes in the exchange rate may be the difference between profit and loss. When promoting, selling a product it is important for an organization to consider the extra financial information including current rates, taxes etc. in the economy of the country.

- Interest rate
- Inflation rate
- Growth in spending power
- Rate of people in a pensionable age
- Recession or Boom
- Customer liquidations
- Balances of Sharing

Socio-cultural

The socio-cultural environment looks at the demographic characteristics of the current business environment. It looks at the values, customs and norms of the environment of which a company or organisation is placed. When looking at the socio-cultural environment it is important to consider the social values of the environment. Organizations look at the cultural characteristics of the society and consider all values and customs that are often associated with the culture while they try to market and sell the product or service, such as:

- values, beliefs
- language
- religion
- education
- literacy
- time orientation
- lifestyle.

Technological Factors

The technological environment is becoming a lot more important in the modern day business environment. New technology produces new opportunities for companies and organizations to create, sell and promote a product. Technology is rapidly growing and forever changing. Telecommunication technology e.g. cellphones and laptops are increasing the opportunity within an organization to promote and sell a product. The internet has made information available to the consumer to easily compare current prices of a product or service with the price of the competitors of the same product or service. The internet has also created more opportunity to market the product or service via the use of social media.

- Internet
- E-commerce
- Social Media
- Electronic Media
- Research and Development
- Rate of technological change.

Environmental Factors

The environmental factors of the PESTLE analysis include natural resources that are affected by the processes of selling and marketing products or services. The two main environmental trends that need to be considered when evaluating the natural environment is the increased pollution and growing shortage of raw materials, Government regulations are creating practices that encourage environmental sustainability. A business might for example utilize recyclable and biodegradable packaging, thus making the most of the environmental opportunities to create a sustainable organizational in the current natural environment.

- Competitive advantage
- Waste disposal
- Energy consumption
- Pollution monitoring, etc.

Legal Factors

The legal environment includes the laws and regulations of a state. The laws and regulations will influence the way in which an organization will market or sell the product and services. The legal factors influence trade agreements between different governments and states. The governments that have a well developed public policy about selling and marketing goods may limit competition and place other obligations on retailers.

- Employment law
- Health and safety
- Product safety
- Advertising regulations
- Product labeling
- Labour laws etc.

SWOT Analysis

SWOT or situation analysis is used when without to look at both the internal and external environment. SWOT stands for Strength, Weakness, Opportunity and Threat. The internal factors considered are the strengths and weaknesses where the opportunities and threats are external factors that are all used and considered to help improve the overall decision making process in dynamic strategic situations the business is facing.

The strengths are positive characteristics in the internal business environment which can be capitalized on to increase the overall organisations performance. The weakness are factors of the internal environment which may restrict and interfere with the positive organizational performance. The internal environment factors will include finance, production, research, development and marketing. The opportunities include factors of the external environment that act like stepping stones for the organization in order to achieve their current strategic goals. The threats include the factors that have an effect and may interrupt the organization from achieving the goals. Often threats will come out of the external business environment.

Mesoenvironment

The meso-level is settled between the macro- and the micro- level. This field deals with the design of the specific environment of the enterprises. It is of decisive importance that the layout of the physical infrastructure (transport, communication and power distribution systems) and of the sector policies, especially of the education, research and technology policy, are oriented towards competitiveness. In addition, the design of the trade policy and systems of rules (for example: environmental norms and technical safety standards), which contributes to the development of national advantages of competition, is relevant. Like on the micro-level, on the meso-level new patterns of organisation and steering must be developed. The state shall give impulses and mediate between enterprises, associations, science and intermediate institutions. "The design of locations becomes like that a continuous process on the basis of the efforts of enterprises, science and state as well as of the determined cooperation of private and public agents".

References

- Wernerfelt, B. (1984), A resource-based view of the firm, Strategic Management Journal, Vol. 5, (April–June): pp. 171-180 PDF
- Kaplan, Robert S; Norton, D. P. (1996). The Balanced Scorecard: Translating Strategy into Action. Boston, MA.: Harvard Business School Press. ISBN 978-0-87584-651-4
- Schneiderman, Arthur M. (2006). "Analog Devices: 1986–1992, The First Balanced Scorecard". Arthur M. Schneiderman. Archived from the original on 25 December 2013. Retrieved 28 May 2014
- Abernethy, Margret A; Horne, M.; Lillis, A.M.; Malina, M.A.; Selto, F.H. (2005). "A multi-method approach to building causal performance maps from expert knowledge". Management accounting research. 16 (2): 135–155. doi:10.1016/j.mar.2005.03.003
- Radnor, Z; Lovell, W. (2003). "Defining, justifying and implementing the Balanced Scorecard in the National Health Service". International Journal of Medical Marketing. 3 (3): 174–188. doi:10.1057/palgrave.jmm.5040117
- Chandler, Alfred D. (1962). Strategy and Structure: Chapters in the History of the American Enterprise. Boston, MA.: The MIT Press. ISBN 978-1-61427-508-4
- Rigby, D.; Bilodeau B. (2013). "Bain and Company's Management Tools and Trends Survey 2013". Bain & Company. Archived from the original on 7 April 2014. Retrieved 28 May 2014
- Butler, A.; Letza S. R.; Neale B. (1997). "Linking the Balanced Scorecard to Strategy". Long Range Planning. 30 (2): 242–253. doi:10.1016/s0024-6301(96)00116-1
- Schneiderman, Arthur M. (1999). "Why Balanced Scorecards fail". Journal of Strategic Performance Measurement (January)
- Olve, Nils-Göran; Roy, J.; Wetter, M. (25 Feb 1999). Performance Drivers: A practical guide to using the Balanced Scorecard. New York: John Wiley and Sons. ISBN 978-0-471-98623-2
- "How do I link corporate and individual performance management systems?" (PDF). 2GC Active Management. Archived from the original (PDF) on 1 May 2014. Retrieved 28 May 2014
- Norreklit, Hanne (2000). "The balance on the balanced scorecard – a critical analysis of some of its assumptions". Management Accounting Research. 11 (1): 65–88. doi:10.1006/mare.1999.0121
- Kong, E. (2010). Analysing BSC and IC's usefulness in non-profit organisations. Journal of Intellectual Capital, 11(3), 284-304
- Penrose, Edith (1959). The Theory of the Growth of the Firm. New York: John Wiley and Sons. ISBN 978-0-19-828977-7
- Tang, David (21 October 2014). "Introduction to Strategy Development and Strategy Execution". Flevy. Retrieved 2 November 2014

- Gardiner, P. D.; Simmons, J. E. L. (2003). "Performance measurement tools: The balanced scorecard and the EFQM excellence model". Measuring Business Excellence. 7 (1): 14–29. doi:10.1108/13683040310466690
- Costa, Jorge (1995). "An Empirically- based Review Of The Concept Of Environment Scanning". International Journal of Contemporary Hospitality Management
- Niven, Paul R. (18 April 2002). Balanced Scorecard Step-by-step: Maximizing Performance and Maintaining Results. New York: John Wiley & Sons. ISBN 978-0-471-07872-2
- Elefalke, K (2001). "The Balanced Scorecard of the Swedish Police Service: 7000 officers in total quality management project". Total Quality Management. 12 (7): 958–966. doi:10.1080/09544120120096106

4

Essentials of Company Analysis

Evaluating the theoretical value of a company is very important. This process is carried out by investors to assess products and services and to evaluate securities. This chapter has been carefully written to provide an easy understanding of the varied facets of company analysis.

Company Analysis

Importance of Company Analysis: Analysis possibly helps investors in identifying the economy and then the industries where one can invest. Having done that, one has to look for those companies which offer better return for the investment or stocks of those companies which are likely to outperform others. One should also be able to find the stocks that are available cheap, i.e. the market price is more that the intrinsic value. For estimating the intrinsic value of the company one has to look at two major aspects: the company's business in terms of products, services, capabilities, competitiveness etc. and corresponding business strategy & the resultant financial performance.

Stock Valuation

In financial markets, stock valuation is the method of calculating theoretical values of companies and their stocks. The main use of these methods is to predict future market prices, or more generally, potential market prices, and thus to profit from price movement – stocks that are judged *undervalued* (with respect to their theoretical value) are bought, while stocks that are judged *overvalued* are sold, in the expectation that undervalued stocks will overall rise in value, while overvalued stocks will generally decrease in value.

In the view of fundamental analysis, stock valuation based on fundamentals aims to give an estimate of the intrinsic value of a stock, based on predictions of the future cash flows and profitability of the business. Fundamental analysis may be replaced or augmented by market criteria – what the market will pay for the stock, disregarding intrinsic value. These can be combined as "predictions of future cash flows/profits (fundamental)", together with "what will the market pay for these profits?" These can be seen as "supply and demand" sides – what underlies the supply (of stock), and what drives the (market) demand for stock?

In the view of John Maynard Keynes, stock valuation is not a *prediction* but a *convention,* which serves to facilitate investment and ensure that stocks are liquid, despite being underpinned by an illiquid business and its illiquid investments, such as factories.

Fundamental Criteria (Fair Value)

The most theoretically sound stock valuation method, called income valuation or the discounted cash flow (DCF) method, involves discounting of the profits (dividends, earnings, or cash flows) the stock will bring to the stockholder in the foreseeable future, and a final value on disposal. The discounted rate normally includes a risk premium which is commonly based on the capital asset pricing model.

In July 2010, a Delaware court ruled on appropriate inputs to use in discounted cash flow analysis in a dispute between shareholders and a company over the proper fair value of the stock. In this case the shareholders' model provided value of $139 per share and the company's model provided $89 per share. Contested inputs included the terminal growth rate, the equity risk premium, and beta.

The fundamental valuation is the valuation that people use to justify stock prices. The most common example of this type of valuation methodology is P/E ratio, which stands for Price to Earnings Ratio. This form of valuation is based on historic ratios and statistics and aims to assign value to a stock based on measurable attributes. This form of valuation is typically what drives long-term stock prices.

The other way stocks are valued is based on supply and demand. The more people that want to buy the stock, the higher its price will be. And conversely, the more people that want to sell the stock, the lower the price will be. This form of valuation is very hard to understand or predict, and it often drives the short-term stock market trends.

There are many different ways to value stocks. The key is to take each approach into account while formulating an overall opinion of the stock. If the valuation of a company is lower or higher than other similar stocks, then the next step would be to determine the reasons.

Earnings Per Share (EPS)

EPS is the Net income available to common shareholders of the company divided by the number of shares outstanding. Usually there will be two types of EPS listed: a GAAP (Generally Accepted Accounting Principles) EPS and a Pro Forma EPS, which means that the income has been adjusted to exclude any one time items as well as some non-cash items like amortization of goodwill or stock option expenses. The most important thing to look for in the EPS figure is the overall quality of earnings. Make sure the company is not trying to manipulate their EPS numbers to make it look like they are more profitable. Also, look at the growth in EPS over the past several quarters / years to understand how volatile their EPS is, and to see if they are an underachiever or an overachiever. In other words, have they consistently beaten expectations or are they constantly restating and lowering their forecasts?

The EPS number that most analysts use is the pro forma EPS. To compute this number, use the net income that excludes any one-time gains or losses and excludes any non-cash expenses like stock options or amortization of goodwill. Then divide this number by the number of fully diluted shares outstanding. Historical EPS figures and forecasts for the next 1–2 years can be found by visiting free financial sites such as Yahoo Finance (enter the ticker and then click on "estimates").

Price to Earnings (P/E)

Now that the analyst has several EPS figures (historical and forecasts), the analyst will be able to look at the most common valuation technique used, the price to earnings ratio, or P/E. To compute this figure, one divides the stock price by the annual EPS figure. For example, if the stock is trading at $10 and the EPS is $0.50, the P/E is 20 times. A complete analysis of the P/E multiple includes a look at the historical and forward ratios.

Historical P/Es are computed by taking the current price divided by the sum of the EPS for the last four quarters, or for the previous year. Historical trends of the P/E should also be considered by viewing a chart of its historical P/E over the last several years (one can find this on most finance sites like Yahoo Finance). Specifically consider what range the P/E has traded in so as to determine whether the current P/E is high or low versus its historical average.

Forward P/Es reflect the future growth of the company into the future. Forward P/Es are computed by taking the current stock price divided by the sum of the EPS estimates for the next four quarters, or for the EPS estimate for next calendar or fiscal year or two.

P/Es change constantly. If there is a large price change in a stock, or if the earnings (EPS) estimates change, the ratio is recomputed.

Growth Rate

Valuations rely very heavily on the expected growth rate of a company. One must look at the historical growth rate of both sales and income to get a feeling for the type of future growth expected. However, companies are constantly changing, as well as the economy, so solely using historical growth rates to predict the future is not an acceptable form of valuation. Instead, they are used as guidelines for what future growth could look like if similar circumstances are encountered by the company. Calculating the future growth rate requires personal investment research. This may take form in listening to the company's quarterly conference call or reading a press release or other company article that discusses the company's growth guidance. However, although companies are in the best position to forecast their own growth, they are often far from accurate, and unforeseen events could cause rapid changes in the economy and in the company's industry.

For any valuation technique, it is important to look at a range of forecast values. For example, if the company being valued has been growing earnings between 5 and 10% each year for the last 5 years, but believes that it will grow 15 –20% this year, a more conservative growth rate of 10–15% would be appropriate in valuations. Another example would be for a company that has been going through restructuring. It may have been growing earnings at 10–15% over the past several quarters or years because of cost cutting, but their sales growth could be only 0–5%. This would signal that their earnings growth will probably slow when the cost cutting has fully taken effect. Therefore, forecasting an earnings growth closer to the 0–5% rate would be more appropriate rather than the 15–20%. Nonetheless, the growth rate method of valuations relies heavily on gut feel to make a forecast. This is why analysts often make inaccurate forecasts, and also why familiarity with a company is essential before making a forecast.

Capital Structure Substitution - asset Pricing Formula

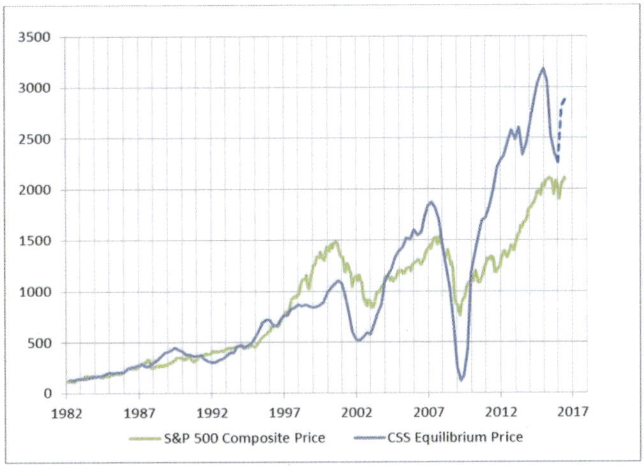

S&P 500 Composite Index compared to the CSS asset pricing formula - July 2016

The capital structure substitution theory (CSS) describes the relationship between earnings, stock price and capital structure of public companies. The equilibrium condition of the CCS theory can be easily rearranged to an asset pricing formula:

$$P_x = \frac{E_x}{R_x[1-T]}$$

where

- P is the current market price of public company x
- E is the earnings-per-share of company x
- R is the nominal interest rate on corporate bonds of company x
- T is the corporate tax rate

The CSS theory suggests that company share prices are strongly influenced by bondholders. As a result of active repurchasing or issuing of shares by company managements, equilibrium pricing is no longer a result of balancing shareholder demand and supply. The asset pricing formula only applies to debt-holding companies.

The asset pricing formula can be used on a market aggregate level as well. The resulting graph shows at what times the S&P 500 Composite was overpriced and at what times it was under-priced relative to the capital structure substitution theory equilibrium. In times when the market is under-priced, corporate buyback programs will allow companies to drive up earnings-per-share, and generate extra demand in the stock market.

Price Earnings to Growth (PEG) Ratio

This valuation technique has really become popular over the past decade or so. It is better than just looking at a P/E because it takes three factors into account; the price, earnings, and earnings growth rates. To compute the PEG ratio, the Forward P/E is divided by the expected earnings growth rate (one can also use historical P/E and historical growth rate to see where it has traded in the past). This will yield a ratio that is usually expressed as a percentage. The theory goes that as the percentage rises over 100% the stock becomes more and more overvalued, and as the PEG ratio falls below 100% the stock becomes more and more undervalued. The theory is based on a belief that P/E ratios should approximate the long-term growth rate of a company's earnings. Whether or not this is true will never be proven and the theory is therefore just a rule of thumb to use in the overall valuation process.

Here is an example of how to use the PEG ratio to compare stocks. Stock A is trading at a forward P/E of 15 and expected to grow at 20%. Stock B is trading at a forward P/E of 30 and expected to grow at 25%. The PEG ratio for Stock A is 75% (15/20) and for Stock B is 120% (30/25). According to the PEG ratio, Stock A is a better purchase because it has a lower PEG ratio, or in other words, you can purchase its future earnings growth for a lower relative price than that of Stock B.

Sum of Perpetuities Method

The PEG ratio is a special case in the sum of perpetuities method (SPM) equation. A generalized version of the Walter model (1956), SPM considers the effects of dividends, earnings growth, as well as the risk profile of a firm on a stock's value. Derived from the compound interest formula using the present value of a perpetuity equation, SPM is an alternative to the Gordon Growth Model. The variables are:

- P is the value of the stock or business
- E is a company's earnings
- G is the company's constant growth rate
- K is the company's risk adjusted discount rate
- D is the company's dividend payment

$$P = \left(\frac{E * G}{K^2}\right) + \left(\frac{D}{K}\right)$$

In a special case where K is equal to 10%, and the company does not pay dividends, SPM reduces to the PEG ratio.

Additional models represent the sum of perpetuities in terms of earnings, growth rate, the risk-adjusted discount rate, and accounting book value.

Return on Invested Capital (ROIC)

This valuation technique measures how much money the company makes each year per dollar of invested capital. Invested Capital is the amount of money invested in the company by both stockholders and debtors. The ratio is expressed as a percent and one looks for a percent that approximates the level of growth that expected. In its simplest definition, this ratio measures the investment return that management is able to get for its capital. The higher the number, the better the return.

To compute the ratio, take the pro forma net income (same one used in the EPS figure mentioned above) and divide it by the invested capital. Invested capital can be estimated by adding together the stockholders equity, the total long and short term debt and accounts payable, and then subtracting accounts receivable and cash (all of these numbers can be found on the company's latest quarterly balance sheet). This ratio is much more useful when comparing it to other companies being valued.

Return on Assets (ROA)

Similar to ROIC, ROA, expressed as a percent, measures the company's ability to make money from its assets. To measure the ROA, take the pro forma net income divided by the total assets. However, because of very common irregularities in balance sheets (due to things like Goodwill, write-offs, discontinuations, etc.) this ratio is not always a good indicator of the company's potential. If the ratio is higher or lower than expected, one should look closely at the assets to see what could be over or understating the figure.

Price to Sales (P/S)

This figure is useful because it compares the current stock price to the annual sales. In other words, it describes how much the stock costs per dollar of sales earned.

Market Cap

Market cap, which is short for market capitalization, is the value of all of the company's stock. To measure it, multiply the current stock price by the fully diluted shares outstanding. Remember, the market cap is only the value of the stock. To get a more complete picture, look at the enterprise value.

Enterprise Value (EV)

Enterprise value is equal to the total value of the company, as it is trading for on the stock market. To compute it, add the market cap and the total net debt of the company. The total net debt is equal to total long and short term debt plus accounts payable, minus accounts receivable, minus cash. The enterprise value is the best approximation of what a company is worth at any point in time because it takes into account the actual stock price instead of balance sheet prices. When analysts say that a company is a "billion dollar" company, they are often referring to its total enterprise value. Enterprise value fluctuates rapidly based on stock price changes.

EV to Sales

This ratio measures the total company value as compared to its annual sales. A high ratio means that the company's value is much more than its sales. To compute it, divide the EV by the net sales for the last four quarters. This ratio is especially useful when valuing companies that do not have earnings, or that are going through unusually rough times. For example, if a company is facing restructuring and it is currently losing money, then the P/E ratio would be irrelevant. However, by applying an EV to Sales ratio, one could compute what that company could trade for when its restructuring is over and its earnings are back to normal.

EBITDA

EBITDA stands for earnings before interest, taxes, depreciation and amortization. It is one of the best measures of a company's cash flow and is used for valuing both public and private companies. To compute EBITDA, use a company's income statement, take the net income and then add back interest, taxes, depreciation, amortization and any other non-cash or one-time charges. This leaves you with a number that approximates how much cash the company is producing. EBITDA is a very popular figure because it can easily be compared across companies, even if not all of the companies are profitable.

EV to EBITDA

This is perhaps one of the best measurements of whether or not a company is cheap or expensive. To compute, divide the EV by EBITDA. The higher the number, the more expensive the company is. However, remember that more expensive companies are often valued higher because they are growing faster or because they are a higher quality company. With that said, the best way to use EV/EBITDA is to compare it to that of other similar companies.

Approximate Valuation Approaches

Average Growth Approximation

Assuming that two stocks have the same earnings growth, the one with a lower P/E is a better value. The P/E method is perhaps the most commonly used valuation method in the stock brokerage industry. By using comparison firms, a target price/earnings (or P/E) ratio is selected for the company, and then the future earnings of the company are estimated. The valuation's fair price is simply estimated earnings times target P/E. This model is essentially the same model as Gordon's model, if k-g is estimated as the dividend payout ratio (D/E) divided by the target P/E ratio.

Constant Growth Approximation

The Gordon model or *Gordon's growth model* is the best known of a class of discounted dividend models. It assumes that dividends will increase at a constant growth rate (less than the discount rate) forever. The valuation is given by the formula:

$$P = D \cdot \sum_{i=1}^{\infty} \left(\frac{1+g}{1+k} \right)^i = D \cdot \frac{1+g}{k-g}.$$

and the following table defines each symbol:

Symbol	Meaning	Units
	estimated stock price	\$ or € or £
D	*last dividend paid*	\$ or € or £
k	*discount rate*	%
g	*the growth rate of the dividends*	%

Dividend growth rate is not known, but earnings growth may be used in its place, assuming that the payout ratio is constant.

Limited High-growth Period Approximation

When a stock has a significantly higher growth rate than its peers, it is sometimes assumed that the earnings growth rate will be sustained for a short time (say, 5 years), and then the growth rate will revert to the mean. This is probably the most rigorous approximation that is practical.

While these DCF models are commonly used, the uncertainty in these values is hardly ever discussed. Note that the models diverge for $k = g$ and hence are extremely sensitive to the difference of dividend growth to discount factor. One might argue that an analyst can justify any value (and that would usually be one close to the current price supporting his call) by fine-tuning the growth/discount assumptions.

Implied Growth Models

One can use the Gordon model or the limited high-growth period approximation model to impute an implied growth estimate. To do this, one takes the average P/E and average growth for a comparison index, uses the current (or forward) P/E of the stock in question, and calculates what growth rate would be needed for the two valuation equations to be equal. This yields an estimate of the "break-even" growth rate for the stock's current P/E ratio. (Note : we are using earnings not dividends here because dividend policies vary and may be influenced by many factors including tax treatment).

Imputed Growth Acceleration Ratio

Subsequently, one can divide this imputed growth estimate by recent historical growth rates. If the resulting ratio is greater than one, it implies that the stock would need to experience accelerated growth relative to its prior recent historical growth to justify its current P/E (higher values suggest potential overvaluation). If the resulting ratio is less than one, it implies that either the market expects growth to slow for this stock or that the stock could sustain its current P/E with lower than historical growth (lower values suggest potential undervaluation). Comparison of the IGAR across stocks in the same industry may give estimates of relative value. IGAR averages across an industry may give estimates of relative expected changes in industry growth (e.g. the market's imputed expectation that an industry is about to "take-off" or stagnate). Naturally, any differences in IGAR between stocks in the same industry may be due to differences in fundamentals, and would require further specific analysis.

Market Criteria (Potential Price)

Some feel that if the stock is listed in a well-organized stock market, with a large volume of transactions, the market price will reflect all known information relevant to the valuation of the stock. This is called the efficient-market hypothesis.

On the other hand, studies made in the field of behavioral finance tend to show that deviations from the fair price are rather common, and sometimes quite large.

Thus, in addition to fundamental economic criteria, market criteria also have to be taken into account market-based valuation. Valuing a stock requires not just an estimate its fair value, but also to determine its potential price range, taking into account market behavior aspects. One of the behavioral valuation tools is the stock image, a coefficient that bridges the theoretical fair value and the market price.

Keynes's View

In the view of noted economist John Maynard Keynes, stock valuation is not an *estimate* of the fair value of stocks, but rather a *convention,* which serves to provide the necessary stability and liquidity for investment, so long as the convention does not break down:

> Certain classes of investment are governed by the average expectation of those who deal on the Stock Exchange as revealed in the price of shares, rather than by the genuine expectations of the professional entrepreneur. How then are these highly significant daily, even hourly, revaluations of existing investments carried out in practice?
>
> In practice, we have tacitly agreed, as a rule, to fall back on what is, in truth, a convention. The essence of this convention – though it does not, of course, work out so simply – lies in assuming that the existing state of affairs will continue indefinitely, except in so far as we have specific reasons to expect a change.
>
> Nevertheless the above conventional method of calculation will be compatible with a considerable measure of continuity and stability in our affairs, so long as we can rely on the maintenance of the convention.
>
> Thus investment becomes reasonably 'safe' for the individual investor over short periods, and hence over a succession of short periods however many, if he can fairly rely on there being no breakdown in the convention and on his therefore having an opportunity to revise his judgment and change his investment, before there has been time for much to happen. Investments which are 'fixed' for the community are thus made 'liquid' for the individual.
>
> —*The General Theory, Chapter 12*

Company Analysis vs. Stock Valuation: Having identified a good company in terms of earnings and growth potential, one has to value the stock of the company separately. It is quite likely that the stock of a good company is priced very high in the market, i.e. market price is higher than the intrinsic value of the stock. The reverse can also be true.

Growth Companies vs. Growth Stocks: Growth companies are those that show more than average growth in sales and earnings. Growth companies can also be defined as those earning rate of return more than the expected rate of return from the investors' point view, i.e. weighted average cost of capital. However growth stocks are those that show higher rate of return than other stocks in the market with similar risk characteristics. Such stocks show a superior risk adjusted rate of return. It is also true that such stocks will not consistently show superior adjusted rate of return. Because of superior performance, there will be more demand for the stocks and the stocks will be priced high in the market. As a result the superior return will vanish and the stocks will show normal return.

Defensive Companies vs. Defensive Stocks: Companies with ability to show earnings while withstanding an economic downturn are known as defensive companies. These companies are characterized with low business and financial risk. Whereas stocks with a negative systematic risk i.e. of β (as per CAPM) are known as defensive stocks. Such stocks are likely to show positive return when market moves downward. Such stocks are to be avoided in a bull phase.

Cyclical Companies vs. Cyclical Stocks: Cyclical companies are those whose sales and earnings will be greatly influenced by aggregate business activity. These companies do well during economic expansion and poorly during economic contraction. Cyclical stocks are those that will experience changes in their rates of return greater than changes in overall market rates of return. Such stocks will have high beta.

Value versus Growth Investing: Growth stocks will have positive earnings surprises and above-average risk adjusted rates of return because the stocks are undervalued. Value stocks appear to be undervalued for reasons besides earnings growth potential. Value stocks usually have low P/E ratio or low P/B ratio.

It is imperative for investors to analyze the companies for their performance and subsequently find the intrinsic value of the stocks of the companies. If the intrinsic value of the stock is higher than the market price, one can take a buy decision.

Strategy Analysis

Strategy refers to a plan of action designed to achieve a particular goal. Firms without proper strategies from time to time can face premature death. Such firms have a passive management that does not explore new opportunities and adapt to the changes happening in the surrounding. Table lists different levels of strategy and corresponding management decisions for a typical firm. All the decisions affect the cash flows of a company, hence are important from analysis and valuation point of view.

Table: Multiple Layers/ Levels of Strategy

Levels of Strategy	Management Decision
Corporate Strategy	Activities to enhance substantial competitive advantage • Selecting the Business to do? • Entering New Market • Exiting/ withdrawal from market
Business Strategy	• Decisions to maximize competitive position within the chosen market
Operational Strategy	• Planning for execution of the goal of the strategic business unit (SBU)

Firm Competitive Strategies: As discussed in Industry Analysis, five competitive forces as suggested by Michael E Porter are: Current rivalry, Threat of new entrants, Potential substitutes and Bargaining power of suppliers. Porter's five force analysis helps in determining potential attractiveness of an industry- insight of margins. One can take a decision about exit from or entry into an industry. With the help of a systematic and structured analysis of market structure and competitive situation, one can define different strategies that reduces power of competitive forces. Company can adopt defensive or offensive competitive strategy. Defensive strategy involves positioning firm so that it its capabilities provide the best means to deflect the effect of competitive forces in the industry. Offensive strategy involves using the company's strength to affect the competitive industry forces, thus improving the firm's relative industry position. Porter also suggested two major strategies:

Low-Cost Strategy: The firm seeks to be the low-cost producer, and hence the cost leader in its industry. This could be because of economies of scale, technology, access to cheap resources etc.

Differentiation Strategy: Firm positions itself as unique in the industry. The differentiating factor needs to be truly unique so that it generates more revenue for the firm compared to other competitors. The incremental revenue because of uniqueness also should exceed the cost of creating that uniqueness.

Business Analysis

Business analysis is a research discipline of identifying business needs and determining solutions to business problems. Solutions often include a software-systems development component, but may also consist of process improvement, organizational change or strategic planning and policy development. The person who carries out this task is called a business analyst or BA.

Business analysts do not work solely on developing software systems. Those who attempt to do so run the risk of developing an incomplete solution.

Although there are different role definitions, depending upon the organization, there does seem to be an area of common ground where most business analysts work. The responsibilities appear to be:

- To investigate business systems, taking a holistic view of the situation. This may include examining elements of the organisation structures and staff development issues as well as current processes and IT systems.
- To evaluate actions to improve the operation of a business system. Again, this may require an examination of organisational structure and staff development needs, to ensure that they are in line with any proposed process redesign and IT system development.
- To document the business requirements for the IT system support using appropriate documentation standards.

In line with this, the core business analyst role could be defined as an internal consultancy role that has the responsibility for investigating business situations, identifying and evaluating options for improving business systems, defining requirements and ensuring the effective use of information systems in meeting the needs of the business.

Sub-disciplines

Business analysis as a discipline includes requirements analysis, sometimes also called requirements engineering. It focuses on ensuring the changes made to an organisation are aligned with its strategic goals. These changes include changes to strategies, structures, policies, business rules, processes, and information systems.

Examples of business analysis includes:

Enterprise Analysis or Company Analysis

Focuses on understanding the needs of the business as a whole, its strategic direction, and identifying initiatives that will allow a business to meet those strategic goals. It also includes:

- Creating and maintaining the business architecture
- Conducting feasibility studies
- Identifying new business opportunities
- Scoping and defining new business opportunities
- Preparing the business case
- Conducting the initial risk assessment

Requirements Planning and Management

Involves planning the requirements development process, determining which requirements are the highest priority for implementation, and managing change.

Requirements Elicitation

Describes techniques for collecting requirements from stakeholders in a project. Techniques for requirements elicitation include:

- Brainstorming
- Document analysis
- Focus group
- Interface analysis
- Interviews
- Workshops
- Reverse engineering
- Surveys
- User task analysis
- Process mapping
- Observation/job shadowing
- Design thinking

Requirements Analysis and Documentation

Describes how to develop and specify requirements in enough detail to allow them to be successfully implemented by a project team.

Analysis

The major forms of analysis are:

- Architecture analysis
- Business process analysis
- Object-oriented analysis
- Structured analysis
- Data warehouse analysis, storage and databases analysis

Documentation

Requirements documentation can take several forms:

- Textual – for example, stories that summarize specific information
- Matrix – for example, a table of requirements with priorities
- Diagrams – for example, how data flows from one structure to the other
- Wireframe – for example, how elements are required in a website,
- Models – for example, 3-D models that describes a character in a computer game

Requirements Communication

Describes techniques for ensuring that stakeholders have a shared understanding of the requirements and how they will be implemented.

Solution Assessment and Validation

Describes how the business analyst can perform correctness of a proposed solution, how to support the implementation of a solution, and how to assess possible shortcomings in the implementation.

Techniques

There are a number of generic business techniques that a business analyst will use when facilitating business change.

Some of these techniques include:

PESTLE

This is used to perform an external environmental analysis by examining the many different external factors affecting an organization.

The six attributes of PESTLE:

Political (current and potential influences from political pressures)

Economic (the local, national and world economy impact)

Sociological (the ways in which a society can affect an organization)

Technological (the effect of new and emerging technology)

Legal (the effect of national and world legislation)

Environmental (the local, national and world environmental issues)

Heptalysis

This is used to perform an in-depth analysis of early stage businesses/ventures on seven important categories:

Market opportunity

Product/solution

Execution plan

Financial engine

Human capital

Potential return

Margin of safety

STEER

It is an analysis that puts into consideration – the following

Socio-cultural

Technological

Economic

Ecological

Regulatory Factors

MOST

This is used to perform an internal environmental analysis by defining the attributes of MOST to ensure that the project you are working on is aligned to each of the four attributes.

The four attributes of MOST

Mission (where the business intends to go)

Objectives (the key goals which will help achieve the mission)

Strategies (options for moving forward)

Tactics (how strategies are put into action)

SWOT

It is used to help focus activities into areas of strength and where the greatest opportunities lie. This is used to identify the dangers that take the form of weaknesses and both internal and external threats.

The four attributes of SWOT analysis:

Strengths – What are the advantages? What is currently done well? (e.g. key area of best-performing activities of your company)

Weaknesses – What should be improved? What is there to overcome? (e.g. key area where you are performing unsatisfactorily)

Opportunities – What good opportunities face the organization? (e.g. key area where your competitors are performing poorly)

Threats – What obstacles does the organization face? (e.g. key area where your competitor will perform well)

CATWOE

This is used to prompt thinking about what the business is trying to achieve. Business perspectives help the business analyst to consider the impact of any proposed solution on the people involved.

There are six elements of CATWOE:

Customers – Who are the beneficiaries of the highest level business process and how does the issue affect them?

Actors – Who is involved in the situation, who will be involved in implementing solutions and what will impact their success?

Transformation Process – What processes or systems are affected by the issue?

World View – What is the big picture and what are the wider impacts of the issue?

Owner – Who owns the process or situation being investigated and what role will they play in the solution?

Environmental Constraints – What are the constraints and limitations that will impact the solution and its success?

de Bono's Six Thinking Hats

This is often used in a brainstorming session to generate and analyse ideas and options. It is useful to encourage specific types of thinking and can be a convenient and symbolic way to request someone to "switch gears". It involves restricting the group to only thinking in specific ways – giving ideas & analysis in the "mood" of the time. Also known as the Six Thinking Hats.

White: Pure facts, logical.

Green: Creative.

Yellow: Bright, optimistic, positive.

Black: Negative, devil's advocate.

Red: Emotional.

Blue: Cold, control.

Not all colors / moods have to be used

Five Whys

Five Whys is used to get to the root of what is really happening in a single instance. For each answer given a further 'why' is asked.

MoSCoW

This is used to prioritize requirements by allocating an appropriate priority, gauging it against the validity of the requirement itself and its priority against other requirements.

MoSCoW comprises:

Must have – or else delivery will be a failure

Should have – otherwise will have to adopt a workaround

Could have – to increase delivery satisfaction

Won't have this time – useful to the exclude requirements from this delivery timeframe

VPEC-T

This technique is used when analyzing the expectations of multiple parties having different views of a system in which they all have an interest in common, but have different priorities and different responsibilities.

Values – constitute the objectives, beliefs and concerns of all parties participating. They may be financial, social, tangible and intangible

Policies – constraints that govern what may be done and the manner in which it may be done

Events – real-world proceedings that stimulate activity

Content – the meaningful portion of the documents, conversations, messages, etc. that are produced and used by all aspects of business activity

Trust – between users of the system and their right to access and change information within it

SCRS

The SCRS approach in business analysis claims that the analysis should flow from the high-level business strategy to the solution, through the current state and the requirements. SCRS stands for:

Strategy

Current State

Requirements

Solution

Roles of Business Analysts

As the scope of business analysis is very wide, there has been a tendency for business analysts to specialize in one of the three sets of activities which constitute the scope of business analysis, the primary role for business analysts is to identify business needs and provide solutions to business problems these are done as being a part of following set of activities.

Strategist

Organizations need to focus on strategic matters on a more or less continuous basis in the modern business world. Business analysts, serving this need, are well-versed in analyzing the strategic profile of the organization and its environment, advising senior management on suitable policies, and the effects of policy decisions.

Architect

Organizations may need to introduce change to solve business problems which may have been identified by the strategic analysis, referred to above. Business analysts contribute by analyzing objectives, processes and resources, and suggesting ways by which re-design (BPR), or improvements (BPI) could be made. Particular skills of this type of analyst are "soft skills", such as knowledge of the business, requirements engineering, stakeholder analysis, and some "hard skills", such as business process modeling. Although the role requires an awareness of technology and its uses, it is not an IT-focused role.

Three elements are essential to this aspect of the business analysis effort: the redesign of core business processes; the application of enabling technologies to support the new core processes; and the management of organizational change. This aspect of business analysis is also called "business process improvement" (BPI), or "reengineering".

IT-Systems analyst

There is the need to align IT Development with the business-system as a whole. A long-standing problem in business is how to get the best return from IT investments, which are generally very expensive and of critical, often strategic, importance. IT departments, aware of the problem, often create a business analyst role to better understand, and define the requirements for their IT systems. Although there may be some overlap with the developer and testing roles, the focus is always on the IT part of the change process, and generally, this type of business analyst gets involved, only when a case for change has already been made and decided upon.

In any case, the term "analyst" is lately considered somewhat misleading, insofar as analysts (i.e. problem investigators) also do design work (solution definers).

Function Within the Organizational Structure

The role of business analysis can exist in a variety of structures within an organizational framework. Because Business Analysts typically act as a liaison between the business and technology functions of a company, the role can be often successful either aligned to a line of business, within IT or sometimes both.

Business Alignment

When Business Analysts report up through the business side, they are often subject matter experts for a specific line of business. These Business Analysts typically work solely on project work for a particular business, pulling in Business Analysts from other areas for cross-functional projects. In this case, there are usually Business Systems Analysts on the IT side to focus on more technical requirements.

IT alignment

In many cases, Business Analysts live solely within IT and they focus on both business and systems requirements for a project, consulting with various subject matter experts (SMEs) to ensure thorough understanding. Depending on the organizational structure, Business

Analysts may be aligned to a specific development lab or they might be grouped together in a resource pool and allocated to various projects based on availability and expertise. The former builds specific subject matter expertise while the latter provides the ability to acquire cross-functional knowledge.

Business analysis center of excellence

Whether business analysts are grouped together or are dispersed in terms of reporting structure, many companies have created business analysis centers of excellence. A center of excellence provides a framework by which all business analysts in an organization conduct their work, usually consisting of processes, procedures, templates and best practices. In addition to providing guidelines and deliverables, it also provides a forum to focus on continuous improvement for the business analysis function.

Goals

Ultimately, business analysis wants to achieve the following outcomes:

- Create solutions
- Give enough tools for robust project management
- Improve efficiency and reduce waste
- Provide essential documentation, like requirements document, project initiation documents and others.

One way to assess these goals is to measure the return on investment (ROI) for all projects. According to Forrester Research, more than $100 billion is spent annually in the U.S. on custom and internally developed software projects. For all of these software development projects, keeping accurate data is important and business leaders are constantly asking for the return or ROI on a proposed project or at the conclusion of an active project. However, asking for the ROI without sufficient data of where value is created or destroyed may result with inaccurate projections.

Reduce Waste and Complete Projects on Time

Project delays are costly in several ways:

- Project costs – For every month of delay, the project team costs and expenses continue to accumulate. When a large part of the development team has been outsourced, the costs will start to add up quickly and are very visible if contracted on a time and materials basis (T&M). Fixed price contracts with external parties limit this risk. For internal resources, the costs of delays are not as readily apparent, unless time spent by resources is being tracked against the project, as labor costs are essentially 'fixed' costs.
- Opportunity costs – Opportunity costs come in two types – lost revenue and unrealized expense reductions. Some projects are specifically undertaken with the purpose of driving new or additional revenues to the bottom line. For every month of delay, a company foregoes a month of this new revenue stream. The purpose of other projects is to improve

efficiencies and reduce costs. Again, each month of failure postpones the realization of these expense reductions by another month. In the vast majority of cases, these opportunities are never captured or analyzed, resulting in misleading ROI calculations. Of the two opportunity costs, the lost revenue is the most egregious – and the effects are greater and longer lasting.

N.B. On a lot of projects (particularly larger ones) the project manager is the one responsible for ensuring that a project is completed on time. The BA's job is more to ensure that if a project is not completed on time then at least the highest priority requirements are met.

Document the Right Requirements

Business analysts want to make sure that they define the requirements in a way that meets the business needs, for example, in IT applications the requirements need to meet end-users' needs. Essentially, they want to define the right application. This means that they must document the right requirements through listening carefully to 'customer' feedback, and by delivering a complete set of clear requirements to the technical architects and coders who will write the program. If a business analyst has limited tools or skills to help him elicit the right requirements, then the chances are fairly high that he will end up documenting requirements that will not be used or that will need to be re-written – resulting in rework as discussed below. The time wasted to document unnecessary requirements not only impacts the business analyst, it also impacts the rest of the development cycle. Coders need to generate application code to perform these unnecessary requirements and testers need to make sure that the wanted features actually work as documented and coded. Experts estimate that 10% to 40% of the features in new software applications are unnecessary or go unused. Being able to reduce the amount of these extra features by even one-third can result in significant savings. An approach of minimalism or "Keep it Simple" and minimum technology supports a reduced cost number for the end result and on going maintenance of the implemented solution.

Improve Project Efficiency

Efficiency can be achieved in two ways: by reducing rework and by shortening project length.

Rework is a common industry headache and it has become so common at many organizations that it is often built into project budgets and time lines. It generally refers to extra work needed in a project to fix errors due to incomplete or missing requirements and can impact the entire software development process from definition to coding and testing. The need for rework can be reduced by ensuring that the requirements gathering and definition processes are thorough and by ensuring that the business and technical members of a project are involved in these processes from an early stage.

Shortening project length presents two potential benefits. For every month that a project can be shortened, project resource costs can be diverted to other projects. This can lead to savings on the current project and lead to earlier start times of future projects (thus increasing revenue potential).

Business Analysis Professional Qualifications

The two most widely recognised Business Analysis Qualifications are:

- BCS Int. Diploma in Business Analysis
- International Institute of Business Analysis (IIBA) Certified Business Analysis Professional

However, after wide consultations with practitioners, employers and other key stakeholders, the IIBA in 2016 introduced new certification levels as follows:

- Level 1 – Entry-level Certificate in Business Analysis (ECBA)
- Level 2 – Certification of Capability in Business Analysis (CCBA)
- Level 3 – Certified Business Analysis Professional (CBAP)
- Level 4 – Certified Business Analysis Thought Leader (CBATL)

PEST Analysis

PEST analysis (political, economic, social and technological) describes a framework of macro-environmental factors used in the environmental scanning component of strategic management. It is part of an external analysis when conducting a strategic analysis or doing market research, and gives an overview of the different macro-environmental factors to be taken into consideration. It is a strategic tool for understanding market growth or decline, business position, potential and direction for operations.

Variants that build on the PEST framework include:

- PESTEL or PESTLE, which adds legal and environmental factors. Popular in the United Kingdom.
- SLEPT adding legal factors.
- STEEPLE and STEEPLED, adding ethics and demographic factors.
- DESTEP, adding demographic and ecological factors.
- SPELIT, adding legal and intercultural factors. Popular in the United States since the mid-2000s.

There is also STEER, which considers socio-cultural, technological, economic, ecological, and regulatory factors, but does not specifically include political factors.

Composition

The basic PEST analysis includes four factors:

- Political factors are basically how the government intervenes in the economy. Specifically, political factors has areas including tax policy, labour law, environmental law, trade restrictions, tariffs, and political stability. Political factors may also include goods and services which the government aims to provide or be provided (merit goods) and those that the government does not want to be provided (demerit goods or merit bads). Furthermore, governments have a high impact on the health, education, and infrastructure of a nation.

- Economic factors include economic growth, interest rates, exchange rates, the inflation rate. These factors greatly affect how businesses operate and make decisions. For example, interest rates affect a firm's cost of capital and therefore to what extent a business grows and expands. Exchange rates can affect the costs of exporting goods and the supply and price of imported goods in an economy.
- Social factors include the cultural aspects and health consciousness, population growth rate, age distribution, career attitudes and emphasis on safety. High trends in social factors affect the demand for a company's products and how that company operates. For example, the ageing population may imply a smaller and less-willing workforce (thus increasing the cost of labour). Furthermore, companies may change various management strategies to adapt to social trends caused from this (such as recruiting older workers).
- Technological factors include technological aspects like R&D activity, automation, technology incentives and the rate of technological change. These can determine barriers to entry, minimum efficient production level and influence the outsourcing decisions. Furthermore, technological shifts would affect costs, quality, and lead to innovation.

Expanding the analysis to PESTLE or PESTEL adds:

- Legal factors include discrimination law, consumer law, antitrust law, employment law, and health and safety law. These factors can affect how a company operates, its costs, and the demand for its products.
- Environmental factors include ecological and environmental aspects such as weather, climate, and climate change, which may especially affect industries such as tourism, farming, and insurance. Furthermore, growing awareness of the potential impacts of climate change is affecting how companies operate and the products they offer, both creating new markets and diminishing or destroying existing ones.

Other factors for the various offshoots include:

- Demographic factors include gender, age, ethnicity, knowledge of languages, disabilities, mobility, home ownership, employment status, religious belief or practice, culture and tradition, living standards and income level.
- Regulatory factors include acts of parliament and associated regulations, international and national standards, local government by-laws, and mechanisms to monitor and ensure compliance with these.

More factors discussed in the SPELIT Power Matrix include:

- Inter-cultural factors considers collaboration in a global setting.
- Other specialized factors discussed in chapter 10 of the SPELIT Power Matrix include the Ethical, Educational, Physical, Religious, and Security environments. The security environment may include either personal, company, or national security.

- Other business-related factors that might be considered in an environmental analysis include Competition, Demographics, Ecological, Geographical, Historical, Organizational, and Temporal (schedule).

Applicability of the Factors

The model's factors will vary in importance to a given company based on its industry and the goods it produces. For example, consumer and B2B companies tend to be more affected by the social factors, while a global defense contractor would tend to be more affected by political factors. Additionally, factors that are more likely to change in the future or more relevant to a given company will carry greater importance. For example, a company which has borrowed heavily will need to focus more on the economic factors (especially interest rates).

Furthermore, conglomerate companies who produce a wide range of products (such as Sony, Disney, or BP) may find it more useful to analyze one department of its company at a time with the PESTEL model, thus focusing on the specific factors relevant to that one department. A company may also wish to divide factors into geographical relevance, such as local, national, and global.

Use of PEST Analysis with other Models

The PEST factors, combined with external micro-environmental factors and internal drivers, can be classified as opportunities and threats in a SWOT analysis. A graphical method for PEST analysis called 'PESTLEWeb' has been developed at Henley Business School in the UK. Research has shown that PESTLEWeb diagrams are considered by users to be more logical, rational and convincing than traditional PEST analysis.

SWOT Analysis

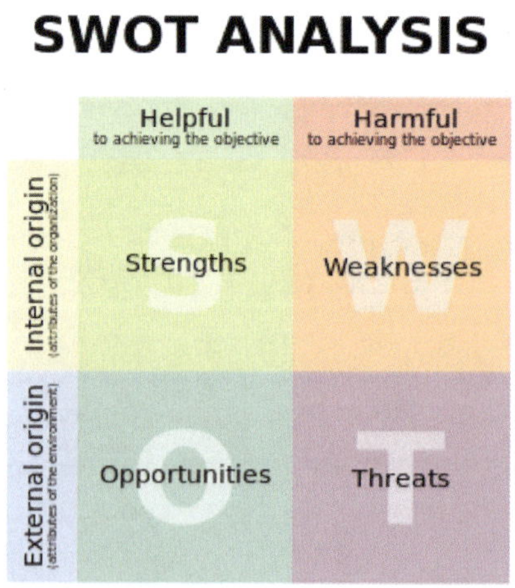

A SWOT analysis, with its four elements in a 2×2 matrix.

SWOT analysis (alternatively SWOT matrix) is an acronym for *strengths*, *weaknesses*, *opportunities*, and *threats* and is a structured planning method that evaluates those four elements of an organization, project or business venture. A SWOT analysis can be carried out for a company, product, place, industry, or person. It involves specifying the objective of the business venture or project and identifying the internal and external factors that are favorable and unfavorable to achieve that objective. Some authors credit SWOT to Albert Humphrey, who led a convention at the Stanford Research Institute (now SRI International) in the 1960s and 1970s using data from Fortune 500 companies. However, Humphrey himself did not claim the creation of SWOT, and the origins remain obscure. The degree to which the internal environment of the firm matches with the external environment is expressed by the concept of strategic fit.

- Strengths: characteristics of the business or project that give it an advantage over others
- Weaknesses: characteristics of the business that place the business or project at a disadvantage relative to others
- Opportunities: elements in the environment that the business or project could exploit to its advantage
- Threats: elements in the environment that could cause trouble for the business or project

Identification of SWOTs is important because they can inform later steps in planning to achieve the objective. First, decision-makers should consider whether the objective is attainable, given the SWOTs. If the objective is *not* attainable, they must select a different objective and repeat the process.

Users of SWOT analysis must ask and answer questions that generate meaningful information for each category (strengths, weaknesses, opportunities, and threats) to make the analysis useful and find their competitive advantage.

Internal and External Factors

So it is said that if you know your enemies and know yourself, you can win a hundred battles without a single loss. If you only know yourself, but not your opponent, you may win or may lose. If you know neither yourself nor your enemy, you will always endanger yourself.

The Art of War by Sun Tzu

SWOT analysis aims to identify the key internal and external factors seen as important to achieving an objective. SWOT analysis groups key pieces of information into two main categories:

1. Internal factors – the *strengths* and *weaknesses* internal to the organization
2. External factors – the *opportunities* and *threats* presented by the environment external to the organization

Analysis may view the internal factors as strengths or as weaknesses depending upon their effect on the organization's objectives. What may represent strengths with respect to one objective may be weaknesses (distractions, competition) for another objective. The factors may include all of the 4Ps as well as personnel, finance, manufacturing capabilities, and so on.

The external factors may include macroeconomic matters, technological change, legislation, and sociocultural changes, as well as changes in the marketplace or in competitive position. The results are often presented in the form of a matrix.

SWOT analysis is just one method of categorization and has its own weaknesses. For example, it may tend to persuade its users to compile lists rather than to think about actual important factors in achieving objectives. It also presents the resulting lists uncritically and without clear prioritization so that, for example, weak opportunities may appear to balance strong threats.

It is prudent not to eliminate any candidate SWOT entry too quickly. The importance of individual SWOTs will be revealed by the value of the strategies they generate. A SWOT item that produces valuable strategies is important. A SWOT item that generates no strategies is not important.

Use

The usefulness of SWOT analysis is not limited to profit-seeking organizations. SWOT analysis may be used in any decision-making situation when a desired end-state (objective) is defined. Examples include non-profit organizations, governmental units, and individuals. SWOT analysis may also be used in pre-crisis planning and preventive crisis management. SWOT analysis may also be used in creating a recommendation during a viability study/survey.

Strategy Building

SWOT analysis can be used effectively to build organizational or personal strategy. Steps necessary to execute strategy-oriented analysis involve identification of internal and external factors (using popular the 2x2 matrix), selection and evaluation of the most important factors, and identification of relations existing between internal and external features.

For instance, strong relations between strengths and opportunities can suggest good conditions in the company and allow using an *aggressive* strategy. On the other hand, strong interactions between weaknesses and threats could be analyzed as a potential warning and advice for using a *defensive* strategy.

Matching and Converting

One way of utilizing SWOT is matching and converting. Matching is used to find competitive advantage by matching the strengths to opportunities. Another tactic is to convert weaknesses or threats into strengths or opportunities. An example of a conversion strategy is to find new markets. If the threats or weaknesses cannot be converted, a company should try to minimize or avoid them.

Corporate Planning

As part of the development of strategies and plans to enable the organization to achieve its objectives, that organization will use a systematic/rigorous process known as corporate planning. SWOT alongside PEST/PESTLE can be used as a basis for the analysis of business and environmental factors.

- Set objectives – defining what the organization is going to do
- Environmental scanning

    - Internal appraisals of the organization's SWOT, this needs to include an assessment of the present situation as well as a portfolio of products/services and an analysis of the product/service life cycle

- Analysis of existing strategies, this should determine relevance from the results of an internal/external appraisal. This may include gap analysis of environmental factors
- Strategic Issues defined – key factors in the development of a corporate plan that the organization must address
- Develop new/revised strategies – revised analysis of strategic issues may mean the objectives need to change
- Establish critical success factors – the achievement of objectives and strategy implementation
- Preparation of operational, resource, projects plans for strategy implementation
- Monitoring results – mapping against plans, taking corrective action, which may mean amending objectives/strategies

Marketing

In many competitor analyses, marketers build detailed profiles of each competitor in the market, focusing especially on their relative competitive strengths and weaknesses using SWOT analysis. Marketing managers will examine each competitor's cost structure, sources of profits, resources and competencies, competitive positioning and product differentiation, degree of vertical integration, historical responses to industry developments, and other factors.

Marketing management often finds it necessary to invest in research to collect the data required to perform accurate marketing analysis. Accordingly, management often conducts market research (alternately marketing research) to obtain this information. Marketers employ a variety of techniques to conduct market research, but some of the more common include:

- Qualitative marketing research such as focus groups
- Quantitative marketing research such as statistical surveys
- Experimental techniques such as test markets
- Observational techniques such as ethnographic (on-site) observation
- Marketing managers may also design and oversee various environmental scanning and competitive intelligence processes to help identify trends and inform the company's marketing analysis.

Below is an example SWOT analysis of a market position of a small management consultancy with specialism in HRM.

Strengths	Weaknesses	Opportunities	Threats
Reputation in marketplace	Shortage of consultants at operating level rather than partner level	Well established position with a well-defined market niche	Large consultancies operating at a minor level
Expertise at partner level in HRM consultancy	Unable to deal with multidisciplinary assignments because of size or lack of ability	Identified market for consultancy in areas other than HRM	Other small consultancies looking to invade the marketplace

In Community Organization

The SWOT analysis has been utilized in community work as a tool to identify positive and negative factors within organizations, communities, and the broader society that promote or inhibit successful implementation of social services and social change efforts. It is used as a preliminary resource, assessing strengths, weaknesses, opportunities, and threats in a community served by a nonprofit or community organization. This organizing tool is best used in collaboration with community workers and/or community members before developing goals and objectives for a program design or implementing an organizing strategy. The SWOT analysis is a part of the planning for social change process and will not provide a strategic plan if used by itself. After a SWOT analysis is completed, a social change organization can turn the SWOT list into a series of recommendations to consider before developing a strategic plan.

SWOT ANALYSIS

	Strengths 1. 2. 3. 4.	Weaknesses 1. 2. 3. 4.
Opportunities 1. 2. 3. 4.	Opportunity-Strength strategies *Use strengths to take advantage of opportunities* 1. 2.	Opportunity-Weakness strategies *Overcome weaknesses by taking advantage of opportunities* 1. 2.
Threats 1. 2. 3. 4.	Threat-Strength strategies *Use strengths to avoid threats* 1. 2.	Threat-Weakness Strategies *Minimize weaknesses and avoid threats* 1. 2.

one example of a SWOT Analysis used in community organizing

SWOT ANALYSIS

Internal		External	
Strengths	Weaknesses	Opportunities	Threats

A simple SWOT Analysis used in Community Organizing

Strengths and Weaknesses: *These are the internal factors within an organization.*

- Human resources - staff, volunteers, board members, target population
- Physical resources - your location, building, equipment

- Financial - grants, funding agencies, other sources of income
- Activities and processes - programs you run, systems you employ
- Past experiences - building blocks for learning and success, your reputation in the community

Opportunities and Threats: *These are external factors stemming from community or societal forces.*

- Future trends in your field or the culture
- The economy - local, national, or international
- Funding sources - foundations, donors, legislatures
- Demographics - changes in the age, race, gender, culture of those you serve or in your area
- The physical environment (Is your building in a growing part of town? Is the bus company cutting routes?)
- Legislation (Do new federal requirements make your job harder...or easier?)
- Local, national, or international events

Although the SWOT analysis was originally designed as an organizational method for business and industries, it has been replicated in various community work as a tool for identifying external and internal support to combat internal and external opposition. The SWOT analysis is necessary to provide direction to the next stages of the change process. It has been utilized by community organizers and community members to further social justice in the context of Social Work practice.

Application in Community Organization

Elements to Consider

Elements to consider in a SWOT analysis include understanding the community that a particular organization is working with. This can be done via public forums, listening campaigns, and informational interviews. Data collection will help inform the community members and workers when developing the SWOT analysis. A needs and assets assessment are tooling that can be used to identify the needs and existing resources of the community. When these assessments are done and data has been collected, an analysis of the community can be made that informs the SWOT analysis.

Steps for Implementation

A SWOT analysis is best developed in a group setting such as a work or community meeting. A facilitator can conduct the meeting by first explaining what a SWOT analysis is as well as identifying the meaning of each term.

One way of facilitating the development of a SWOT analysis includes developing an example SWOT with the larger group then separating each group into smaller teams to present to the larger group after set amount of time. This allows for individuals, who may be silenced in a larger group setting, to contribute. Once the allotted time is up, the facilitator may record all the factors of each group onto a large document such as a poster board, and then the large group, as a collective, can go work through each of the threats and weaknesses to explore options that may be used to combat negative forces with the strengths and opportunities present within the organization and community. A SWOT meeting allows participants to creatively brainstorm, identify obstacles, and possibly strategize solutions/way forward to these limitations.

When to use SWOT Analysis

The uses of a SWOT analysis by a community organization are as follows: to organize information, provide insight into barriers that may be present while engaging in social change processes, and identify strengths available that can be activated to counteract these barriers.

A SWOT analysis can be used to:

- Explore new solutions to problems
- Identify barriers that will limit goals/objectives
- Decide on direction that will be most effective
- Reveal possibilities and limitations for change
- To revise plans to best navigate systems, communities, and organizations
- As a brainstorming and recording device as a means of communication
- To enhance "credibility of interpretation" to be utilized in presentation to leaders or key supporters.

Benefits

The SWOT analysis in social work practice framework is beneficial because it helps organizations decide whether or not an objective is obtainable and therefore enables organizations to set achievable goals, objectives, and steps to further the social change or community development effort. It enables organizers to take visions and produce practical and efficient outcomes that effect long-lasting change, and it helps organizations gather meaningful information to maximize their potential. Completing a SWOT analysis is a useful process regarding the consideration of key organizational priorities, such as gender and cultural diversity and fundraising objectives.

Limitations

Some findings from Menon et al. (1999) and Hill and Westbrook (1997) have suggested that SWOT may harm performance and that "no-one subsequently used the outputs within the later stages of the strategy".

Other critiques include the misuse of the SWOT analysis as a technique that can be quickly designed without critical thought leading to a misrepresentation of strengths, weaknesses, opportunities, and threats within an organization's internal and external surroundings.

Another limitation includes the development of a SWOT analysis simply to defend previously decided goals and objectives. This misuse leads to limitations on brainstorming possibilities and "real" identification of barriers. This misuse also places the organization's interest above the well-being of the community. Further, a SWOT analysis should be developed as a collaborative with a variety of contributions made by participants including community members. The design of a SWOT analysis by one or two community workers is limiting to the realities of the forces, specifically external factors, and devalues the possible contributions of community members.

Choosing Company based on Operating/ Financial Characteristics

Lessons from Select Authors: Experts or authors have from time to time provided insights into selecting companies or stocks for investment. We quote the suggestions / advice from two such experts, Peter Lynch and Warren Buffet. The suggestions provided by such experts are not specific to a time frame, thus applicable always.

Peter Lynch, earlier associated with Fidelity Investments has suggested the following attributes to look for while analyzing firms.

- Firm's product should not be faddish. Consumers should continue to purchase over time.
- Firm should have some long-run comparative advantage over its rivals.
- Firm's industry or product has market stability. There should be less potential for entry by other players.
- Firm can benefit from cost reductions.
- Firms that buy back shares show there are putting money into the firm.
- Lynch has suggests categorizing the companies by six story types:

Slow Growers: Large and aging companies that are expected to grow only slightly faster than th-eeconomy as a whole, but often paying large regular dividends. These are not among his favorites.

Stalwarts: Large companies that are still able to grow, with annual earnings growth rates of around 10% to 12%; If purchased at a good price, Lynch says he expects good but not enormous re-turns--certainly no more than 50% in two years and possibly less. These firms also offer downside protection during recessions.

Fast-Growers: Small, aggressive new firms with annual earnings growth of 20% to 25% a year. These do not have to be in fast-growing industries, and in fact Lynch prefers those that are not. Fast-growers are among Lynch's favorites, and he says that an investor's biggest gains will come from this type of stock. However, they also carry considerable risk.

Cyclicals: Companies in which sales and profits tend to rise and fall in somewhat predictable patterns based on the economic cycle; examples include companies in the auto industry, airlines and steel. Lynch warns that these firms can be mistaken for stalwarts by inexperienced investors, but share prices of cy-clicals can drop dramatically during hard times. Thus, timing is crucial when investing in these firms, and Lynch says that investors must learn to detect the early signs that business is starting to turn down.

Turnarounds: Companies that have been battered down or depressed--Lynch calls these "no-growers"; his examples include Chrysler, Penn Central and General Public Utilities (owner of Three Mile Island). The stocks of successful turnarounds can move back up quickly, and Lynch points out that of all the categories, these upturns are least related to the general market.

Asset opportunities: Companies that have assets that Wall Street analysts and others have overlooked. Lynch points to several general areas where asset plays can often be found--metals and oil, newspapers and TV stations, and patented drugs. However, finding these hidden assets requires a real working knowledge of the company that owns the assets, and Lynch points out that within this category, the "local" edge--your own knowledge and experience--can be used to greatest advantage.

Warren Buffet has suggested four tents, viz. Business Tenets; Management Tenets; Financial Tenets; Market Tenets;

Business Tenets:

- Is the business simple and understandable?
- Does the business have a consistent operating history?
- Does the business have favorable long-term prospects?

Management Tenets:

- Is management rational?
- Is management candid with its shareholders?

Financial Tenets:

- Focus on return on equity, not earnings per share
- Calculate "owner earnings"
- Look for companies with high profit margins
- For every dollar retained, make sure the company has created at least one dollar of market value

Market Tenets:

- What is the intrinsic value of the business?
- Can the business be purchased at a significant discount to its fundamental intrinsic value?

Financial Analysis of Companies

Estimating Intrinsic Value: After selecting a group of companies, one has to value the company or stock. The valuation methods are listed here for easy reference.

A. Present value of cash flows (PVCF)

1. Present value of dividends (DDM)
2. Present value of free cash flow to equity (FCFE)
3. Present value of free cash flow to firm (FCFF)

B. Relative valuation techniques

1. Price earnings ratio (P/E)
2. Price cash flow ratios (P/CF)
3. Price book value ratios (P/BV)
4. Price sales ratio (P/S)

Table below provides the P/E and P/B ratios of stocks that are part of BSE Sensex. Such ratios are on a particular date and thus vary from time to time. These relative valuation measures should be compared for firms in a particular industry. Comparing the ratios across industries might be misleading.

Table Price-Earning and Price-Book Value Ratio Sensex Companies as on 21 June 2010

#	Company Name	P/E	P/B	#	Company Name	P/E	P/B
1	A C C Ltd.	10.31	2.58	17	Mahindra & Mahindra Ltd.	18.45	4.54
2	Bharat Heavy Electricals Ltd.	28.18	7.47	18	Maruti Suzuki India Ltd.	15.91	3.41
3	Bharti Airtel Ltd.	10.66	2.74	19	N T P C Ltd.	18.99	2.26
4	Cipla Ltd.	27.66	4.47	20	Oil & Natural Gas Corpn. Ltd.	15.38	2.91
5	D L F Ltd.	63.82	3.75	21	Reliance Communications Ltd.	77.47	0.74
6	H D F C Bank Ltd.	31.17	4.27	22	Reliance Industries Ltd.	21.46	2.71
7	Hero Honda Motors Ltd.	18.11	10.53	23	Reliance Infrastructure Ltd.	25.25	2.19
8	Hindalco Industries Ltd.	16.29	1.03	24	State Bank Of India	16.53	2.3
9	Hindustan Unilever Ltd.	27.02	15.65	25	Sterlite Industries (India) Ltd.	55.88	2.78
10	HDFC Limited	30.68	5.6	26	Tata Consultancy Services Ltd.	28.78	10.26
11	I C I C I Bank Ltd.	24.97	1.95	27	Tata Motors Ltd.	13.24	2.44
12	I T C Ltd.	28.1	8.19	28	Tata Power Co. Ltd.	45.46	2.76
13	Infosys Technologies Ltd.	27.75	7.3	29	Tata Steel Ltd.	8.87	1.19
14	Jaiprakash Associates Ltd.	14.77	3.65	30	Wipro Ltd.	20.73	6.37
15	Jindal Steel & Power Ltd.	43.19	9.43		**Average**	**27.34**	**4.72**
16	Larsen & Toubro Ltd.	35	6.18		**Median**	**25.11**	**3.53**

Historical Financial Analysis: analysis of financial reports is one of the intricate part of security analysis. Financial statements are supposed to depict a true and fair view of the company. The major financial statements are income statement, balance sheet and cash flow statement. Different techniques for analyzing financial statements are discussed in Session 9 & 10. One has to analyse the company performance for profitability, efficiency, liquidity, solveny and capital. market standing. As part of financial statement analysis, normalization and adjustments need to be done so that the statements are comparable across the companies in a particular group. Since financial statements are the outputs of financial accounting/ reporting system, subjectivity creeps into such reports because of accounting policies being followed by a particular company. Hence one should look at the notes to accounts which are part of financial statements. As rightly told, profit is an opinion. Financial statement analysis may not reveal the possible frauds or misrepresentation in financial reporting strategy by the companies. Hence one should make a special attempt in finding out such things.

Fraud and Red Flags in Financial Reporting

Carefully done, financial statement analysis can reveal unusual patterns that are difficult to rationalize- questions all 'red flags'. Numbers on their own may not make any sense. Questioning the number can help.

Some indications of red flags:

- Assets utilization ratios that provide early warning signal.
- Unexplained changes are reasons for suspicious activities
- Unreasonable growth goals that can not be financed easily

Red flags in Financial Reporting

- Unexplained changes in policies & estimates especially in doom days
- Unexplained transactions to boost profit
- Very consistent margin, growth rate and stable or consistent increasing cash and bank balance
- Unusual increase in debtors and inventories in relation to sales
- Unusual increase in intangible assets
- Reduction in managed cost- like advertisement to boost cost
- One time profit from non-operating assets
- Unexplained focus or shift towards non-core business
- Significant changes in segment revenue & margin
- Improper method adopt in asset valuation
- Increasing gap between accounting income and taxable income
- Increasing gap between reputed income and cash from operation
- Unexplained write-off

- R&D partnership
- Presence of special purpose vehicles/ enterprises (SPVs/ SPEs)
- Weak governance structure
- Complex ownership and financial structure

The list has no end. One has to be careful enough while interpreting the results of a company and suggesting an investment decision based on the same.

Measures of Value-Added

Economic Value Added

In corporate finance, economic value added (EVA) is an estimate of a firm's economic profit, or the value created in excess of the required return of the company's shareholders. EVA is the net profit less the equity cost of the firm's capital. The idea is that value is created when the return on the firm's economic capital employed exceeds the cost of that capital. This amount can be determined by making adjustments to GAAP accounting. There are potentially over 160 adjustments but in practice only several key ones are made, depending on the company and its industry. EVA is a service mark of Stern Value Management.

Calculation

EVA is net operating profit after taxes (or NOPAT) less a capital charge, the latter being the product of the cost of capital and the economic capital. The basic formula is:

$$\begin{aligned} \text{EVA} &= (\text{ROIC} - \text{WACC}) \cdot (\text{total assets} - \text{current liability}) \\ &= \text{NOPAT} - \text{WACC} \cdot (\text{total assets} - \text{current liability}) \end{aligned}$$

where:

- $\text{ROIC} = \dfrac{\text{NOPAT}}{\text{total assets} - \text{current liability}}$, is the return on invested capital;
- (WACC) is the weighted average cost of capital (WACC);
- $(\text{total assets} - \text{current liability})$ is the economic capital employed (total assets – current liability);
- NOPAT is the net operating profit after tax, with adjustments and translations, generally for the amortization of goodwill, the capitalization of brand advertising and other non-cash items.

EVA calculation:

EVA = net operating profit after taxes – a capital charge [the residual income method] therefore EVA = NOPAT – (c × capital), or alternatively

EVA = (r × capital) – (c × capital) so that

EVA = (r – c) × capital *[the spread method, or excess return method]*

where

r = rate of return, and

c = cost of capital, or the weighted average cost of capital (WACC).

NOPAT is profits derived from a company's operations after cash taxes but before financing costs and non-cash bookkeeping entries. It is the total pool of profits available to provide a cash return to those who provide capital to the firm.

Capital is the amount of cash invested in the business, net of depreciation. It can be calculated as the sum of interest-bearing debt and equity or as the sum of net assets less non-interest-bearing current liabilities (NIBCLs).

The capital charge is the cash flow required to compensate investors for the riskiness of the business given the amount of economic capital invested.

The cost of capital is the minimum rate of return on capital required to compensate investors (debt and equity) for bearing risk, their opportunity cost.

Another perspective on EVA can be gained by looking at a firm's return on net assets (RONA). RONA is a ratio that is calculated by dividing a firm's NOPAT by the amount of capital it employs (RONA = NOPAT/Capital) after making the necessary adjustments of the data reported by a conventional financial accounting system.

EVA = (RONA – required minimum return) × net investments

If RONA is above the threshold rate, EVA is positive.

Comparison with other Approaches

Other approaches along similar lines include residual income valuation (RI) and residual cash flow. Although EVA is similar to residual income, under some definitions there may be minor technical differences between EVA and RI (for example, adjustments that might be made to NOPAT before it is suitable for the formula below). Residual cash flow is another, much older term for economic profit. In all three cases, *money cost of capital* refers to the amount of money rather than the proportional cost (% cost of capital); at the same time, the adjustments to NOPAT are unique to EVA.

Although in concept, these approaches are in a sense nothing more than the traditional, commonsense idea of "profit", the utility of having a more precise term such as EVA is that it makes a clear separation from dubious accounting adjustments that have enabled businesses such as Enron to report profits while actually approaching insolvency.

Other measures of shareholder value include:

- Added value
- Market value added
- Total shareholder return

Market Value Added

The firm's market value added, or MVA, is the discounted sum (present value) of all future expected economic value added:

$$MVA = V - K_0 = \sum_{t=1}^{\infty} \frac{EVA_t}{(1+c)^t}$$

Note that MVA = PV of EVA.

More enlightening is that since MVA = NPV of free cash flow (FCF) it follows therefore that the

NPV of FCF = PV of EVA;

since after all, EVA is simply the re-arrangement of the FCF formula.

Process-based Costing

In 2012, Mocciaro Li Destri, Picone & Minà proposed a performance and cost measurement system that integrates the EVA criteria with process-based costing (PBC). The EVA-PBC methodology allows us to implement the EVA management logic not only at the firm level, but also at lower levels of the organization. EVA-PBC methodology plays an interesting role in bringing strategy back into financial performance measures.

Market Value Added

Market value added (MVA) is the difference between the current market value of a firm and the capital contributed by investors. If MVA is positive, the firm has added value. If it is negative, the firm has destroyed value. The amount of value added needs to be greater than the firm's investors could have achieved investing in the market portfolio, adjusted for the leverage (beta coefficient) of the firm relative to the market.

Basic Formula

The formula for MVA is:

$$MVA = V - K$$

where:

- *MVA* is market value added

- V is the market value of the firm, including the value of the firm's equity and debt
- K is the capital invested in the firm

MVA is the present value of a series of EVA values. MVA is economically equivalent to the traditional NPV measure of worth for evaluating an after-tax cash flow profile of a project if the cost of capital is used for discounting.

Net Present Value

In finance, the net present value (NPV) or net present worth (NPW) is a measurement of the profitability of an undertaking that is calculated by subtracting the present values (PV) of cash outflows (including initial cost) from the present values of cash inflows over a period of time. Incoming and outgoing cash flows can also be described as benefit and cost cash flows, respectively.

Time value of money dictates that time affects the value of cash flows. In other words, a lender may give you 99 cents for the promise of receiving $1.00 a month from now, but the promise to receive that same dollar 20 years in the future would be worth much less today to that same person (lender), even if the payback in both cases was equally certain. This decrease in the current value of future cash flows is based on the market dictated rate of return. More technically, cash flows of *nominal* equal value over a time series result in different *effective* value cash flows that make future cash flows less valuable over time. If for example there exists a time series of identical cash flows, the cash flow in the present is the most valuable, with each future cash flow becoming less valuable than the previous cash flow. A cash flow today is more valuable than an identical cash flow in the future because a present flow can be invested immediately and begin earning returns, while a future flow cannot.

Net present value (NPV) is determined by calculating the costs (negative cash flows) and benefits (positive cash flows) for each period of an investment. The period is typically one year, but could be measured in quarter-years, half-years or months. After the cash flow for each period is calculated, the present value (PV) of each one is achieved by discounting its future value at a periodic rate of return (the rate of return dictated by the market). NPV is the sum of all the discounted future cash flows. Because of its simplicity, NPV is a useful tool to determine whether a project or investment will result in a net profit or a loss. A positive NPV results in profit, while a negative NPV results in a loss. The NPV measures the excess or shortfall of cash flows, in present value terms, above the cost of funds. In a theoretical situation of unlimited capital budgeting a company should pursue every investment with a positive NPV. However, in practical terms a company's capital constraints limit investments to projects with the highest NPV whose cost cash flows, or initial cash investment, do not exceed the company's capital. NPV is a central tool in discounted cash flow (DCF) analysis and is a standard method for using the time value of money to appraise long-term projects. It is widely used throughout economics, finance, and accounting.

In the case when all future cash flows are positive, or incoming (such as the principal and coupon payment of a bond) the only outflow of cash is the purchase price, the NPV is simply the PV of future cash flows minus the purchase price (which is its own PV). NPV can be described as the "difference amount" between the sums of discounted cash inflows and cash outflows. It compares the present value of money today to the present value of money in the future, taking inflation and returns into account.

The NPV of a sequence of cash flows takes as input the cash flows and a discount rate or discount curve and outputs a price. The converse process in DCF analysis—taking a sequence of cash flows and a price as input and inferring as output a discount rate (the discount rate which would yield the given price as NPV)—is called the yield and is more widely used in bond trading.

Formula

Each cash inflow/outflow is discounted back to its present value (PV). Then all are summed. Therefore, NPV is the sum of all terms,

$$\frac{R_t}{(1+i)^t}$$

where

t – the time of the cash flow

i – the discount rate, i.e. the return that could be earned per unit of time on an investment with similar risk

R_t – the net cash flow i.e. cash inflow – cash outflow, at time *t*. For educational purposes, R_0 is commonly placed to the left of the sum to emphasize its role as (minus) the investment.

The result of this formula is multiplied with the Annual Net cash in-flows and reduced by Initial Cash outlay the present value but in cases where the cash flows are not equal in amount, then the previous formula will be used to determine the present value of each cash flow separately. Any cash flow within 12 months will not be discounted for NPV purpose, nevertheless the usual initial investments during the first year R_0 are summed up a negative cash flow.

Given the (period, cash flow) pairs (t, R_t) where N is the total number of periods, the net present value NPV is given by:

$$NPV(i, N) = \sum_{t=0}^{N} \frac{R_t}{(1+i)^t}$$

Many computer-based spreadsheet programs have built-in formula for PV and NPV.

The Discount Rate

The rate used to discount future cash flows to the present value is a key variable of this process.

A firm's weighted average cost of capital (after tax) is often used, but many people believe that it is appropriate to use higher discount rates to adjust for risk, opportunity cost, or other factors. A variable discount rate with higher rates applied to cash flows occurring further along the time span might be used to reflect the yield curve premium for long-term debt.

Another approach to choosing the discount rate factor is to decide the rate which the capital needed for the project could return if invested in an alternative venture. If, for example, the capital required for Project A can earn 5% elsewhere, use this discount rate in the NPV calculation to allow a direct comparison to be made between Project A and the alternative. Related to this concept is to use the firm's reinvestment rate. Re-investment rate can be defined as the rate of return for the firm's investments on average. When analyzing projects in a capital constrained environment, it may be appropriate to use the reinvestment rate rather than the firm's weighted average cost of capital as the discount factor. It reflects opportunity cost of investment, rather than the possibly lower cost of capital.

An NPV calculated using variable discount rates (if they are known for the duration of the investment) may better reflect the situation than one calculated from a constant discount rate for the entire investment duration.

For some professional investors, their investment funds are committed to target a specified rate of return. In such cases, that rate of return should be selected as the discount rate for the NPV calculation. In this way, a direct comparison can be made between the profitability of the project and the desired rate of return.

To some extent, the selection of the discount rate is dependent on the use to which it will be put. If the intent is simply to determine whether a project will add value to the company, using the firm's weighted average cost of capital may be appropriate. If trying to decide between alternative investments in order to maximize the value of the firm, the corporate reinvestment rate would probably be a better choice.

Using variable rates over time, or discounting "guaranteed" cash flows differently from "at risk" cash flows, may be a superior methodology but is seldom used in practice. Using the discount rate to adjust for risk is often difficult to do in practice (especially internationally) and is difficult to do well. An alternative to using discount factor to adjust for risk is to explicitly correct the cash flows for the risk elements using rNPV or a similar method, then discount at the firm's rate.

Use in Decision Making

NPV is an indicator of how much value an investment or project adds to the firm. With a particular project, if R_t is a positive value, the project is in the status of positive cash inflow in the time of t. If R_t is a negative value, the project is in the status of discounted cash outflow in the time of t. Appropriately risked projects with a positive NPV could be accepted. This does not necessarily mean that they should be undertaken since NPV at the cost of capital may not account for opportunity cost, i.e., comparison with other available investments. In financial theory, if there is a choice between two mutually exclusive alternatives, the one yielding the higher NPV should be selected. A positive net present value indicates that the projected earnings generated by a project or investment (in present dollars) exceeds the anticipated costs (also in present dollars). Generally, an investment with a positive NPV will be a profitable one and one with a negative NPV will result in a net loss. This concept is the basis for the Net Present Value Rule, which dictates that the only investments that should be made are those with positive NPV values.

If...	It means...	Then...
NPV > 0	the investment would add value to the firm	the project may be accepted
NPV < 0	the investment would subtract value from the firm	the project may be rejected
NPV = 0	the investment would neither gain nor lose value for the firm	We should be indifferent in the decision whether to accept or reject the project. This project adds no monetary value. Decision should be based on other criteria, e.g., strategic positioning or other factors not explicitly included in the calculation.

Interpretation as Integral Transform

The time-discrete formula of the net present value

$$NPV(i,N) = \sum_{t=0}^{N} \frac{R_t}{1+i^t}$$

can also be written in a continuous variation

$$NPV(i) = \int_{t=0}^{\infty} (1+i)^{-t} \cdot r(t)dt$$

where

> $r(t)$ is the rate of flowing cash given in money per time, and $r(t) = 0$ when the investment is over.

Net present value can be regarded as Laplace- respectively Z-transformed cash flow with the integral operator including the complex number s which resembles to the interest rate i from the real number space or more precisely $s = \ln(1 + i)$.

$$F(s) = \{\mathcal{L}f\}(s) = \int_0^{\infty} e^{-st} f(t)dt$$

From this follow simplifications known from cybernetics, control theory and system dynamics. Imaginary parts of the complex number s describe the oscillating behaviour (compare with the pork cycle, cobweb theorem, and phase shift between commodity price and supply offer) whereas real parts are responsible for representing the effect of compound interest (compare with damping).

Example

A corporation must decide whether to introduce a new product line. The company will have immediate costs of 100,000 at $t = 0$. Recall, a cost is a negative for outgoing cash flow, thus this cash flow is represented as -100,000. The company assumes the product will provide equal benefits of 10,000 for each of 12 years beginning at $t = 1$. For simplicity, assume the company will have no outgoing cash flows after the initial 100,000 cost. This also makes the simplifying assumption that the net cash received or paid is lumped into a single transaction occurring *on the last day* of each year. At the end of the 12 years the product no longer provides any cash flow and is discontinued without any additional costs. Assume that the effective annual discount rate is 10%.

The present value (value at $t = 0$) can be calculated for each year:

Year	Cash flow	Present value
$T = 0$	-	−100,000
$T = 1$	-	9,090.91
$T = 2$	-	8,264.46
$T = 3$	-	7,513.15
$T = 4$	-	6,830.13
$T = 5$	-	6,209.21
$T = 6$	-	5,644.74
$T = 7$	-	5,131.58
$T = 8$	-	4,665.07
$T = 9$	-	4,240.98
$T = 10$	-	3,855.43
$T = 11$	-	3,504.94
$T = 12$	-	3,186.31

The total present value of the incoming cash flows is 68,136.91. The total present value of the outgoing cash flows is simply the 100,000 at time $t = 0$. Thus:

$$\text{NPV} = \text{PV(Benefits)} - \text{PV(Costs)}$$

In this example:

$$\text{NPV} = 68{,}136.91 - 100{,}000$$

$$\text{NPV} = -31{,}863.09$$

Observe that as t increases the present value of each cash flow at t decreases. For example, the final incoming cash flow has a future value of 10,000 at $t = 12$ but has a present value (at $t = 0$) of 3,186.31. The opposite of discounting is compounding. Taking the example in reverse, it is the equivalent of investing 3,186.31 at $t = 0$ (the present value) at an interest rate of 10% compounded for 12 years, which results in a cash flow of 10,000 at $t = 12$ (the future value).

The importance of NPV becomes clear in this instance. Although the incoming cash flows (10,000 x 12 = 120,000) appear to exceed the outgoing cash flow (100,000), the future cash flows are not adjusted using the discount rate. Thus, the project appears misleadingly profitable. When the cash flows are discounted however, it indicates the project would result in a net loss of 31,863.09. Thus, the NPV calculation indicates that this project should be disregarded because investing in this project is the equivalent of a loss of 31,863.09 at $t = 0$. The concept of time value of money indicates that cash flows in different periods of time cannot be accurately compared unless they have been adjusted to reflect their value at the same period of time (in this instance, $t = 0$). It is the present value of each future cash flow that must be determined in order to provide any meaningful comparison between cash flows at different periods of time. There are a few inherent assumptions in this type of analysis:

1. The *investment horizon* of all possible investment projects considered are equally acceptable to the investor (e.g. a 3-year project is not necessarily preferable vs. a 20-year project.)
2. The 10% discount rate is the appropriate (and stable) rate to discount the expected cash flows from each project being considered. Each project is assumed equally speculative.
3. The shareholders cannot get above a 10% return on their money if they were to directly assume an equivalent level of risk. (If the investor could do better elsewhere, no projects should be undertaken by the firm, and the excess capital should be turned over to the shareholder through dividends and stock repurchases.)

More realistic problems would also need to consider other factors, generally including: smaller time buckets, the calculation of taxes (including the cash flow timing), inflation, currency exchange fluctuations, hedged or unhedged commodity costs, risks of technical obsolescence, potential future competitive factors, uneven or unpredictable cash flows, and a more realistic salvage value assumption, as well as many others.

A more simple example of the net present value of incoming cash flow over a set period of time, would be winning a Powerball lottery of $500 million. If one does not select the “CASH” option they will be paid $25,000,000 dollars per year for 20 years, a total of $500,000,000, however, if one does select the “CASH” option, they will receive a one-time lump sum payment of approximately $285 million, the NPV of $500,000,000 paid over time.

Common Pitfalls

- If, for example, the R_t are generally negative late in the project (*e.g.*, an industrial or mining project might have clean-up and restoration costs), then at that stage the company owes money, so a high discount rate is not cautious but too optimistic. Some people see this as a problem with NPV. A way to avoid this problem is to include explicit provision for financing any losses after the initial investment, that is, explicitly calculate the cost of financing such losses.
- Another common pitfall is to adjust for risk by adding a premium to the discount rate. Whilst a bank might charge a higher rate of interest for a risky project, that does not mean that this is a valid approach to adjusting a net present value for risk, although it can be a reasonable approximation in some specific cases. One reason such an approach may not work well can be seen from the following: if some risk is incurred resulting in some losses, then a discount rate in the NPV will reduce the effect of such losses below their true financial cost. A rigorous approach to risk requires identifying and valuing risks explicitly, *e.g.*, by actuarial or Monte Carlo techniques, and explicitly calculating the cost of financing any losses incurred.

- Yet another issue can result from the compounding of the risk premium. R is a composite of the risk free rate and the risk premium. As a result, future cash flows are discounted by both the risk-free rate as well as the risk premium and this effect is compounded by each subsequent cash flow. This compounding results in a much lower NPV than might be otherwise calculated. The certainty equivalent model can be used to account for the risk premium without compounding its effect on present value.
- Another issue with relying on NPV is that it does not provide an overall picture of the gain or loss of executing a certain project. To see a percentage gain relative to the investments for the project, usually, Internal rate of return or other efficiency measures are used as a complement to NPV.
- Non-specialist users frequently make the error of computing NPV based on cash flows after interest. This is wrong because it double counts the time value of money. Free cash flow should be used as the basis for NPV computations.

History

Net present value as a valuation methodology dates at least to the 19th century. Karl Marx refers to NPV as fictitious capital, and the calculation as "capitalising," writing:

The forming of a fictitious capital is called capitalising. Every periodically repeated income is capitalised by calculating it on the average rate of interest, as an income which would be realised by a capital at this rate of interest.

In mainstream neo-classical economics, NPV was formalized and popularized by Irving Fisher, in his 1907 *The Rate of Interest* and became included in textbooks from the 1950s onwards, starting in finance texts.

Alternative Capital Budgeting Methods

- Adjusted present value (APV): adjusted present value, is the net present value of a project if financed solely by ownership equity plus the present value of all the benefits of financing.
- Accounting rate of return (ARR): a ratio similar to IRR and MIRR
- Cost-benefit analysis: which includes issues other than cash, such as time savings.
- Internal rate of return (IRR): which calculates the rate of return of a project while disregarding the absolute amount of money to be gained.
- Modified internal rate of return (MIRR): similar to IRR, but it makes explicit assumptions about the reinvestment of the cash flows. Sometimes it is called Growth Rate of Return.
- Payback period: which measures the time required for the cash inflows to equal the original outlay. It measures risk, not return.
- Real option: which attempts to value managerial flexibility that is assumed away in NPV.
- Equivalent annual cost (EAC): a capital budgeting technique that is useful in comparing two or more projects with different lifespans.

References

- Brown, Christian; Abraham, Fred (October 2012). "Sum of Perpetuities Method for Valuing Stock Prices". Journal of Economics. 38 (1): 59–72. Retrieved 20 October 2012
- Lawrence P. Carr; Alfred J. Nanni Jr. (28 July 2009). Delivering Results: Managing What Matters. Springer Science & Business Media. p. 44. ISBN 978-1-4419-0621-2
- Quincy, Ronald. "SWOT Analysis: Raising capacity of your organization". Rutgers School of Social Work. Retrieved 2013-02-25
- Hill, T. & R. Westbrook (1997). "SWOT Analysis: It's Time for a Product Recall". Long Range Planning. 30 (1): 46–52. doi:10.1016/S0024-6301(96)00095-7
- Walter, James (March 1956). "Dividend Policies and Common Stock Prices". Journal of Finance. 11 (1): 29–41. JSTOR 2976527. doi:10.1111/j.1540-6261.1956.tb00684.x
- Armstrong. M. A handbook of Human Resource Management Practice (10th edition) 2006, Kogan Page , London ISBN 0-7494-4631-5
- Kurt, Daniel (2003-11-24). "Net Present Value (NPV) Definition | Investopedia". Investopedia. Retrieved 2016-05-05
- . Westhues, Anne; Jean Lafrance; Glen Schmidt (2001). "A SWOT analysis of social work education in Canada". Social Work Education: The International Journal. 20 (1): 35–56
- White, Gerald I.; Sondhi, Ashwinpaul; Fried, Dov (1998). The Analysis and Use of Financial Statements. John Wiley & Sons, Inc. ISBN 0-471-11186-4
- Grubbström, Robert W. (1967). "On the Application of the Laplace Transform to Certain Economic Problems". Management Science. 13: 558–567. doi:10.1287/mnsc.13.7.558
- Menon, A.; et al. (1999). "Antecedents and Consequences of Marketing Strategy Making". Journal of Marketing. American Marketing Association. 63 (2): 18–40. JSTOR 1251943. doi:10.2307/1251943
- Berk, Johnathan; DeMarzo, Peter; Stangeland, David (2015). Corporate Finance (3rd Canadian ed.). Toronto: Pearson Canada. p. 64. ISBN 978-0133552683
- Steven Buser: LaPlace Transforms as Present Value Rules: A Note, The Journal of Finance, Vol. 41, No. 1, March, 1986, pp. 243-247
- FASB, 2001. Improving Business Reporting: Insights into Enhancing Voluntary Disclosures. Retrieved on April 20, 2012

5

Fundamentals of Security Analysis

Security analysis is the analysis of the monetary contracts that occur between parties. It can be categorized into equities and debt securities or in a combination of both. The chapter closely examines the key concepts of technical analysis to provide an extensive understanding of the subject.

Security Analysis

Security analysis is the analysis of tradeable financial instruments called securities. These are usually classified into debt securities, equities, or some hybrid of the two. Tradeable credit derivatives are also securities. Commodities or futures contracts are not securities. They are distinguished from securities by the fact that their performance is not dependent on the management or activities of an outside or third party. Options on these contracts are however considered securities, since performance is now dependent on the activities of a third party. The definition of what is and what is not a security comes directly from the language of a United States Supreme Court decision in the case of SEC v. W. J. Howey Co.. Security analysis is typically divided into fundamental analysis, which relies upon the examination of fundamental business factors such as financial statements, and technical analysis, which focuses upon price trends and momentum. Quantitative analysis may use indicators from both areas.

Technical Analysis

In finance, technical analysis is an analysis methodology for forecasting the direction of prices through the study of past market data, primarily price and volume. Behavioral economics and quantitative analysis use many of the same tools of technical analysis, which, being an aspect of active management, stands in contradiction to much of modern portfolio theory. The efficacy of both technical and fundamental analysis is disputed by the efficient-market hypothesis which states that stock market prices are essentially unpredictable.

History

The principles of technical analysis are derived from hundreds of years of financial market data. Some aspects of technical analysis began to appear in Amsterdam-based businessman Joseph de la Vega's accounts of the Dutch financial markets in the 17th century. In Asia, technical analysis is said to be a method developed by Homma Munehisa during the early 18th century which evolved into the use of candlestick techniques, and is today a technical analysis charting tool. In the 1920s and 1930s Richard W. Schabacker published several books which continued the work of Charles Dow and William Peter Hamilton in their books *Stock Market Theory and Practice* and *Technical*

Market Analysis. In 1948 Robert D. Edwards and John Magee published *Technical Analysis of Stock Trends* which is widely considered to be one of the seminal works of the discipline. It is exclusively concerned with trend analysis and chart patterns and remains in use to the present. Early technical analysis was almost exclusively the analysis of charts, because the processing power of computers was not available for the modern degree of statistical analysis. Charles Dow reportedly originated a form of point and figure chart analysis.

Dow theory is based on the collected writings of Dow Jones co-founder and editor Charles Dow, and inspired the use and development of modern technical analysis at the end of the 19th century. Other pioneers of analysis techniques include Ralph Nelson Elliott, William Delbert Gann and Richard Wyckoff who developed their respective techniques in the early 20th century. More technical tools and theories have been developed and enhanced in recent decades, with an increasing emphasis on computer-assisted techniques using specially designed computer software.

General Description

Fundamental analysts examine earnings, dividends, assets, quality, ratio, new products, research and the like. Technicians employ many methods, tools and techniques as well, one of which is the use of charts. Using charts, technical analysts seek to identify price patterns and market trends in financial markets and attempt to exploit those patterns.

Technicians using charts search for archetypal price chart patterns, such as the well-known head and shoulders or double top/bottom reversal patterns, study technical indicators, moving averages, and look for forms such as lines of support, resistance, channels, and more obscure formations such as flags, pennants, balance days and cup and handle patterns.

Technical analysts also widely use market indicators of many sorts, some of which are mathematical transformations of price, often including up and down volume, advance/decline data and other inputs. These indicators are used to help assess whether an asset is trending, and if it is, the probability of its direction and of continuation. Technicians also look for relationships between price/volume indices and market indicators. Examples include the moving average, relative strength index, and MACD. Other avenues of study include correlations between changes in Options (implied volatility) and put/call ratios with price. Also important are sentiment indicators such as Put/Call ratios, bull/bear ratios, short interest, Implied Volatility, etc.

There are many techniques in technical analysis. Adherents of different techniques (for example, Candlestick analysis -the oldest form of technical analysis developed by a Japanese grain trader-, Harmonics, Dow theory, and Elliott wave theory) may ignore the other approaches, yet many traders combine elements from more than one technique. Some technical analysts use subjective judgment to decide which pattern(s) a particular instrument reflects at a given time and what the interpretation of that pattern should be. Others employ a strictly mechanical or systematic approach to pattern identification and interpretation.

Contrasting with technical analysis is *fundamental analysis*, the study of economic factors that influence the way investors price financial markets. Technical analysis holds that prices already reflect all the underlying fundamental factors. Uncovering the trends is what technical indicators are designed to do, although neither technical nor fundamental indicators are perfect. Some traders use technical or fundamental analysis exclusively, while others use both types to make trading decisions.

Characteristics

Technical analysis employs models and trading rules based on price and volume transformations, such as the relative strength index, moving averages, regressions, inter-market and intra-market price correlations, business cycles, stock market cycles or, classically, through recognition of chart patterns.

Technical analysis stands in contrast to the fundamental analysis approach to security and stock analysis. In the fundamental equation M = P/E technical analysis is the examination of M (multiple). Multiple encompasses the psychology generally abounding, i.e. the extent of willingness to buy/sell. Also in M is the ability to pay as, for instance, a spent-out bull can't make the market go higher and a well-heeled bear won't. Technical analysis analyzes price, volume, psychology, money flow and other market information, whereas fundamental analysis looks at the facts of the company, market, currency or commodity. Most large brokerage, trading group, or financial institutions will typically have both a technical analysis and fundamental analysis team.

Technical analysis is widely used among traders and financial professionals and is very often used by active day traders, market makers and pit traders. In the 1960s and 1970s it was widely dismissed by academics. In a recent review, Irwin and Park reported that 56 of 95 modern studies found that it produces positive results but noted that many of the positive results were rendered dubious by issues such as data snooping, so that the evidence in support of technical analysis was inconclusive; it is still considered by many academics to be pseudoscience. Academics such as Eugene Fama say the evidence for technical analysis is sparse and is inconsistent with the *weak form* of the efficient-market hypothesis. Users hold that even if technical analysis cannot predict the future, it helps to identify trends, tendencies, and trading opportunities.

In the foreign exchange markets, its use may be more widespread than fundamental analysis. This does not mean technical analysis is more applicable to foreign markets, but that technical analysis is more recognized as to its efficacy there than elsewhere. While some isolated studies have indicated that technical trading rules might lead to consistent returns in the period prior to 1987, most academic work has focused on the nature of the anomalous position of the foreign exchange market. It is speculated that this anomaly is due to central bank intervention, which obviously technical analysis is not designed to predict. Recent research suggests that combining various trading signals into a Combined Signal Approach may be able to increase profitability and reduce dependence on any single rule.

Principles

A fundamental principle of technical analysis is that a market's price reflects all relevant information, so their analysis looks at the history of a security's trading pattern rather than external drivers such as economic, fundamental and news events. Therefore, price action tends to repeat itself due to investors collectively tending toward patterned behavior – hence technical analysis focuses on identifiable trends and conditions.

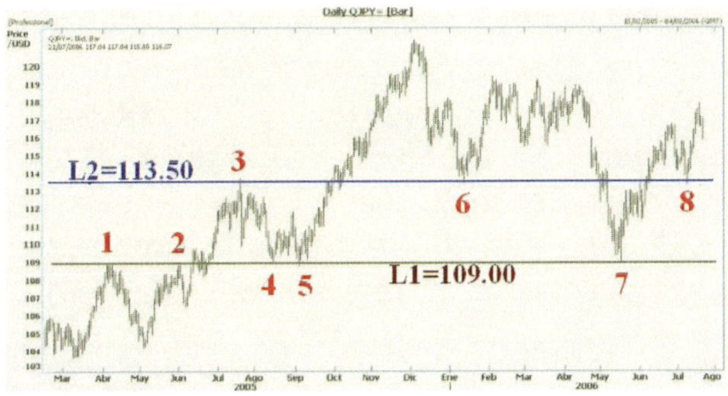

Stock chart showing levels of support (4,5,6, 7, and 8) and resistance (1, 2, and 3); levels of resistance tend to become levels of support and vice versa.

Market Action Discounts Everything

Based on the premise that all relevant information is already reflected by prices, technical analysts believe it is important to understand what investors think of that information, known and perceived.

Prices Move in Trends

Technical analysts believe that prices trend directionally, i.e., up, down, or sideways (flat) or some combination. The basic definition of a price trend was originally put forward by Dow theory.

An example of a security that had an apparent trend is AOL from November 2001 through August 2002. A technical analyst or trend follower recognizing this trend would look for opportunities to sell this security. AOL consistently moves downward in price. Each time the stock rose, sellers would enter the market and sell the stock; hence the "zig-zag" movement in the price. The series of "lower highs" and "lower lows" is a tell tale sign of a stock in a down trend. In other words, each time the stock moved lower, it fell below its previous relative low price. Each time the stock moved higher, it could not reach the level of its previous relative high price.

Note that the sequence of lower lows and lower highs did not begin until August. Then AOL makes a low price that does not pierce the relative low set earlier in the month. Later in the same month, the stock makes a relative high equal to the most recent relative high. In this a technician sees strong indications that the down trend is at least pausing and possibly ending, and would likely stop actively selling the stock at that point.

History Tends to Repeat Itself

Technical analysts believe that investors collectively repeat the behavior of the investors that preceded them. To a technician, the emotions in the market may be irrational, but they exist. Because investor behavior repeats itself so often, technicians believe that recognizable (and predictable) price patterns will develop on a chart. Recognition of these patterns can allow the technician to select trades that have a higher probability of success.

Technical analysis is not limited to charting, but it always considers price trends. For example, many technicians monitor surveys of investor sentiment. These surveys gauge the attitude of market participants, specifically whether they are bearish or bullish. Technicians use these surveys to help determine whether a trend will continue or if a reversal could develop; they are most likely to anticipate a change when the surveys report extreme investor sentiment. Surveys that show overwhelming bullishness, for example, are evidence that an uptrend may reverse; the premise being that if most investors are bullish they have already bought the market (anticipating higher prices). And because most investors *are* bullish and invested, one assumes that few buyers remain. This leaves more potential sellers than buyers, despite the bullish sentiment. This suggests that prices will trend down, and is an example of contrarian trading.

Recently, Kim Man Lui, Lun Hu, and Keith C.C. Chan have suggested that there is statistical evidence of association relationships between some of the index composite stocks whereas there is no evidence for such a relationship between some index composite others. They show that the price behavior of these Hang Seng index composite stocks is easier to understand than that of the index.

Industry

The industry is globally represented by the International Federation of Technical Analysts(IFTA), which is a federation of regional and national organizations. In the United States, the industry is represented by both the Market Technicians Association (MTA) and the American Association of Professional Technical Analysts (AAPTA). The United States is also represented by the Technical Security Analysts Association of San Francisco (TSAASF). In the United Kingdom, the industry is represented by the Society of Technical Analysts (STA). In Canada the industry is represented by the Canadian Society of Technical Analysts. In Australia, the industry is represented by the Australian Technical Analysts Association (ATAA), (which is affiliated to IFTA) and the Australian Professional Technical Analysts (APTA) Inc.

Professional technical analysis societies have worked on creating a body of knowledge that describes the field of Technical Analysis. A body of knowledge is central to the field as a way of defining how and why technical analysis may work. It can then be used by academia, as well as regulatory bodies, in developing proper research and standards for the field. The Market Technicians Association (MTA) has published a body of knowledge, which is the structure for the MTA's Chartered Market Technician (CMT) exam.

Systematic Trading

Neural Networks

Since the early 1990s when the first practically usable types emerged, artificial neural networks (ANNs) have rapidly grown in popularity. They are artificial intelligence adaptive software systems that have been inspired by how biological neural networks work. They are used because they can learn to detect complex patterns in data. In mathematical terms, they are universal function approximators, meaning that given the right data and configured correctly, they can capture and model any input-output relationships. This not only removes the need for human interpretation of charts or the series of rules for generating entry/exit signals, but also provides a bridge to fundamental analysis, as the variables used in fundamental analysis can be used as input.

As ANNs are essentially non-linear statistical models, their accuracy and prediction capabilities can be both mathematically and empirically tested. In various studies, authors have claimed that neural networks used for generating trading signals given various technical and fundamental inputs have significantly outperformed buy-hold strategies as well as traditional linear technical analysis methods when combined with rule-based expert systems.

While the advanced mathematical nature of such adaptive systems has kept neural networks for financial analysis mostly within academic research circles, in recent years more user friendly neural network software has made the technology more accessible to traders. However, large-scale application is problematic because of the problem of matching the correct neural topology to the market being studied.

Backtesting

Systematic trading is most often employed after testing an investment strategy on historic data. This is known as backtesting. Backtesting is most often performed for technical indicators, but can be applied to most investment strategies (e.g. fundamental analysis). While traditional backtesting was done by hand, this was usually only performed on human-selected stocks, and was thus prone to prior knowledge in stock selection. With the advent of computers, backtesting can be performed on entire exchanges over decades of historic data in very short amounts of time.

The use of computers does have its drawbacks, being limited to algorithms that a computer can perform. Several trading strategies rely on human interpretation, and are unsuitable for computer processing. Only technical indicators which are entirely algorithmic can be programmed for computerised automated backtesting.

Combination with other Market Forecast Methods

John Murphy states that the principal sources of information available to technicians are price, volume and open interest. Other data, such as indicators and sentiment analysis, are considered secondary.

However, many technical analysts reach outside pure technical analysis, combining other market forecast methods with their technical work. One advocate for this approach is John Bollinger, who coined the term *rational analysis* in the middle 1980s for the intersection of technical analysis and fundamental analysis. Another such approach, fusion analysis, overlays fundamental analysis with technical, in an attempt to improve portfolio manager performance.

Technical analysis is also often combined with quantitative analysis and economics. For example, neural networks may be used to help identify intermarket relationships.

Investor and newsletter polls, and magazine cover sentiment indicators, are also used by technical analysts.

Empirical Evidence

Whether technical analysis actually works is a matter of controversy. Methods vary greatly, and different technical analysts can sometimes make contradictory predictions from the same data. Many investors claim that they experience positive returns, but academic appraisals often find that it has little predictive power. Of 95 modern studies, 56 concluded that technical analysis had positive results, although data-snooping bias and other problems make the analysis difficult. Nonlinear prediction using neural networks occasionally produces statistically significant prediction results. A Federal Reserve working paper regarding support and resistance levels in short-term foreign exchange rates "offers strong evidence that the levels help to predict intraday trend interruptions," although the "predictive power" of those levels was "found to vary across the exchange rates and firms examined".

Technical trading strategies were found to be effective in the Chinese marketplace by a recent study that states, "Finally, we find significant positive returns on buy trades generated by the contrarian version of the moving-average crossover rule, the channel breakout rule, and the Bollinger band trading rule, after accounting for transaction costs of 0.50 percent."

An influential 1992 study by Brock et al. which appeared to find support for technical trading rules was tested for data snooping and other problems in 1999; the sample covered by Brock et al. was robust to data snooping.

Subsequently, a comprehensive study of the question by Amsterdam economist Gerwin Griffioen concludes that: "for the U.S., Japanese and most Western European stock market indices the recursive out-of-sample forecasting procedure does not show to be profitable, after implementing little transaction costs. Moreover, for sufficiently high transaction costs it is found, by estimating CAPMs, that technical trading shows no statistically significant risk-corrected out-of-sample forecasting power for almost all of the stock market indices." Transaction costs are particularly applicable to "momentum strategies"; a comprehensive 1996 review of the data and studies concluded that even small transaction costs would lead to an inability to capture any excess from such strategies.

In a paper published in the Journal of Finance, Dr. Andrew W. Lo, director MIT Laboratory for Financial Engineering, working with Harry Mamaysky and Jiang Wang found that:

Technical analysis, also known as "charting", has been a part of financial practice for many decades, but this discipline has not received the same level of academic scrutiny and acceptance as more traditional approaches such as fundamental analysis. One of the main obstacles is the highly subjective nature of technical analysis – the presence of geometric shapes in historical price charts is often in the eyes of the beholder. In this paper, we propose a systematic and automatic approach to technical pattern recognition using nonparametric kernel regression, and apply this method to a large number of U.S. stocks from 1962 to 1996 to evaluate the effectiveness of technical analysis. By comparing the unconditional empirical distribution of daily stock returns to the conditional distribution – conditioned on specific technical indicators such as head-and-shoulders or double-bottoms – we find that over the 31-year sample period, several technical indicators do provide incremental information and may have some practical value.

In that same paper Dr. Lo wrote that "several academic studies suggest that ... technical analysis may well be an effective means for extracting useful information from market prices." Some techniques such as Drummond Geometry attempt to overcome the past data bias by projecting support and resistance levels from differing time frames into the near-term future and combining that with reversion to the mean techniques.

Thomas DeMark's indicators enjoy a remarkable endorsement in the financial industry. A recent work has investigated the predictive power of three DeMark indicators (Sequential, Combo and

Setup Trend), over 21 commodity futures markets and 10 years of data. Market entry signals have been tested by comparing conditional returns (i.e. conditioned on the entry signals) to unconditional returns. For the period from Jan. 2004 to Jan. 2014, the tests suggest statistically significant predictive power on a wide range of commodity futures.

Efficient Market Hypothesis

The efficient-market hypothesis (EMH) contradicts the basic tenets of technical analysis by stating that past prices cannot be used to profitably predict future prices. Thus it holds that technical analysis cannot be effective. Economist Eugene Fama published the seminal paper on the EMH in the *Journal of Finance* in 1970, and said "In short, the evidence in support of the efficient markets model is extensive, and (somewhat uniquely in economics) contradictory evidence is sparse."

Technicians say that EMH ignores the way markets work, in that many investors base their expectations on past earnings or track record, for example. Because future stock prices can be strongly influenced by investor expectations, technicians claim it only follows that past prices influence future prices. They also point to research in the field of behavioral finance, specifically that people are not the rational participants EMH makes them out to be. Technicians have long said that irrational human behavior influences stock prices, and that this behavior leads to predictable outcomes. Author David Aronson says that the theory of behavioral finance blends with the practice of technical analysis:

By considering the impact of emotions, cognitive errors, irrational preferences, and the dynamics of group behavior, behavioral finance offers succinct explanations of excess market volatility as well as the excess returns earned by stale information strategies.... cognitive errors may also explain the existence of market inefficiencies that spawn the systematic price movements that allow objective TA [technical analysis] methods to work.

EMH advocates reply that while individual market participants do not always act rationally (or have complete information), their aggregate decisions balance each other, resulting in a rational outcome (optimists who buy stock and bid the price higher are countered by pessimists who sell their stock, which keeps the price in equilibrium). Likewise, complete information is reflected in the price because all market participants bring their own individual, but incomplete, knowledge together in the market.

Random Walk Hypothesis

The random walk hypothesis may be derived from the weak-form efficient markets hypothesis, which is based on the assumption that market participants take full account of any information contained in past price movements (but not necessarily other public information). In his book *A Random Walk Down Wall Street*, Princeton economist Burton Malkiel said that technical forecasting tools such as pattern analysis must ultimately be self-defeating: "The problem is that once such a regularity is known to market participants, people will act in such a way that prevents it from happening in the future." Malkiel has stated that while momentum may explain some stock price movements, there is not enough momentum to make excess profits. Malkiel has compared technical analysis to "astrology".

In the late 1980s, professors Andrew Lo and Craig McKinlay published a paper which cast doubt on the random walk hypothesis. In a 1999 response to Malkiel, Lo and McKinlay collected empirical papers that questioned the hypothesis' applicability that suggested a non-random and possibly predictive component to stock price movement, though they were careful to point out that rejecting random walk does not necessarily invalidate EMH, which is an entirely separate concept from RWH. In a 2000 paper, Andrew Lo back-analyzed data from U.S. from 1962 to 1996 and found that "several technical indicators do provide incremental information and may have some practical value". Burton Malkiel dismissed the irregularities mentioned by Lo and McKinlay as being too small to profit from.

Technicians say that the EMH and random walk theories both ignore the realities of markets, in that participants are not completely rational and that current price moves are not independent of previous moves. Some signal processing researchers negate the random walk hypothesis that stock market prices resemble Wiener processes, because the statistical moments of such processes and real stock data vary significantly with respect to window size and similarity measure. They argue that feature transformations used for the description of audio and biosignals can also be used to predict stock market prices successfully which would contradict the random walk hypothesis.

The random walk index (RWI) is a technical indicator that attempts to determine if a stock's price movement is random in nature or a result of a statistically significant trend. The random walk index attempts to determine when the market is in a strong uptrend or downtrend by measuring price ranges over N and how it differs from what would be expected by a random walk (randomly going up or down). The greater the range suggests a stronger trend.

Scientific Technical Analysis

Caginalp and Balenovich in 1994 used their asset-flow differential equations model to show that the major patterns of technical analysis could be generated with some basic assumptions. Some of the patterns such as a triangle continuation or reversal pattern can be generated with the assumption of two distinct groups of investors with different assessments of valuation.The major assumptions of the models are that the finiteness of assets and the use of trend as well as valuation in decision making. Many of the patterns follow as mathematically logical consequences of these assumptions.

One of the problems with conventional technical analysis has been the difficulty of specifying the patterns in a manner that permits objective testing.

Japanese candlestick patterns involve patterns of a few days that are within an uptrend or downtrend. Caginalp and Laurent were the first to perform a successful large scale test of patterns. A mathematically precise set of criteria were tested by first using a definition of a short term trend by smoothing the data and allowing for one deviation in the smoothed trend. They then considered eight major three-day candlestick reversal patterns in a non-parametric manner and defined the patterns as a set of inequalities. The results were positive with an overwhelming statistical confidence for each of the patterns using the data set of all S&P 500 stocks daily for the five-year period 1992-1996.

Among the most basic ideas of conventional technical analysis is that a trend, once established, tends to continue. However, testing for this trend has often led researchers to conclude that stocks are a random walk. One study, performed by Poterba and Summers, found a small trend effect that was too small to be of trading value. As Fisher Black noted, "noise" in trading price data makes it difficult to test hypotheses.

One method for avoiding this noise was discovered in 1995 by Caginalp and Constantine who used a ratio of two essentially identical closed-end funds to eliminate any changes in valuation. A closed-end fund (unlike an open-end fund) trades independently of its net asset value and its shares cannot be redeemed, but only traded among investors as any other stock on the exchanges. In this study, the authors found that the best estimate of tomorrow's price is not yesterday's price (as the efficient market hypothesis would indicate), nor is it the pure momentum price (namely, the same relative price change from yesterday to today continues from today to tomorrow). But rather it is almost exactly halfway between the two.

Starting from the characterization of the past time evolution of market prices in terms of price velocity and price acceleration, an attempt towards a general framework for technical analysis has been developed, with the goal of establishing a principled classification of the possible patterns characterizing the deviation or defects from the random walk market state and its time translational invariant properties. The classification relies on two dimensionless parameters, the Froude number characterizing the relative strength of the acceleration with respect to the velocity and the time horizon forecast dimensionalized to the training period. Trend-following and contrarian patterns are found to coexist and depend on the dimensionless time horizon. Using a renormalisation group approach, the probabilistic based scenario approach exhibits statistically signifificant predictive power in essentially all tested market phases.

A survey of modern studies by Park and Irwin showed that most found a positive result from technical analysis.

In 2011, Caginalp and DeSantis have used large data sets of closed-end funds, where comparison with valuation is possible, in order to determine quantitatively whether key aspects of technical analysis such as trend and resistance have scientific validity. Using data sets of over 100,000 points they demonstrate that trend has an effect that is at least half as important as valuation. The effects of volume and volatility, which are smaller, are also evident and statistically significant. An important aspect of their work involves the nonlinear effect of trend. Positive trends that occur within approximately 3.7 standard deviations have a positive effect. For stronger uptrends, there is a negative effect on returns, suggesting that profit taking occurs as the magnitude of the uptrend increases. For downtrends the situation is similar except that the "buying on dips" does not take place until the downtrend is a 4.6 standard deviation event. These methods can be used to examine investor behavior and compare the underlying strategies among different asset classes.

In 2013, Kim Man Lui and T Chong pointed out that the past findings on technical analysis mostly reported the profitability of specific trading rules for a given set of historical data. These past studies had not taken the human trader into consideration as no real-world trader would mechanically adopt signals from any technical analysis method. Therefore, to unveil the truth of technical analysis, we should get back to understand the performance between experienced and novice traders. If the market really walks randomly, there will be no difference between these two kinds of traders. However, it is found by experiment that traders who are more knowledgeable on technical analysis significantly outperform those who are less knowledgeable.

Ticker-tape Reading

Until the mid-1960s, "tape reading" was a popular form of technical analysis. It consisted of reading market information such as price, volume, order size, and so on from a paper strip which ran through a machine called a stock ticker. Market data was sent to brokerage houses and to the homes and offices of the most active speculators. This system fell into disuse with the advent of electronic information panels in the late 60's, and later computers, which allow for the easy preparation of charts.

Quotation Board

Another form of technical analysis used so far was via interpretation of stock market data contained in quotation boards, that in the times before electronic screens, were huge chalkboards located in the stock exchanges, with data of the main financial assets listed on exchanges for analysis of their movements. It was manually updated with chalk, with the updates regarding some of these data being transmitted to environments outside of exchanges (such as brokerage houses, bucket shops, etc.) via the aforementioned tape, telegraph, telephone and later telex.

This analysis tool was used both, on the spot, mainly by market professionals for day trading and scalping, as well as by general public through the printed versions in newspapers showing the data of the negotiations of the previous day, for swing and position trades.

Despite to continue appearing in print in newspapers, as well as computerized versions in some websites, analysis via quotation board is another form of technical analysis that has fallen into disuse by the majority.

Charting Terms and Indicators

Concepts

- Average true range – averaged daily trading range, adjusted for price gaps.
- Breakout – the concept whereby prices forcefully penetrate an area of prior support or resistance, usually, but not always, accompanied by an increase in volume.
- Chart pattern – distinctive pattern created by the movement of security prices on a chart
- Cycles – time targets for potential change in price action (price only moves up, down, or sideways)
- Dead cat bounce – the phenomenon whereby a spectacular decline in the price of a stock is immediately followed by a moderate and temporary rise before resuming its downward movement
- Elliott wave principle and the golden ratio to calculate successive price movements and retracements
- Fibonacci ratios – used as a guide to determine support and resistance

- Momentum – the rate of price change
- Point and figure analysis – A priced-based analytical approach employing numerical filters which may incorporate time references, though ignores time entirely in its construction
- Resistance – a price level that may prompt a net increase of selling activity
- Support – a price level that may prompt a net increase of buying activity
- Trending – the phenomenon by which price movement tends to persist in one direction for an extended period of time

Types of Charts

- Candlestick chart – Of Japanese origin and similar to OHLC, candlesticks widen and fill the interval between the open and close prices to emphasize the open/close relationship. In the West, often black or red candle bodies represent a close lower than the open, while white, green or blue candles represent a close higher than the open price.
- Line chart – Connects the closing price values with line segments.
- Open-high-low-close chart – OHLC charts, also known as bar charts, plot the span between the high and low prices of a trading period as a vertical line segment at the trading time, and the open and close prices with horizontal tick marks on the range line, usually a tick to the left for the open price and a tick to the right for the closing price.
- Point and figure chart – a chart type employing numerical filters with only passing references to time, and which ignores time entirely in its construction.

Overlays

Overlays are generally superimposed over the main price chart.

- Bollinger bands – a range of price volatility
- Channel – a pair of parallel trend lines
- Ichimoku kinko hyo – a moving average-based system that factors in time and the average point between a candle's high and low
- Moving average – an average over a window of time before and after a given time point that is repeated at each time point in the given chart. A moving average can be thought of as a kind of dynamic trend-line.
- Parabolic SAR – Wilder's trailing stop based on prices tending to stay within a parabolic curve during a strong trend
- Pivot point – derived by calculating the numerical average of a particular currency's or stock's high, low and closing prices
- Resistance – a price level that may act as a ceiling above price

- Support – a price level that may act as a floor below price
- Trend line – a sloping line described by at least two peaks or two troughs
- Zig Zag – This chart overlay that shows filtered price movements that are greater than a given percentage.

Breadth Indicators

These indicators are based on statistics derived from the broad market.

- Advance–decline line – a popular indicator of market breadth.
- McClellan Oscillator - a popular closed-form indicator of breadth.
- McClellan Summation Index - a popular open-form indicator of breadth.

Price-based Indicators

These indicators are generally shown below or above the main price chart.

- Average directional index – a widely used indicator of trend strength.
- Commodity Channel Index – identifies cyclical trends.
- MACD – moving average convergence/divergence.
- Momentum – the rate of price change.
- Relative strength index (RSI) – oscillator showing price strength.
- Relative Vigor Index (RVI) – oscillator measures the conviction of a recent price action and the likelihood that it will continue.
- Stochastic oscillator – close position within recent trading range.
- Trix – an oscillator showing the slope of a triple-smoothed exponential moving average.

Volume-based Indicators

- Accumulation/distribution index – based on the close within the day's range.
- Money Flow – the amount of stock traded on days the price went up.
- On-balance volume – the momentum of buying and selling stocks.

Trading with Mixing Indicators

- MACD & Average directional index
- MACD & Super Trend
- MACD & Moving average

Assumptions of Technical Analysis

Following are the four assumptions that support the basic approach of technical analysis:

1. The market value of any good or service is determined solely by the interaction of supply and demand
2. Supply and demand are governed by numerous factors, both rational and irrational
3. Disregarding minor fluctuations, the prices for individual securities and the overall value of the market tend to move in trends, which persist for appreciable lengths of time
4. Prevailing trends change in reaction to shifts in supply and demand relationships and these shifts can be detected in the action of the market

Difference Between Technical Analysis and Fundamental Analysis

These two terms refer to different approaches for investment decision by using different methodologies and research techniques for forecasting the future trends of price movement. Fundamental analysis is an investment strategy or philosophy which attempts to measure the intrinsic value of a financial asset like stock by studying everything from the macro economic and industry conditions to the internal management and financial condition of companies. Technical analysis on the other hand is the evaluation of financial assets historical market statistics such as past prices, volatility, trading volume to measure a financial assets future price. It does not look in to the intrinsic value rather it uses charts to identify patterns and trends that may suggest what a financial asset like stock will do in the future.

Technical analysts believe that there is no point of evaluating the fundamentals as the all fundamental information must have already reflected in the stock's price. Fundamental analysis takes a relatively long-term approach as compared to the short term approach of the technical analysts. In other words the basic difference between fundamental and technical analysts can be seen as the difference between investing versus trading. However, in the world of stock analysis, which strategy works best is always debated and perhaps the combination of both gives the suggestive results.

Advantages and Challenges of Technical Analysis

1. Not heavily dependent on financial accounting statements

- Problems with accounting statements:
    - Lack information needed by security analysts
    - Accounting Standards allows firms to select reporting procedures, resulting in difficulty comparing statements from two firms
    - Non-quantifiable factors do not show up in financial statements

2. Fundamental analyst must process new information and quickly determine a new intrinsic value, but technical analyst merely has to recognize a movement to a new equilibrium

3. Technicians trade when a move to a new equilibrium is underway but a fundamental analyst finds undervalued securities that may not adjust their prices as quickly

Challenges to Technical Analysis

1. Assumptions of Technical Analysis
   - Empirical tests of Efficient Market Hypothesis (EMH) show that prices do not move in trends
2. Technical Trading rules
   - The past may not be repeated
   - Patterns may become self-fulfilling prophecies
   - A successful rule will gain followers and become less successful
   - Rules require a great deal of subjective judgement

Technical Indicators

Stock cycles typically go through a peak and trough. For instance, let us analyse the following chart of a typical stock price cycle:

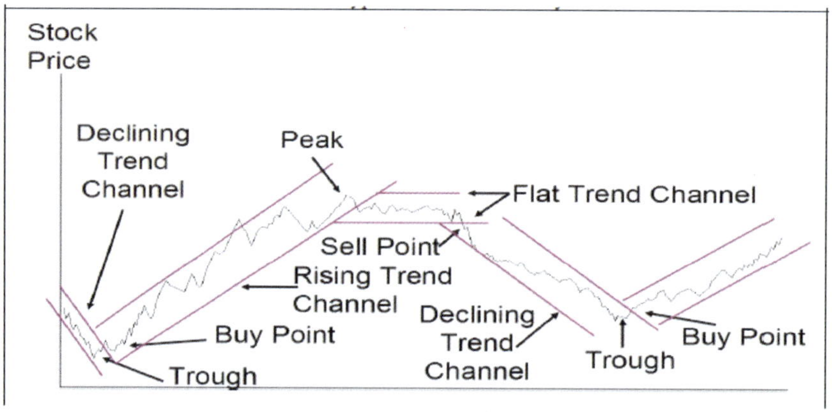

Typical Stock Market Cycle

Here in the above chart we can see a rising trend channel, a flat trend channel, a declining trend channel, and indications of when a technical analyst would want to trade.

Technical Trading Rules

Following are the some of the trading rules that are the major tools for technical analysis:

1. Trading Rules: Contrary-opinion or trading against crowd

Many analysts rely on rules developed from the premise that the majority of investors are wrong as the market approaches peaks and troughs. Technicians try to determine whether investors are strongly bullish or bearish and then trade in the opposite direction.

Under this popular trading strategy technical analysts follow certain technical indicators:

1. Mutual fund cash positions: Mutual funds assumed to act incorrectly before a market turning point. Low liquidity or low cash positions with mutual funds imply funds fully invested (bullish) and market is near or at peak. On the other hand high liquidity implies funds are bearish and thus considered a good time to buy.

2. Credit balances in brokerage accounts: Credit balances in the brokerage account increases when investors sell stocks and leave the proceeds for future investments. Technical analysts look for the build-up of credit balances as a bullish indicator as the investors expect to reinvest the money in the short term. On the other hand a lower credit balance is an indicator of bearish indicator as it suggests lower purchasing power or a sell signal as the market approaches a peak.

3. Investment advisory opinions: If a large proportion of investment advisory services gives an indication of sell signals and are bearish with respect to future market movement, the technical analysts considers this as the approach of a bull market signal in the near future.

4. Ratio of trading volume: The ratio of trading volume is considered a measure of speculative activity when the market is in the boom phase or an over-bought phase. Recently rather than its absolute value of high or low the direction of volume ratio is considered as better proxy for market movement.

5. Put –Call Ratio: A higher put/call ratio indicates a pervasive bearish attitude which technicians consider a bullish indicator.

6. Future traders bullish on stock exchange futures: As per the contrary investment strategy when the 70 % percent of speculators are bullish the contrary opinion technicians say it is bearish market and on the opposite when this declines to 30% it becomes a bullish signal

7. Confidence index: Ratio of average yield on top 10 grade corporate bonds divided by the yield on Stock markets' average of 40 bonds. This ratio is positively related to the contrary investment opinion strategy i.e., if it shows a high value then it indicates a bullish sign and if it is low it gives the bearish sign.

8. T-Bill-Eurodollar yield spread: It measures the investor's confidence among alternative economic assets. If it shows a declining trend, the stock market experiences a trough shortly.

9. Debit balances in margin/brokerage accounts: An increase in debit balances implies buying and it is considered a bullish sign while decline in debt balance would indicate selling by the investors and would be a bearish indicator. It indicates investors confidence in the market to invest while borrowing money.

10. Williams percent range (Williams %R): This technical indicator was named after it was developed by Larry Williams. This attempts to measure overbought and oversold market conditions with the value of %R falls between a value of 100 and 0. The trading rule for this indicator follows a simple approach: If value of %R ≤ 20%, then it indicates overbought market and when the value of % R ≥ 80% the market is considered as oversold.

Instruments of Technical Analysis

Several other instruments that are commonly used by technical analysts for determining the future movement of stock prices are as follows:

- Charting Stocks: Bar Charts, Japanese Candlestick Charts, Point and Figure Charts
- Major Chart Patterns: Tend lines
- Price-based Indicators
- Volume-based Indicators
- Dow Theory or Elliot Wave

Charting the Market

Chartists use bar charts, candlestick, or point and figure charts to look for patterns which may indicate future price movements. They also analyze volume and other psychological indicators (breadth, % of bulls vs % of bears, put/call ratio, etc.). Strict chartists don't care about fundamentals at all.

(A) Bar OHLC Chart

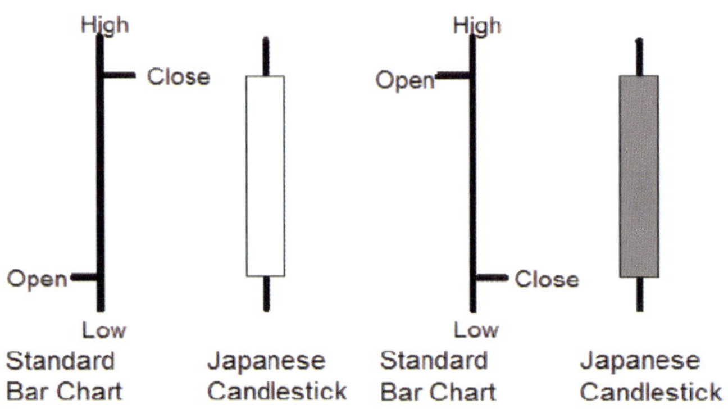

(B) Point & Figure Charts

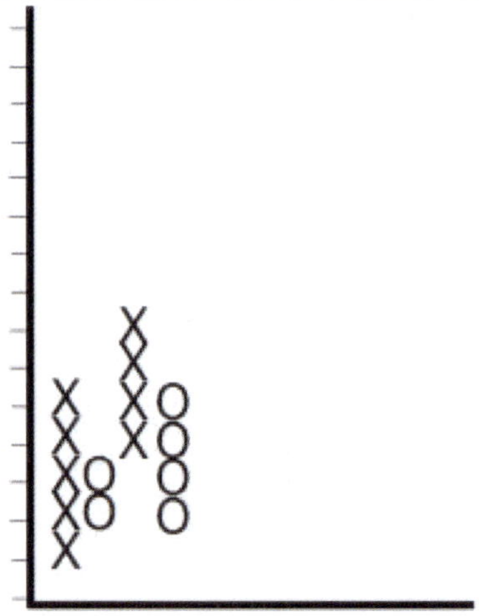

- Drawing Bar (OHLC) Charts: In a open high low close (OHLC) chart Each bar is composed of 4 elements: Open, High, Low, Close Note that the candlestick body is empty (white) on up days, and filled (some colour) on down days.
- Drawing Point & Figure Charts: Point and figure charts are independent of time. An X represents an up move. An O represents a down move. The Box Size is the number of points needed to make an X or O. The Reversal is the price change needed to recognize a change in direction. Typically, P&F charts use a 1-point box and a 3-point reversal.

Candlestick Chart

A candlestick chart (also called Japanese candlestick chart) is a style of financial chart used to describe price movements of a security, derivative, or currency. Each "candlestick" typically shows one day; so for example a one-month chart may show the 20 trading days as 20 "candlesticks".

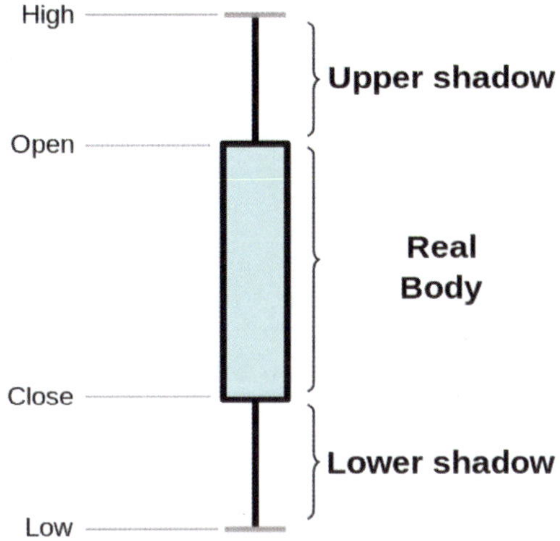

A single candlestick chart. The Low and High caps are usually not present but may be added to ease reading.

It is like a combination of line-chart and a bar-chart: each bar represents all four important pieces of information for that day: the open, the close, the high and the low. Being densely packed with information, they tend to represent trading patterns over short periods of time, often a few days or a few trading sessions.

Candlestick charts are most often used in technical analysis of equity and currency price patterns. They appear superficially similar to box plots, but are unrelated.

History

Candlestick charts are thought to have been developed in the 18th century by Munehisa Homma, a Japanese rice trader of financial instruments. They were introduced to the Western world by Steve Nison in his book, *Japanese Candlestick Charting Techniques*. They are often used today in stock analysis along with other analytical tools such as Fibonacci analysis (Fibonacci retracement).

In *Beyond Candlesticks*, Nison says, "However, based on my research, it is unlikely that Homma used candle charts. As will be seen later, when I discuss the evolution of the candle charts, it was more likely that candle charts were developed in the early part of the Meiji period in Japan (in the late 1800s)."

Description

Candlesticks are usually composed of the body (black or white), and an upper and a lower shadow (wick): the area between the open and the close is called the *real body*, price excursions above and below the real body are called *shadows*. The wick illustrates the highest and lowest traded prices of a security during the time interval represented. The body illustrates the opening and closing trades. If the security closed higher than it opened, the body is white or unfilled, with the opening price at the bottom of the body and the closing price at the top.

If the security closed lower than it opened, the body is black, with the opening price at the top and the closing price at the bottom. A candlestick need not have either a body or a wick.

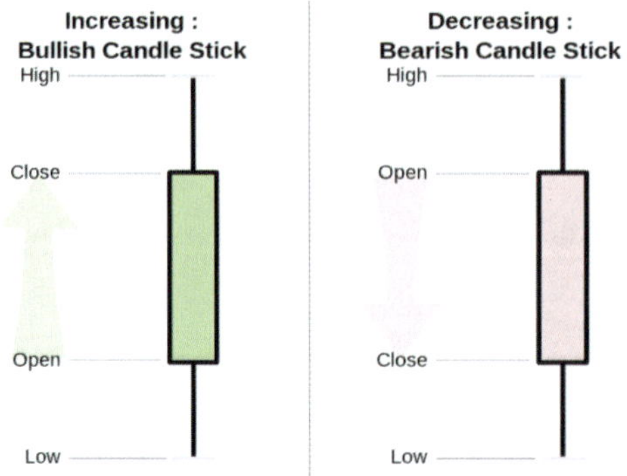

In trading, the trend of the candlestick chart is critical and often shown with colors.

To better highlight price movements, modern candlestick charts (especially those displayed digitally) often replace the black or white of the candlestick body with colors such as red (for a lower closing) and blue or green (for a higher closing).

Candlestick Patterns

In addition to the rather simple patterns depicted in the topic above, there are more complex and difficult patterns which have been identified since the charting method's inception. Complex patterns can be colored or highlighted for better visualization.

Rather than using the open-high-low-close for a given time period (for example, 5 minute, 1 hour, 1 day, 1 month, 1 year), candlesticks can also be constructed using the open-high-low-close of a specified volume range (for example, 1,000; 100,000; 1 million shares per candlestick).

Generally, the longer the body of the candle, the more intense the trading. A hollow body signifies that the stock closed higher than its opening value. A filled body signifies vice versa.

Usage

Candlestick charts are a visual aid for decision making in stock, foreign exchange, commodity, and option trading. For example, when the bar is white and high relative to other time periods, it means buyers are very bullish. The opposite is true for a black bar. Candlestick charts serve as a cornerstone of technical analysis. The main usage of a candlestick patterns is to identify trends. Looking at a candlestick, you can identify an asset's opening and closing prices, highs and lows, and overall range for a specific time frame.

Heikin Ashi Candlesticks

Heikin-Ashi (平均足, Japanese for 'average bar') candlesticks are a weighted version of candlesticks calculated with the following formula:

- Close = (open + high + low + close) / 4

- High = maximum of high, open, or close (whichever is highest)
- Low = minimum of low, open, or close (whichever is lowest)
- Open = (open of previous bar + close of previous bar) / 2

Heikin-Ashi candlesticks must be used with caution with regards to the price as the body doesn't necessarily sync up with the actual open/close. Unlike with regular candlesticks, a long wick shows more strength, whereas the same period on a standard chart might show a long body with little or no wick. Depending on the software or user preference, Heikin-Ashi may be used to chart the price (instead of line, bar, or candlestick), as an indicator overlaid on a regular chart, or as an indicator plotted on a separate window.

Point and Figure Chart

Point and figure (P&F) is a charting technique used in technical analysis. Point and figure charting does not plot price against time as time-based charts do. Instead it plots price against changes in direction by plotting a column of Xs as the price rises and a column of Os as the price falls.

History

The technique is over 100 years old. "Hoyle" was the first to write about it and showed charts in his 1898 book, The Game in Wall Street. The first book/manual dedicated to Point and Figure was written by Victor Devilliers in 1933. Chartcraft Inc, in the USA, popularized the system in the 1940s. Cohen founded Chartcraft and wrote on point and figure charting in 1947. Chartcraft published further pioneering books on P&F charting, namely those by Burke, Aby and Zieg. Chartcraft Inc is still running today, providing daily point and figure services for the US market under the name of Investors Intelligence. Veteran Mike Burke still works for Chartcraft, having started back in 1962 under the guidance of Cohen. Burke went on to train other point and figure gurus, such as Thomas Dorsey who would go on to write authoritative texts on the subject.

A detailed history can be found in Jeremy du Plessis' 'The Definitive Guide to Point and Figure' where many references and examples are cited.

Du Plessis describes the historical development of these charts from a price recording system to a charting method. Traders kept track of prices by writing them down in columns. They noticed patterns in their price record and started referring to them first as 'fluctuation charts' and then as 'figure charts'. They started using Xs instead of numbers and these charts became known as 'point charts'. Traders used both point charts and figure charts together and referred to them as their point and figure charts, which is where Du Plessis suggests the name point and figure came from. Modern point and figure charts are drawn with Xs and Os where columns of Xs are rising prices and columns of Os are falling prices, although many traditionalists such as David Fuller and Louise Yamada still use the Xs only point method of plotting.

Advantages of Point and Figure

Point and Figure charts are based primarily on price action, not time. If there are no significant price moves over time, P&F charts will show no new data. This difference can make P&F charts ideal for detecting directional patterns and trends in a condensed format.

How to Draw

The correct way to draw a point and figure chart is to plot every price change but practicality has rendered this difficult to do for a large quantity of stocks so many point and figure chartists use the summary prices at the end of each day. Some prefer to use the day's closing price and some prefer to use the day's high or low depending on the direction of the last column. The high/low method was invented by A.W. Cohen in his 1947 book, 'How to Use the Three-Point Reversal Method of Point & Figure Stock Market Timing' and has a large following.

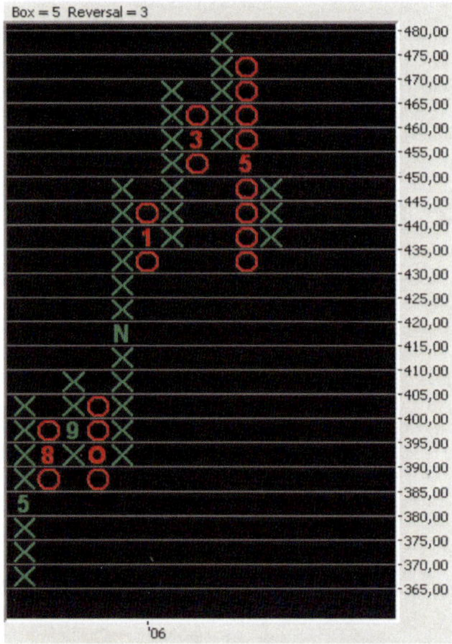

Sample point and figure chart with box size set to $5 and reversal threshold set to 3 box sizes.

The charts are constructed by deciding on the value represented by each X and O. Any price change below this value is ignored so point and figure acts as a filter to filter out the smaller price changes. The charts change column when the price changes direction by the value of a certain number of Xs or Os. Traditionally this was one and is called a 1 box reversal chart. More common is three, called a 3 box reversal chart.

45 Degree Trend Lines

Because point and figure charts are plotted on squared paper, 45 degree lines may be used to define up trends and down trends from important highs and lows on the chart allowing objective analysis of trends.

Price Targets

Also in common usage are two methods of obtaining price targets from point and figure charts. The vertical method measures the length of the thrust off a high or low and projects the thrust to obtain a target. The horizontal method measures the width of a congestion pattern and uses that to obtain a target.

Computerization

In the US, Chartcraft used an IBM S/360 in the 1960s to produce point and figure charts.

Point and figure charts were automated in the UK in the early 1980s by the Indexia company run by Jeremy Du Plessis. This automation increased the popularity and usage of point and figure charts because hundreds of charts could be viewed and altered quickly and easily. At the same time a method of log scaling point and figure charts was devised, where the value of the Xs and Os was set to a percentage rather than a price. This allowed the sensitivity of Point and Figure charts to remain constant no matter what the price level.

Kaufman, in *New Trading Systems and Methods*, 2005, documents research he and Kermit Zeig performed over many years computerizing point and figure charting. LeBeau and Lucas also developed computerized point and figure charts in *Technical Traders Guide to Computer Analysis of the Futures Markets*.

P&F charts are now widely presented in many trading applications either as a native component or as a third-party plug-in, script, or external technical indicator.

Line Chart

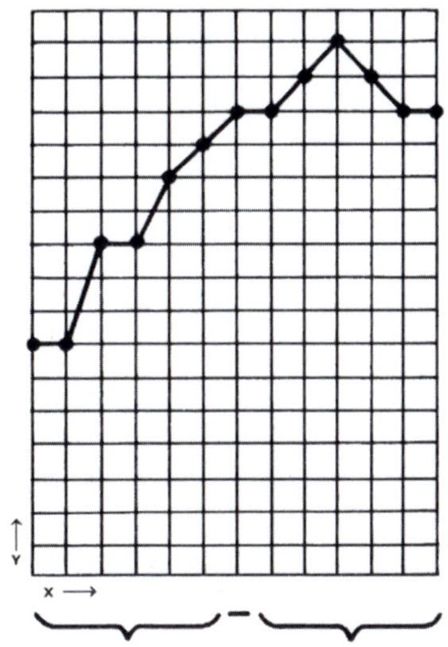

This simple graph shows data over intervals with connected points

A line chart or line graph is a type of chart which displays information as a series of data points called 'markers' connected by straight line segments. It is a basic type of chart common in many fields. It is similar to a scatter plot except that the measurement points are ordered (typically by their x-axis value) and joined with straight line segments. A line chart is often used to visualize a trend in data over intervals of time – a time series – thus the line is often drawn chronologically. In these cases they are known as run charts.

History

Some of the earliest known line charts are generally credited to Francis Hauksbee, Nicolaus Samuel Cruquius, Johann Heinrich Lambert and William Playfair.

Example

In the experimental sciences, data collected from experiments are often visualized by a graph. For example, if one were to collect data on the speed of a body at certain points in time, one could visualize the data by a data table such as the following:

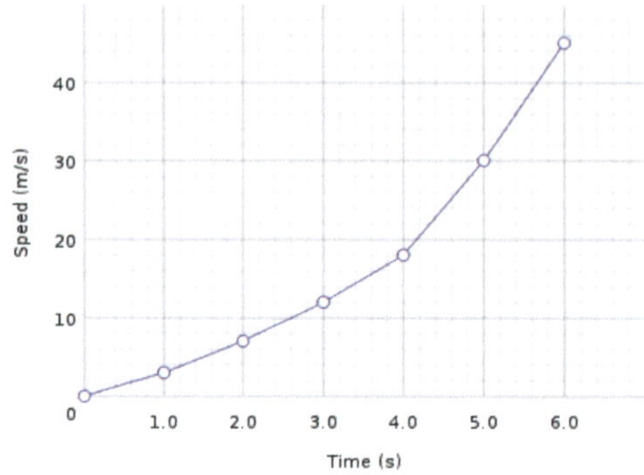

Graph of Speed Vs Time

Elapsed Time (s)	Speed ($m\,s^{-1}$)
0	0
1	3
2	7
3	12
4	20
5	30
6	45.6

The table "visualization" is a great way of displaying exact values, but can be a poor way to understand the underlying patterns that those values represent. Because of these qualities, the table display is often erroneously conflated with the data itself; whereas it is just another visualization of the data.

Understanding the process described by the data in the table is aided by producing a graph or line chart of *Speed versus Time*. Such a visualisation appears in the figure to the right.

Mathematically, if we denote time by the variable t, and speed by v, then the function plotted in the graph would be denoted $\mathrm{v(t)}$ indicating that v (the dependent variable) is a function of t.

Best-fit

Charts often include an overlaid mathematical function depicting the best-fit trend of the scattered data. This layer is referred to as a best-fit layer and the graph containing this layer is often referred to as a line graph.

It is simple to construct a "best-fit" layer consisting of a set of line segments connecting adjacent data points; however, such a "best-fit" is usually not an ideal representation of the trend of the underlying scatter data for the following reasons:

1. It is highly improbable that the discontinuities in the slope of the best-fit would correspond exactly with the positions of the measurement values.

2. It is highly unlikely that the experimental error in the data is negligible, yet the curve falls exactly through each of the data points.

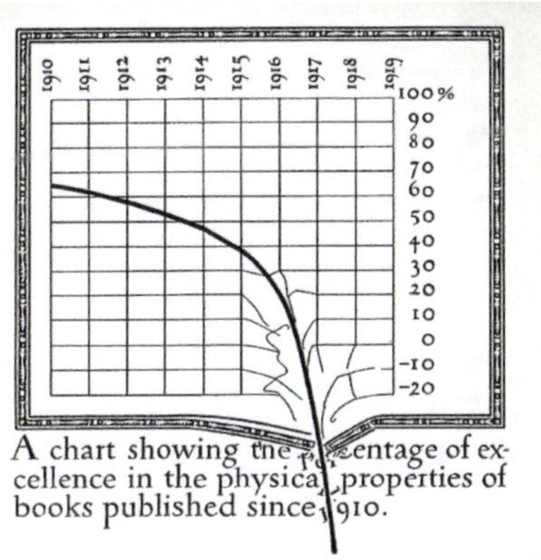

A parody line graph published in 1919.

In either case, the best-fit layer can reveal trends in the data. Further, measurements such as the gradient or the area under the curve can be made visually, leading to more conclusions or results from the data.

A true best-fit layer should depict a continuous mathematical function whose parameters are determined by using a suitable error-minimization scheme, which appropriately weights the error in the data values. Such curve fitting functionality is often found in graphing software or spreadsheets. Best-fit curves may vary from simple linear equations to more complex quadratic, polynomial, exponential, and periodic curves.

Basic Technical Tools and Indicators

Dow Theory

This theory was first stated by Charles Dow in a series of columns in the Wall Street Journal, December 19, 1900. Dow (and later Hamilton and Rhea) believed that market trends forecast trends in the economy. A change in the trend of the Stock Index must be confirmed by a trend change in the Index in order to generate a valid signal. The major postulate of this theory is derived from the assumption that markets tend to move in similar ways over time.

Dow Theory postulates three types of price movements namely: primary or major tends, secondary or incremental trends and short-term movements or ripples. Primary Trend also called as "the tide" by Dow, is the trend that defines the long-term direction (up to several years). Primary trend represent the broad underlying trend of the market and can last from a few months to many years and also referred as bull and bear markets. Once the primary trend has been identified, it will remain in effect until proven otherwise. Secondary Trend also called as "the waves" by Dow, is shorter-term departures from the primary trend (weeks to months). Secondary trend run counter to the primary trend and are reactionary in nature. For example, in a bull market (primary trend) a secondary move is considered a correction, and in a bear market, secondary moves are sometimes called reaction rallies. Day to day fluctuations or short term fluctuations. Daily fluctuations, while important when viewed as a group on a historical basis, but it might be dangerous and unreliable individually due to the randomness of the movements.

Dow Theory also suggests for three types of market trends: Uptrends occur when in successive rallies security price close at levels higher than previous rallies or lowers to levels higher than previous lows. Downtrends occur when market moves successive lower lows and lower highs. Corrections occur when market moves in one direction and then retreat in the opposite direction for short span of time and then continue in its original direction.

IOC Corporation , NSE: IOC, Price movement from May 2011 to May 2012.

Dow Theory

The third premise of Dow Theory is that each market trends have three phases namely: accumulation phase, public participation phase and excess phase. Lets consider the case of an uptrend in the market. In the accumulation phase expert traders and major market participants take active positions in the market to send the signal of future positive price change. The public participation phase is the stage when the public at large joins the experts trading move and thus results rapid price change.

Simple Moving Averages

A moving average is simply the average price (usually the closing price) over the last N periods. They are used to smooth out fluctuations of less than N periods.

Price Patterns

Technicians look for many patterns in the time series of prices. These patterns are reputed to provide information regarding the size and timing of subsequent price moves. But it is worth to remember that the efficient market hypothesis (EMH) says these patterns are illusions, and have no real meaning. In fact, they can be seen in a randomly generated price series.

1. Head and Shoulders (H&S): This formation is characterized by two small peaks on either side of a larger peak. This is a reversal pattern, meaning that it signifies a change in the trend.
2. Double Tops and Bottoms: These formations are similar to the H&S formations, but there is no head. These are reversal patterns with the same measuring implications as the H&S.
3. Rounded Tops & Bottoms: Rounding formations are characterized by a slow reversal of trend.
4. Triangles: Triangles are continuation formations in three flavours such as: ascending, descending and symmetrical. Typically, triangles should break out about half to three- quarters of the way through the formation.

5. Broadening Formations: These formations are like reverse triangles. These formations usually signal a reversal of the trend.

Following table gives a graphical representation of above mentioned trend patterns.

Different Types of Patterns in the Time Series of Prices

(1) Head and Shoulders (H&S)

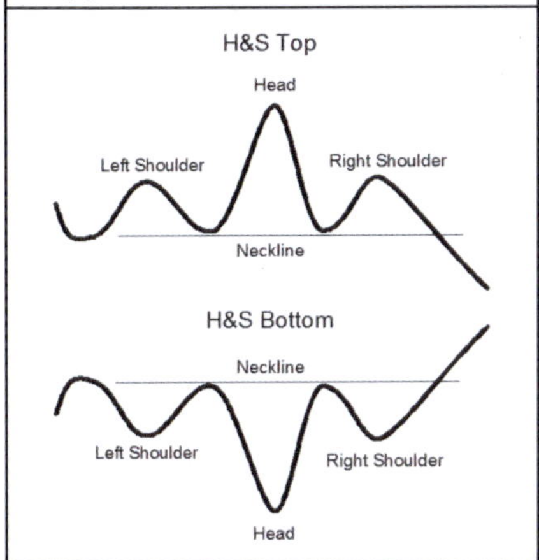

(2) Double Tops and Bottoms

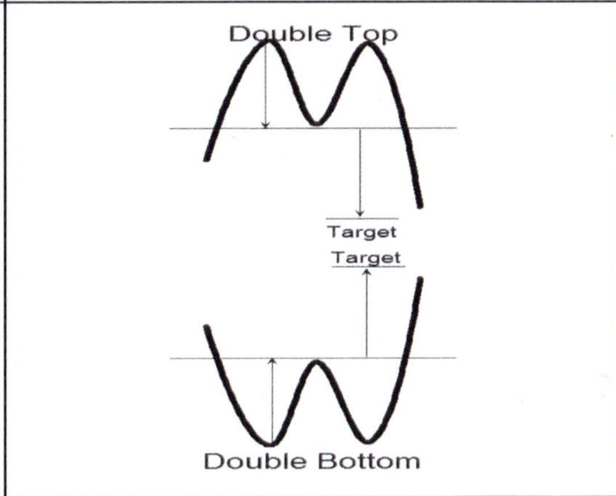

(3) Rounded Tops & Bottoms

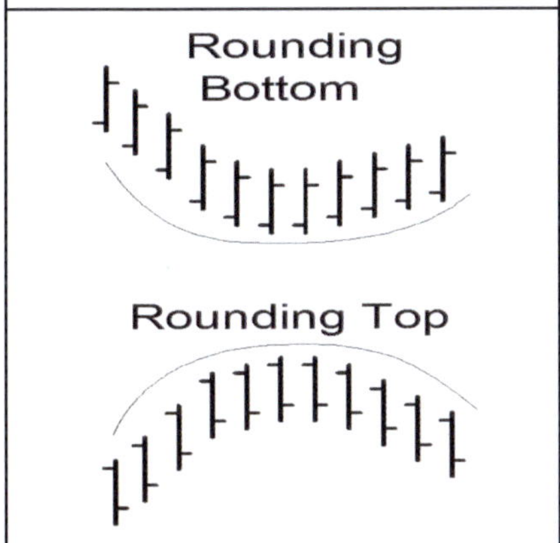

(4) Triangles

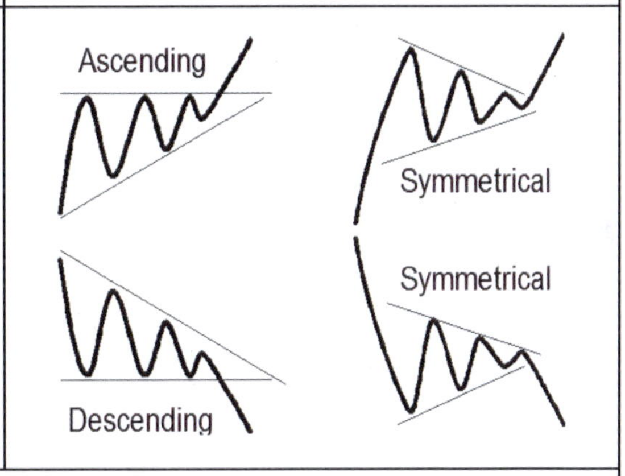

(5) Broadening Formations

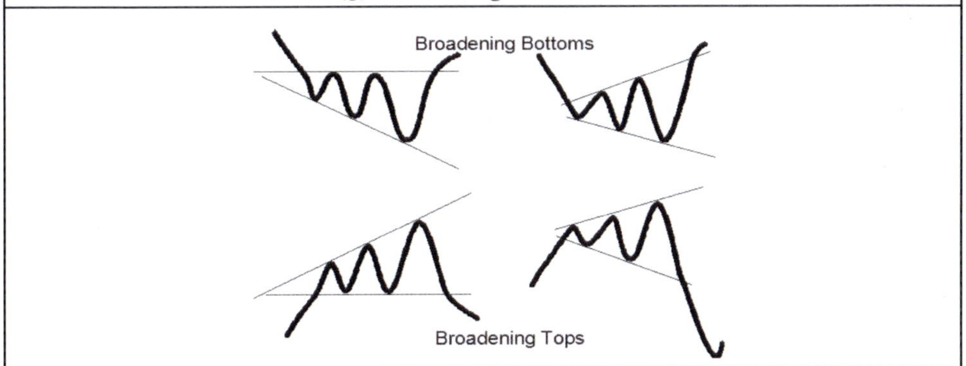

Moving Average Convergence/Divergence

Moving average convergence/divergence (MACD) was developed by Gerald Appel as a way to keep

track of a moving average crossover system. Appel defined MACD as the difference between a 12-day and 26-day moving average. A 9-day moving average of this difference is used to generate signals. When this signal line goes from negative to positive, a buy signal is generated and when it goes from positive to negative, a sell signal is generated. MACD is best used in choppy (trend-less) markets, and is subject to whipsaws (in and out rapidly with little or no profit).

On Balance Volume

On Balance Volume (OBV) was developed by Joseph Granville, one of the most famous technicians of the 1960's and 1970's. OBV is calculated by adding volume on up days, and subtracting volume on down days as Granville believed that "volume leads price." To use OBV, you generally look for OBV to show a change in trend (a divergence from the price trend). If the stock is in an uptrend, but OBV turns down, that is a signal that the price trend may soon reverse.

Bollinger Bands

Bollinger bands were created by John Bollinger (former FNN technical analyst, and regular guest on CNBC). Bollinger Bands are based on a moving average of the closing price. They are two standard deviations above and below the moving average. A buy signal is given when the stock price closes below the lower band, and a sell signal is given when the stock price closes above the upper band. When the bands contract, that is a signal that a big move is coming, but it is impossible to say if it will be up or down. The buy signals are far more reliable than the sell signals.

Trend Line (Technical Analysis)

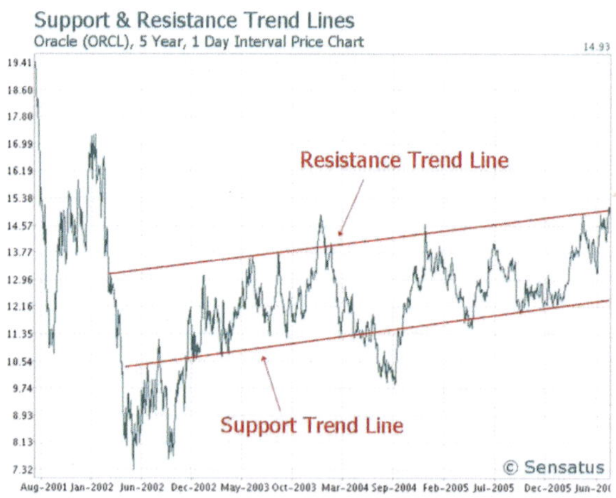

Trend lines on a price chart.

In finance, a trend line is a bounding line for the price movement of a security. It is formed when a diagonal line can be drawn between a minimum of three or more price pivot points. A line can be drawn between any two points, but it does not qualify as a trend line until tested. Hence the need for the third point, the test. Trend lines are commonly used to decide entry and exit timing when trading securities. They can also be referred to as a Dutch line, as the concept was first used in Holland.

A support trend line is formed when a securities price decreases and then rebounds at a pivot point that aligns with at least two previous support pivot points. Similarly a resistance trend line is formed when a securities price increases and then rebounds at a pivot point that aligns with at least two previous resistance pivot points. Stock often begin or end trending because of a stock catalyst such as a product launch or change in management.

Trend lines are a simple and widely used technical analysis approach to judging entry and exit investment timing. To establish a trend line historical data, typically presented in the format of a chart such as the above price chart, is required. Historically, trend lines have been drawn by hand on paper charts, but it is now more common to use charting software that enables trend lines to be drawn on computer based charts. There are some charting software that will automatically generate trend lines, however most traders prefer to draw their own trend lines.

When establishing trend lines it is important to choose a chart based on a price interval period that aligns with your trading strategy. Short term traders tend to use charts based on interval periods, such as 1 minute (i.e. the price of the security is plotted on the chart every 1 minute), with longer term traders using price charts based on hourly, daily, weekly and monthly interval periods.

However, time periods can also be viewed in terms of years. For example, below is a chart of the S&P 500 since the earliest data point until April 2008. While the Oracle example above uses a linear scale of price changes, long term data is more often viewed as logarithmic: e.g. the changes are really an attempt to approximate percentage changes than pure numerical value.

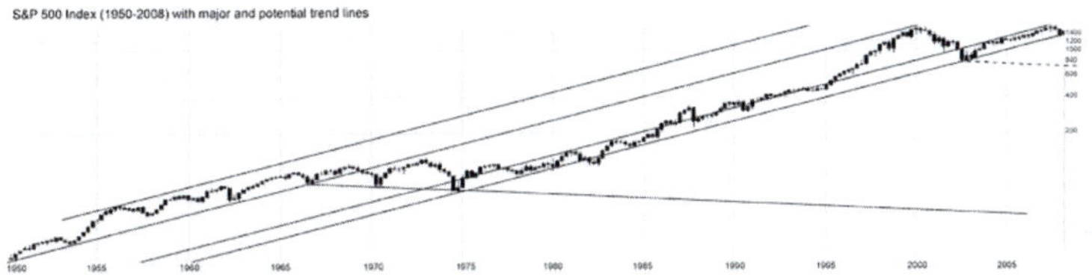

Previous chart from 1950 to about 1990, showing how linear scale obscures details by compressing the data.

Trend lines are typically used with price charts, however they can also be used with a range of technical analysis charts such as MACD and RSI. Trend lines can be used to identify positive and negative trending charts, whereby a positive trending chart forms an upsloping line when the support and the resistance pivots points are aligned, and a negative trending chart forms a downsloping line when the support and resistance pivot points are aligned.

Trend lines are used in many ways by traders. If a stock price is moving between support and resistance trend lines, then a basic investment strategy commonly used by traders, is to buy a stock at support and sell at resistance, then short at resistance and cover the short at support. The logic behind this, is that when the price returns to an existing principal trend line it may be an opportunity to open new positions in the direction of the trend, in the belief that the trend line will hold and the trend will continue further. A second way is that when price action breaks through the principal trend line of an existing trend, it is evidence that the trend may be going to fail, and a trader may consider trading in the opposite direction to the existing trend, or exiting positions in the direction of the trend.

Relative Strength Index

The relative strength index (RSI) is a technical indicator used in the analysis of financial markets. It is intended to chart the current and historical strength or weakness of a stock or market based on the closing prices of a recent trading period. The indicator should not be confused with relative strength.

The RSI is classified as a momentum oscillator, measuring the velocity and magnitude of directional price movements. Momentum is the rate of the rise or fall in price. The RSI computes momentum as the ratio of higher closes to lower closes: stocks which have had more or stronger positive changes have a higher RSI than stocks which have had more or stronger negative changes.

The RSI is most typically used on a 14-day timeframe, measured on a scale from 0 to 100, with high and low levels marked at 70 and 30, respectively. Shorter or longer timeframes are used for alternately shorter or longer outlooks. More extreme high and low levels—80 and 20, or 90 and 10—occur less frequently but indicate stronger momentum.

The relative strength index was developed by J. Welles Wilder and published in a 1978 book, *New Concepts in Technical Trading Systems*, and in *Commodities* magazine (now *Futures* magazine) in the June 1978 issue. It has become one of the most popular oscillator indices.

The RSI provides signals that tell investors to buy when the currency is oversold and to sell when it is overbought.

Calculation

For each trading period an upward change *U* or downward change *D* is calculated. Up periods are characterized by the close being higher than the previous close:

$$U = \text{close}_{\text{now}} - \text{close}_{\text{previous}}$$

$$D = 0$$

Conversely, a down period is characterized by the close being lower than the previous period's close (note that D is nonetheless a positive number),

$$\text{U} = 0$$

$$\text{D} = \text{close}_{\text{previous}} - \text{close}_{\text{now}}$$

If the last close is the same as the previous, both *U* and *D* are zero. The average *U* and *D* are calculated using an *n*-period smoothed or modified moving average (SMMA or MMA) which is an exponentially smoothed Moving Average with $\alpha = 1/\text{period}$. Some commercial packages, like AIQ, use a standard exponential moving average (EMA) as the average instead of Wilder's SMMA.

Wilder originally formulated the calculation of the moving average as: newval = (prevval * (period - 1) + newdata) / period. This is fully equivalent to the aforementioned exponential smoothing. New data is simply divided by period which is equal to the alpha calculated value of 1/period. Previous average values are modified by (period -1)/period which in effect is period/period - 1/period and finally 1 - 1/period which is 1 - alpha.

The ratio of these averages is the *relative strength* or *relative strength factor*:

$$\text{RS} = \frac{\text{SMMA(U,n)}}{\text{SMMA(D,n)}}$$

If the average of D values is zero, then according to the equation, the RS value will approach infinity, so that the resulting RSI, as computed below, will approach 100.

The relative strength factor is then converted to a relative strength index between 0 and 100:

$$RSI = 100 - \frac{100}{1 + RS}$$

The smoothed moving averages should be appropriately initialized with a simple moving average using the first n values in the price series.

Interpretation

Basic Configuration

Relative strength index 14-period

The RSI is presented on a graph above or below the price chart. The indicator has an upper line, typically at 70, a lower line at 30, and a dashed mid-line at 50.

Principles

Wilder posited that when price moves up very rapidly, at some point it is considered overbought. Likewise, when price falls very rapidly, at some point it is considered oversold. In either case, Wilder deemed a reaction or reversal imminent.

The level of the RSI is a measure of the stock's recent trading strength. The slope of the RSI is directly proportional to the velocity of a change in the trend. The distance traveled by the RSI is proportional to the magnitude of the move.

Wilder believed that tops and bottoms are indicated when RSI goes above 70 or drops below 30. Traditionally, RSI readings greater than the 70 level are considered to be in overbought territory, and RSI readings lower than the 30 level are considered to be in oversold territory. In between the 30 and 70 level is considered neutral, with the 50 level a sign of no trend.

Divergence

Wilder further believed that divergence between RSI and price action is a very strong indication that a market turning point is imminent. Bearish divergence occurs when price makes a new high but the RSI makes a lower high, thus failing to confirm. Bullish divergence occurs when price makes a new low but RSI makes a higher low.

Overbought and Oversold Conditions

Wilder thought that "failure swings" above 70 and below 30 on the RSI are strong indications of market reversals. For example, assume the RSI hits 76, pulls back to 72, then rises to 77. If it falls below 72, Wilder would consider this a "failure swing" above 70.

Finally, Wilder wrote that chart formations and areas of support and resistance could sometimes be more easily seen on the RSI chart as opposed to the price chart. The center line for the relative strength index is 50, which is often seen as both the support and resistance line for the indicator.

If the relative strength index is below 50, it generally means that the stock's losses are greater than the gains. When the relative strength index is above 50, it generally means that the gains are greater than the losses.

Uptrends and Downtrends

In addition to Wilder's original theories of RSI interpretation, Andrew Cardwell has developed several new interpretations of RSI to help determine and confirm trend. First, Cardwell noticed that uptrends generally traded between RSI 40 and 80, while downtrends usually traded between RSI 60 and 20. Cardwell observed when securities change from uptrend to downtrend and vice versa, the RSI will undergo a "range shift."

Example of RSI Indicator Divergence

Next, Cardwell noted that bearish divergence: 1) only occurs in uptrends, and 2) mostly only leads to a brief correction instead of a reversal in trend. Therefore, bearish divergence is a sign confirming an uptrend. Similarly, bullish divergence is a sign confirming a downtrend.

Reversals

Finally, Cardwell discovered the existence of positive and negative reversals in the RSI. Reversals are the opposite of divergence. For example, a positive reversal occurs when an uptrend price correction results in a higher low compared to the last price correction, while RSI results in a lower low compared to the prior correction. A negative reversal happens when a downtrend rally results in a lower high compared to the last downtrend rally, but RSI makes a higher high compared to the prior rally.

In other words, despite stronger momentum as seen by the higher high or lower low in the RSI, price could not make a higher high or lower low. This is evidence the main trend is about to resume. Cardwell noted that positive reversals only happen in uptrends while negative reversals only occur in downtrends, and therefore their existence confirms the trend.

Cutler's RSI

A variation called Cutler's RSI is based on a simple moving average of *U* and *D*, instead of the exponential average above. Cutler had found that since Wilder used a smoothed moving average to calculate RSI, the value of Wilder's RSI depended upon where in the data file his calculations started. Cutler termed this Data Length Dependency. Cutler's RSI is not data length dependent, and returns consistent results regardless of the length of, or the starting point within a data file.

$$RS = \frac{SMA(U,n)}{SMA(D,n)}$$

Cutler's RSI generally comes out slightly different from the normal Wilder RSI, but the two are similar, since SMA and SMMA are also similar.

Support and Resistance

In stock market technical analysis, support and resistance is a concept that the movement of the price of a security will tend to stop and reverse at certain predetermined price levels. These levels are denoted by multiple touches of price without a breakthrough of the level.

Support Versus Resistance

A support level is a level where the price tends to find support as it falls. This means that the price is more likely to "bounce" off this level rather than break through it. However, once the price has breached this level, by an amount exceeding some noise, it is likely to continue falling until meeting another support level.

A resistance level is the opposite of a support level. It is where the price tends to find resistance as it rises. Again, this means that the price is more likely to "bounce" off this level rather than break through it. However, once the price has breached this level, by an amount exceeding some noise, it is likely to continue rising until meeting another resistance level.

Reactive vs Proactive Support and Resistance

Proactive support and resistance methods are "predictive" in that they often outline areas where price has not actually been. They are based upon current price action that, through analysis, has been shown to be predictive of future price action. Proactive support and resistance methods include Measured Moves, Swing Ratio Projection/Confluence (Static (Square of Nine), Dynamic (Fibonacci)), Calculated Pivots, Volatility Based, Trendlines and Moving averages, VWAP, Market Profile (VAH, VAL and POC).

Reactive support and resistance are the opposite: they are formed directly as a result of price action or volume behaviour. They include Volume Profile, Price Swing lows/highs, Initial Balance, Open Gaps, certain Candle Patterns (e.g. Engulfing, Tweezers) and OHLC.

A price histogram is useful in showing at what price a market has spent more relative time. Psychological levels near round numbers often serve as support and resistance.

Identifying Support and Resistance Levels

Support and resistance levels can be identified by trend lines (technical analysis). Some traders believe in using pivot point calculations.

The more often a support/resistance level is "tested" (touched and bounced off by price), the more significance is given to that specific level.

If a price breaks past a support level, that support level often becomes a new resistance level. The opposite is true as well; if price breaks a resistance level, it will often find support at that level in the future.

Psychological Support and Resistance levels form an important part of a trader's technical analysis. As price reaches a value ending in 50 (ex. 1.2050) or 00 (ex. 1.3000), people often see these levels as a strong potential for interruption in the current movement. The price may hit the line and reverse, it could hover around the level as Bulls and Bears fought for supremacy, or it may punch straight through. A trader should always exercise caution when approaching 00 levels in general, and 50 levels if it has previously acted as Support or Resistance.

Using Support and Resistance Levels

This is an example of support switching roles with resistance, and vice versa:

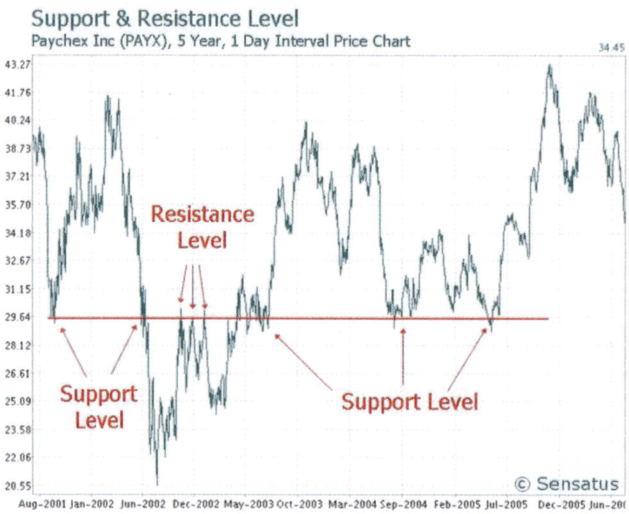

If a stock price is moving between support and resistance levels, then a basic investment strategy commonly used by traders, is to buy a stock at support and sell at resistance, then short at resistance and cover the short at support as per the following example:

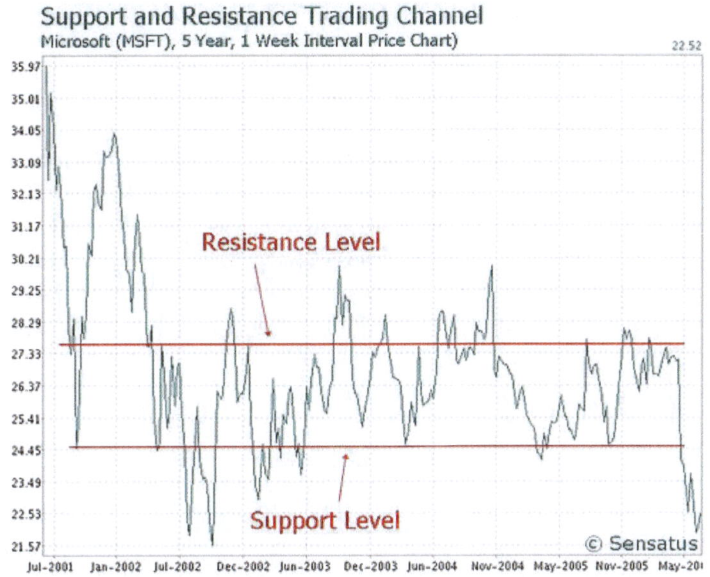

When judging entry and exit investment timing using support or resistance levels, it is important to choose a chart based on a price interval period that aligns with your trading strategy timeframe. Short term traders tend to use charts based on interval periods, such as 1 minute (i.e. the price of the security is plotted on the chart every 1 minute). Longer term traders typically use price charts based on hourly, daily, weekly or monthly interval periods. Typically traders use shorter term interval charts when making a final decisions on when to invest, such as the following example based on 1 week of historical data with price plotted every 15 minutes. In this example, the early signs that the stock was coming out of a downtrend was when it started to form support at $30.48 and then started to form higher highs and higher lows. This signals a change from negative to positive trending.

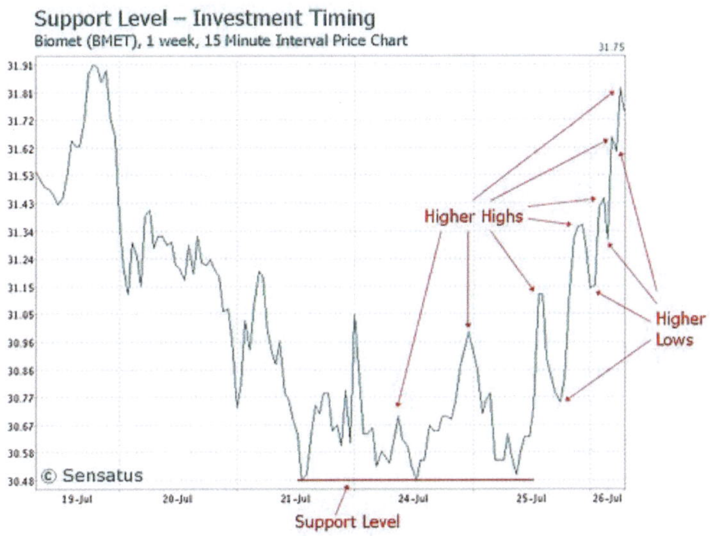

Pivot Point (Technical Analysis)

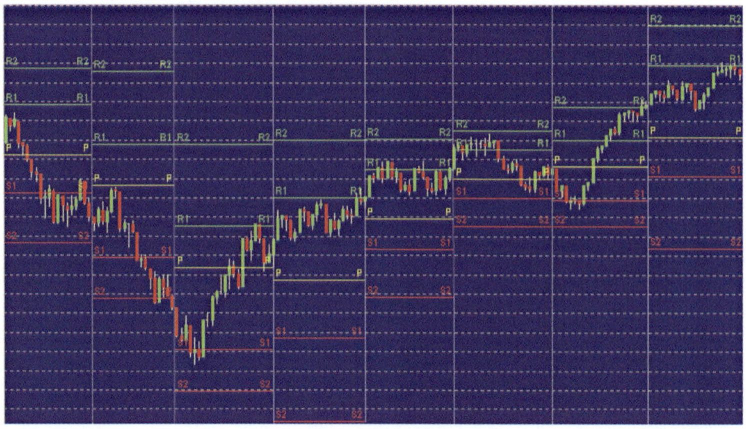

Monthly pivot point chart of the Dow Jones Industrial Average for the first 8 months of 2009, showing sets of first and second levels of resistance (green) and support (red). The pivot point levels are highlighted in yellow. Trading below the pivot point, particularly at the beginning of a trading period sets a bearish market sentiment and often results in further price decline, while trading above it, bullish price action may continue for some time.

In financial markets, a pivot point is a price level that is used by traders as a possible indicator of market movement. A pivot point is calculated as an average of significant prices (high, low, close) from the performance of a market in the prior trading period. If the market in the following period trades above the pivot point it is usually evaluated as a bullish sentiment, whereas trading below the pivot point is seen as bearish.

It is customary to calculate additional levels of support and resistance, below and above the pivot point, respectively, by subtracting or adding price differentials calculated from previous trading ranges of the market.

A pivot point and the associated support and resistance levels are often turning points for the direction of price movement in a market. In an up-trending market, the pivot point and the resistance levels may represent a ceiling level in price above which the uptrend is no longer sustainable and a reversal may occur. In a declining market, a pivot point and the support levels may represent a low price level of stability or a resistance to further decline.

Calculation

Several methods exist for calculating the pivot point (*P*) of a market. Most commonly, it is the arithmetic average of the high (*H*), low (*L*), and closing (*C*) prices of the market in the prior trading period:

$$P = (H + L + C) / 3.$$

Sometimes, the average also includes the previous period's or the current period's opening price (*O*):

$$P = (O + H + L + C) / 4.$$

In other cases, traders like to emphasize the closing price, $P = (H + L + C + C) / 4$, or the current periods opening price, $P = (H + L + O + O) / 4$.

Support and Resistance Levels

Price support and resistance levels are key trading tools in any market. Their roles may be interchangeable, depending on whether the price level is approached in an up-trending or a down-trending market. These price levels may be derived from many market assumptions and conventions. In pivot point analysis, several levels, usually three, are commonly recognized below and above the pivot point. These are calculated from the range of price movement in the previous trading period, added to the pivot point for resistances and subtracted from it for support levels.

The first and most significant level of support (S_1) and resistance (R_1) is obtained by recognition of the upper and the lower halves of the prior trading range, defined by the trading above the pivot point (H – P), and below it (P – L). The first resistance on the up-side of the market is given by the lower width of prior trading added to the pivot point price and the first support on the down-side is the width of the upper part of the prior trading range below the pivot point.

- $R_1 = P + (P - L) = 2 \times P - L$
- $S_1 = P - (H - P) = 2 \times P - H$

Thus, these levels may simply be calculated by subtracting the previous low (L) and high (H) price, respectively, from twice the pivot point value:

The second set of resistance (R_2) and support (S_2) levels are above and below, respectively, the first set. They are simply determined from the full width of the prior trading range (H – L), added to and subtracted from the pivot point, respectively:

- $R_2 = P + (H - L)$
- $S_2 = P - (H - L)$

Commonly a third set is also calculated, again representing another higher resistance level (R_3) and a yet lower support level (S_3). The method of the second set is continued by doubling the range added and subtracted from the pivot point:

- $R_3 = H + 2 \times (P - L) = R_1 + (H - L)$
- $S_3 = L - 2 \times (H - P) = S_1 - (H - L)$

This concept is sometimes, albeit rarely, extended to a fourth set in which the tripled value of the trading range is used in the calculation.

Qualitatively, the second and higher support and resistance levels are always located symmetrically around the pivot point, whereas this is not the case for the first levels, unless the pivot point happens to divide the prior trading range exactly in half.

Trading Tool

The pivot point itself represents a level of highest resistance or support, depending on the overall market condition. If the market is directionless (*undecided*), prices may fluctuate greatly around this level until a price breakout develops. Trading above or below the pivot point indicates the overall market sentiment. It is a leading indicator providing advanced signaling of potentially new market highs or lows within a given time frame.

The support and resistance levels calculated from the pivot point and the previous market width may be used as exit points of trades, but are rarely used as entry signals. For example, if the market is up-trending and breaks through the pivot point, the first resistance level is often a good target to close a position, as the probability of resistance and reversal increases greatly.

Many traders recognize the half-way levels between any of these levels as additional, but weaker resistance or support areas. The half-way (*middle*) point between the pivot point and R_1 is designated *M+*, between R_1 and R_2 is *M++*, and below the pivot point the middle points are labeled as *M−* and *M−−*. In the 5-day intra-day chart of the SPDR Gold Trust (above) the middle points can clearly be identified as support in days 1, 3, and 4, and as resistance in days 2 and 3.

References

- Candlestick Charting Explained: Timeless Techniques for Trading Stocks and Futures, Gregory L. Morris, McGraw-Hill, 2006, ISBN 0-07-146154-X / 9780071461542
- Deng, S.; Sakurai, A. (2013-03-01). "Foreign Exchange Trading Rules Using a Single Technical Indicator from Multiple Timeframes". 2013 27th International Conference on Advanced Information Networking and Applications Workshops: 207–212. doi:10.1109/WAINA.2013.7
- Edwards, Robert D.; Magee, John (1948). "14". Technical Analysis of Stock Trends. Springfield, MA, USA: Stock Trend Service. p. 505. ISBN 1-880408-00-7
- Michael Friendly (2008). "Milestones in the history of thematic cartography, statistical graphics, and data visualization". pp 13–14. Retrieved 7 July 2008
- John J. Murphy (2009). The Visual Investor: How to Spot Market Trends (2nd ed.). John Wiley and Sons. p. 100. ISBN 9780470382059
- Schabacker, R. (2005-01-01). Technical Analysis and Stock Market Profits. Harriman House Limited. ISBN 9781897597569
- Stanley, James. "The Hidden Patterns of Support and Resistance in the Forex Market". Yahoo! Finance. Retrieved 13 August 2015
- Achelis (2006-12-01). Technical Analysis From A To Z. McGraw-Hill Education (India) Pvt Limited. ISBN 9780070636576
- Amiri, M.; Zandieh, M.; Vahdani, B.; Soltani, R.; Roshanaei, V. (January 2010). "An integrated eigenvector–DEA–TOPSIS methodology for portfolio risk evaluation in the FOREX spot market". Expert Systems with Applications. 37 (1): 509–516. doi:10.1016/j.eswa.2009.05.041
- Gil Morales & Chris Kacher, Trade Like an O'Neil Disciple: How We Made 18,000% in the Stock Market, John Wiley & Sons (2010), ISBN 978-0470616536

Permissions

All chapters in this book are published with permission under the Creative Commons Attribution Share Alike License or equivalent. Every chapter published in this book has been scrutinized by our experts. Their significance has been extensively debated. The topics covered herein carry significant information for a comprehensive understanding. They may even be implemented as practical applications or may be referred to as a beginning point for further studies.

We would like to thank the editorial team for lending their expertise to make the book truly unique. They have played a crucial role in the development of this book. Without their invaluable contributions this book wouldn't have been possible. They have made vital efforts to compile up to date information on the varied aspects of this subject to make this book a valuable addition to the collection of many professionals and students.

This book was conceptualized with the vision of imparting up-to-date and integrated information in this field. To ensure the same, a matchless editorial board was set up. Every individual on the board went through rigorous rounds of assessment to prove their worth. After which they invested a large part of their time researching and compiling the most relevant data for our readers.

The editorial board has been involved in producing this book since its inception. They have spent rigorous hours researching and exploring the diverse topics which have resulted in the successful publishing of this book. They have passed on their knowledge of decades through this book. To expedite this challenging task, the publisher supported the team at every step. A small team of assistant editors was also appointed to further simplify the editing procedure and attain best results for the readers.

Apart from the editorial board, the designing team has also invested a significant amount of their time in understanding the subject and creating the most relevant covers. They scrutinized every image to scout for the most suitable representation of the subject and create an appropriate cover for the book.

The publishing team has been an ardent support to the editorial, designing and production team. Their endless efforts to recruit the best for this project, has resulted in the accomplishment of this book. They are a veteran in the field of academics and their pool of knowledge is as vast as their experience in printing. Their expertise and guidance has proved useful at every step. Their uncompromising quality standards have made this book an exceptional effort. Their encouragement from time to time has been an inspiration for everyone.

The publisher and the editorial board hope that this book will prove to be a valuable piece of knowledge for students, practitioners and scholars across the globe.

Index